LIMERICK'S
Fighting Story
1916 — 21

CLARE

TIPPERARY

NEWMARKET ON FERGUS

SIXMILEBRIDGE

BUNRATTY

RIVER SHANNON

LIMERICK CITY

PALLASKENRY

MID LIMK.

CAHERCONLISH

DROMKEEN
PALLASGREEN

ANNACARTY

ASHKEATON

GLIN

BALLYHAHILL

WEST LIMK.

GRANGE

BRUFF
KNOCKLONG

EMLY

TIPPERARY

BALLINGARRY

LACKELLY

KERRY

NEWCASTLE WEST

BRUREE

KILMALLOCK

EAST LIMK.

TEMPLEGLANTAINE

ROCKHILL

TANKARDSTOWN

BALLYLANDERS

CAHIR

TOURNAFULLA

KILFINNANE

ANGLESBOROUGH

CORK

SHRAHERLA

KILBEHENY

GLENACURRANE

MITCHELSTOWN

NEWMARKET

TO KANTURK

BALLYVONAIRE

BUTTEVANT

TO MITCHELSTOWN

TO FERMOY

KILDORRERY

TO KILWORTH

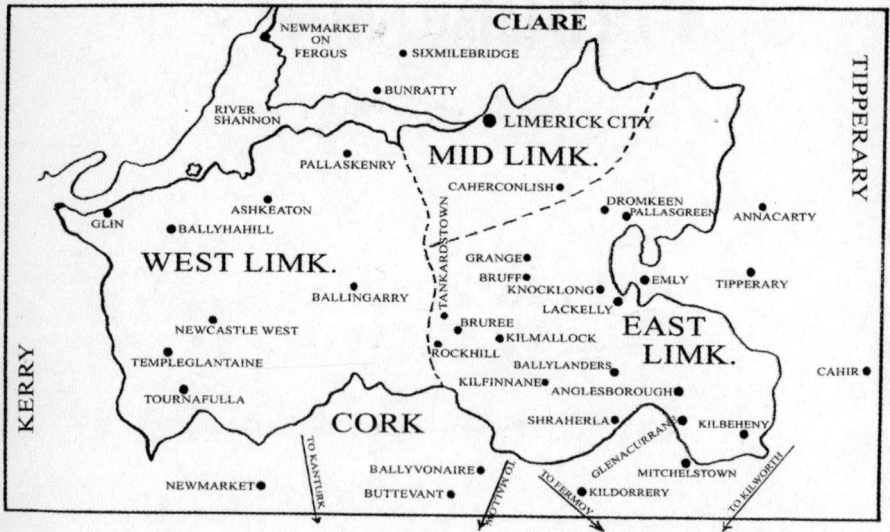

MAP OF LIMERICK DETAILING BRIGADE AREAS

LIMERICK'S
Fighting Story
1916 — 21

Told By The
Men Who Made It

With a Unique Pictorial Record of the Period

INTRODUCTION BY RUÁN O'DONNELL

SERIES EDITOR: BRIAN Ó CONCHUBHAIR

MERCIER PRESS
IRISH PUBLISHER – IRISH STORY

MERCIER PRESS

Cork

www. mercierpress. ie

Trade enquiries to CMD Booksource,
55a Spruce Avenue, Stillorgan Industrial Park,
Blackrock, County Dublin

Originally published by *The Kerryman*, 1948

This edition published by Mercier Press, 2009

© Preface: Brian Ó Conchubhair, 2009

© Introduction: Ruán O'Donnell, 2009

© Text: Mercier Press, 2009

ISBN: 978 1 85635 642 8

10 9 8 7 6 5 4 3 2 1

A CIP record for this title is available from the British Library

Printed and bound in the EU.

CONTENTS

PREFACE (2009)

As we approach the centenary of the 1916 Easter Rising and the Irish War of Independence/Anglo-Irish War (1919–1921), interest among scholars and the general public in these historic events gathers unrelenting pace. Recent years have witnessed a slew of books, articles, documentaries and films, emerge at home and abroad all dealing with the events and controversies involved in the struggle for political independence in the period 1916–1922. While many of these projects have re-evaluated and challenged the standard nationalist narrative that dominated for so long, and indeed have contributed to a more nuanced and complex appreciation of the events in question, the absence of the famous *Fighting Story* series – initially published by *The Kerryman* newspaper and subsequently republished by Anvil Books – is a notable and regrettable absence. First published in Christmas and special editions of *The Kerryman* newspaper in the years before the Second World War, the articles subsequently appeared in four independent collections entitled *Rebel Cork's Fighting Story, Kerry's Fighting Story, Limerick's Fighting Story* and *Dublin's Fighting Story* between 1947–49. The choice of counties reflecting the geographical intensity of the campaign as Dr Peter Hart explains in his new introduction to *Rebel Cork's Fighting Story*: 'The Munster IRA … was much more active than anywhere else except Longford, Roscommon and Dublin city.' Marketed as authentic accounts and as 'gripping episodes' by 'the men who made it', the series was dramatically described as 'more graphic than anything written of late war zones', with 'astonishing pictures' and sold 'at the very moderate price of two shillings'. Benefiting from *The Kerryman*'s wide distribution network and a competitive price, the books proved immediately popular at home and abroad, so much so that many, if not most, of the books, were purchased by, and for, the Irish Diaspora. This competitive price resulted in part from the fact that 'the producers were content to reduce their own profit and to produce the booklet at little above the mere cost of production'. Consequently, however, the volumes quickly disappeared from general circulation. Dr Ruán O'Donnell explains in the new introduction to *Limerick's Fighting Story*, 'The shelf life … was reduced by the poor production values they shared. This was a by-product of the stringent economies of their day when pricing, paper quality, binding and distribution costs had to be considered [which] rendered copies vulnerable to deterioration and unsuited to library utilisation.'

The books targeted not only the younger generation, who knew about those times by hearsay only, but also the older generation who 'will recall vividly a memorable era and the men who made it'. Professor Diarmaid Ferriter notes in the new introduction to *Dublin's Fighting Story* that these volumes answered the perceived need for Volunteers to record their stories in their own words in addition to ensuring the proper education and appreciation of a new generation for their predecessors' sacrifices. The narrative, he writes 'captures the excitement and the immediacy of the Irish War of Independence and the belief that the leaders of the revolution did not urge people to take dangerous courses they were not themselves prepared to take'. These four books deserve reprinting therefore not only for the important factual information they contain, and the resource they offer scholars of various disciplines, but also because of the valuable window they open on the mentality of the period. As Professor J.J. Lee observes in the introduction to *Kerry's Fighting Story*, for anyone 'trying to reconstruct in very different times the historical reality of what it felt like at the time, there is no substitute for contemporary accounts, however many questions these accounts may raise. We know what was to come. Contemporaries did not.' The insight these books offer on IRA organisation at local level suggest to Dr Peter Hart 'why IRA units were so resilient under pressure, and how untrained, inexperienced men could be such formidable soldiers … Irish guerrillas fought alongside their brothers, cousins, school and teammates, and childhood friends – often in the very lanes, fields and streets where they had spent their lives together'. In addition these texts reveal the vital roles, both active and passive, women played in the struggle of Irish Independence.

The establishment of Anvil Books in 1962 saw a reissuing of certain volumes, Cork and Limerick in particular. The link between *The Kerryman* and Anvil Books was Dan Nolan (1910–1989). Son of Thomas Nolan, and nephew of Daniel Nolan and Maurice Griffin, he was related to all three founders of *The Kerryman* newspaper that commenced publishing in 1904. His obituary in that newspaper describes how he 'was only a nipper when he looked down the barrels of British guns as His Majesty's soldiers tried to arrest the proprietors of *The Kerryman* for refusing to publish recruitment advertisements. And he saw the paper and its employees being harassed by the Black and Tans.' On graduating from Castleknock College, he joined the paper's staff in 1928 replacing his recently deceased uncle, Maurice Griffin. His father's death in 1939 saw Dan Nolan become the paper's managing director and his tenure would, in due course, see a marked improvement in its commercial performance: circulation increased and ultimately exceeded 40,000 copies per week, and advertisement revenue also increased significantly. Under his stewardship *The Kerryman*, according to Séamus McConville in an obituary in the paper, 'became solidly established as the unchallenged leader in sales and stature among provincial newspapers'. Recognising his talent, the Provincial Newspaper Association elected him president in 1951. Among his projects were the Rose of Tralee Festival, Tralee Racecourse and Anvil Books. Founded in 1962 with Nolan and Rena Dardis as co-directors, Anvil Books established itself as the pre-eminent publisher of memoirs and accounts dealing with the Irish War of Independence. Indeed the first book published by Anvil

Books was a 1962 reprint of *Rebel Cork's Fighting Story* in a print run of 10,000 copies.

Conscious, no doubt, of the potential for controversy the original foreword was careful not to present the *Fighting Stories* as 'a detailed or chronological history of the fight for independence', and acknowledged 'that in the collection of data about such a period errors and omissions can easily occur and so they will welcome the help of readers who may be able to throw more light upon the various episodes related in the series. Such additional information will be incorporated into the second edition of the booklets which the present rate of orders would seem to indicate will be called for in the very near future.' Subsequent editions of *Rebel Cork's Fighting Story* and *Limerick's Fighting Story* did appear in print with additional material as O'Donnell discusses in his enlightening introduction to *Limerick's Fighting Story*, but the proposed *Tipperary's Fighting Story*, as advertised in the Limerick volume with a suggested publication date of 1948 and a plea for relevant information or pictures, never materialised. This 2009 edition adheres to the original texts as first published by *The Kerryman* rather than the later editions by Anvil Books. A new preface, introduction and index frame the original texts that remain as first presented other than the silent correction of obvious typographical errors.

The preface to the final book, *Dublin's Fighting Story*, concluded by noting that the publishers 'would be satisfied if the series serves to preserve in the hearts of the younger generation that love of country and devotion to its interests which distinguished the men whose doings are related therein'. The overall story narrated in these four books is neither provincial nor insular, nor indeed limited to Ireland, but as Lee remarks in *Kerry's Fighting Story*, it is rather 'like that of kindred spirits elsewhere, at home and abroad, an example of the refusal of the human spirit to submit to arbitrary power'. The hasty and almost premature endings of several chapters may be attributed to the legacy of the Irish Civil War whose shadow constantly hovers at the edges threatening to break into the narrative, and in fact does intrude in a few instances. Lee opines that writers avoided the Civil War as it 'was still too divisive, still too harrowing, a nightmare to be recalled into public memory. Hence the somewhat abrupt ending of several chapters at a moment when hopes were still high and the horrors to come yet unimagined.'

Ireland at the start of the twenty-first century is a very different place than it was when these books were first published. Irish historiography has undergone no less a transformation and to bridge the gap four eminent historians have written new introductions that set the four *Fighting Stories* in the context of recent research and shifts in Irish historiography. Yet Lee's assessment in reference to Kerry holds true for each of the four volumes: 'Whatever would happen subsequently, and however perspectives would inevitably be affected by hindsight, for better and for worse, *Kerry's Fighting Story* lays the foundation for all subsequent studies of these foundation years of an independent Irish state.' As we move toward the centenary of 1916, the War of Independence, the Anglo-Irish Treaty and the Civil War, it is appropriate and fitting that these key texts be once again part of the public debate of those events and it is sincerely hoped that as Ruán O'Donnell states: 'This new life of a classic of its genre will facilitate a fresh evaluation of its unique perspectives on the genesis of the modern Irish state.'

Dr Brian Ó Conchubhair
Series Editor
University of Notre Dame
Easter 2009

ACKNOWLEDGEMENTS

I AM GRATEFUL not only to the scholars who penned the new introductions for their time and expertise, but also to the following who assisted in numerous ways: Beth Bland, Angela Carothers, Aedín Ní Bhroithe-Clements (Hesburgh Library), Professor Mike Cronin, Rena Dardis, Ken Garcia, Dr Michael Griffin, Alan Hayes, Dr Liam Mac Peaircín, Dyann Mahorr, Don and Patrica Nolan, Nora Noonan, Seán Seosamh Ó Conchubhair, Interlibrary Loans at the Hesburgh Library, University of Notre Dame, and Eoin Purcell, Wendy Logue and the staff at Mercier Press. The Limerick map appears in a later version of *Limerick's Fighting Story: From 1916 to the Truce with Britain*, edited by Colonel J.M. MacCarthy also published by Anvil Books. *Táim an-bhuíoch do gach éinne atá luaite thuas, m'athair ach go háirithe as a chuid foighne agus as a chuid saineolais a roinnt liom go fial agus do Thara uair amháin eile a d'fhulaing go foighneach agus an obair seo ar bun agam.*

DR BRIAN Ó CONCHUBHAIR

INTRODUCTION (2009)

THE HISTORIOGRAPHY OF the War of Independence has yet to attain the critical mass necessary to adequately contextualise the position of Limerick during the revolutionary period. The only twentieth-century county level overview was *Limerick's Fighting Story*. If by no means a comprehensive volume, the book contained invaluable material and has been mined by interim histories of the times. The book comprised a nexus where the generally disparate actions of the IRA's Mid-Limerick and East Limerick brigades, organised to the east of the River Maigue, were connected to those of the West Limerick brigade on the opposite bank.

The first paperback edition was printed by *The Kerryman* newspaper in Tralee in 1948. No editor was named, in keeping with the egalitarian policy of anonymity observed by several similar releases on the conflict. The full title of the publication, *Limerick's Fighting Story, 1916-21, Told by the Men Who Made It*, was not merely descriptive but also declaratory in this regard.[1] The second revised edition, however, was credited to its editor, Colonel J.M. MacCarthy, in 1966. While the main title remained unchanged, the subtitle was replaced with another reading *From 1916 to the Truce with Britain*. This referenced an uncomfortable truth known to all adult contemporaries: the Truce may have terminated conflict with British forces but did not herald the end point of a revolutionary cycle set in motion in 1916. Given that the Irish secondary school curriculum did not then encompass the Civil War, potential readers may have been reassured that the thematic range of the book would eschew painful and competing narratives of 1922–23.

Whereas the initial release of *Limerick's Fighting Story* coincided with the Republic of Ireland Act (1948), the second edition appeared at a time when the fiftieth anniversary of the 1916 Rising stimulated an outpouring of republican assertion, rhetoric, nostalgia and celebration. The last prisoners of the IRA's 1956–62 'Border Campaign' had been released and the quest for civil rights in the North of Ireland had not reached the intensity it attained in 1968–69. The collection contained important historical content on republican affairs in 1916, which fully merited its re-release by the Anvil Books' imprint of *The Kerryman* newspaper.[2]

Inevitably, MacCarthy's membership of the Free State army during the Civil War gave rise to accusations that he had produced a partisan version of events. In actuality, his major excision from the original was a chapter by a man who wrote himself into the account of the attack on Ballylanders barracks.[3] MacCarthy neither disparaged nor ignored those he fought against in the Civil War. Any disposition to do so was probably lessened by the cut-off date of the Truce when the IRA was a united entity. Indeed, the conspicuous dearth of allusions to Civil War allegiance is indicative of a desire to avoid divisive issues.

The shelf life of both paperback texts was reduced by the poor production values they shared. This was a by-product of the stringent economies of their day when pricing, paper quality, binding and distribution costs had to be considered. Another title of Limerick interest, Florence O'Donoghue's *No Other Law* appeared in 1954 courtesy of *The Irish Press*. This biography of the Limerick born leader of anti-Treaty IRA during the Civil War was not republished until 1986 when Anvil once again took the initiative.[4] *Limerick's Fighting Story* also went out of print and, if not particularly rare due to a relatively high issue, weak binding rendered copies vulnerable to deterioration and unsuited to library utilisation.[5]

Significantly, the Limerick volume was one of a wider 'fighting story' series. While all planned titles did not appear, those that did represented advances into pioneering territory. Far from standing alone and making pretensions to definitive status, the rationale of the set was to create a skeletal framework which subsequent and kindred volumes would flesh out. The fact that the collation and editing of the accounts was left in the hands of prominent veterans of the period was also pertinent. In many respects, the volumes are closer to synoptic memoirs in sequence than standard historical narratives, although this was generally disguised by using anonymous contributors.

The first edition was sufficiently well received commercially and critically to suggest a second, albeit after a lapse of almost twenty years. While certainly discussed in Munster republican circles, the main criticism of the text was confined to the records of the Bureau of Military History, which at that time were inaccessible. The major difference between the two editions was the acknowledgement of the many contributors in the MacCarthy variant. Whereas the original edition of *Limerick's Fighting Story* featured some thirty-six articles, nineteen of which were written anonymously or under a pseudonym, the MacCarthy edition of the Limerick volume comprised thirty-three short chapters by seventeen writers. Unusually, all but two of the contributors are explicitly credited in MacCarthy's edition indicating that both 'Lindisfarne' and 'Volunteer' preferred obscurity. Transparency militated against the repetition of the problem in the first edition where one or two unnamed authors had elevated themselves at the expense of others. MacCarthy was deeply engaged and provided the preface and six chapters. Donnachadh O'Hannigan, one of the most prominent IRA leaders in the Limerick sector (to whom MacCarthy had acted as adjutant) also wrote two chapters. A presentation copy given by MacCarthy to the O'Hannigan family noted that his comrade could well have written a great deal extra. The inscription read: 'in tribute to his old comrade-in-arms ... who figures so prominently in this book (and who figured even more than the limited scope of the volume could adequately record)'.[6] It is unclear why this did not occur, although the desirability of including other voices may have been a concern.

A number of nationally famous names were represented in both editions, not least Madge Daly of Limerick city's best known Irish Republican Brotherhood (IRB) dynasty. Piaras Béaslaí of IRA general headquarters contributed a general foreword and a chapter on 1916 martyr Edward Daly, brother of Madge and brother-in-law of Tom Clarke. The collective intimacy of the group is illustrated by the fact that Madge Daly had also known Seán Heuston when he was in the Limerick city Na Fianna Éireann along with Con Colbert of Athea, Limerick. Heuston and Colbert were shot in Kilmainham, Dublin, in the aftermath of the 1916 Rising.[7]

Interweaved strands of personal contact provide much of the anecdotal wealth of both books and permeate the bulk of the segments concerning the advent and course of the War of Independence in Limerick. Survivors of a coterie which had coalesced under the banner of the republican movement were reunited in print to relate the stories of episodes and individuals of which they had direct knowledge. The primacy of the first-hand perspective not only informed the selection of incidents discussed, but also strongly influenced their evaluations of the past. The uneven division of labour and imperfect chronology did not evince a project driven by a stringent or sophisticated editorial line. The tone of the book is emphatically republican, unapologetic and at times verges on hagiographic veneration of its subjects. If typical of the heroic phase of Irish history writing, the harsh content imparted ensured that it was by no means a romantic fantasy.

Chapter titles signal from the outset that the IRA rescue of Seán Hogan was 'daring' whereas killings carried out by the British army in Castleconnell were 'cold-blooded murders'. Yet MacCarthy included unflattering truths such as the loss of vital weapons dumps and misfired ambushes. No attempt is made to gloss over the fact that many Volunteers recruited during the 1918 'Conscription Crisis' could not be retained. More seriously, it is acknowledged that a security lapse in the foothills of the Galtee Mountains created a situation in which chance alone saved the East Limerick flying column from encirclement and probable disaster. Contributors must have been conscious that their representation of incidents was open to repudiation. Dan Breen's precociously early volume, *My Fight for Irish Freedom*, had elicited a vociferous backlash following publication in 1924. As late as 1948 Tom Barry drafted a blunt corrective to allegedly erroneous comments published in 1926 by Piaras Béaslaí.[8] Whereas the authors of *Limerick's Fighting Story* could consider subtle elisions and minor exaggerations, gross misrepresentation of basic facts was impossible. Multiple writers spread the responsibility for creating a fair record whilst creating a mutual interest in the composite product. At a time when individual reputations were in focus this methodology cultivated a degree of moral authority.[9]

The book was intended to sit amongst the limited bibliography of the War of Independence. In the course of a wider themed chapter, O'Hannigan referred to a report of the Dromkeen ambush he had prepared for *An t-Óglach*, an illegal and ephemeral IRA publication which few could have accessed.[10] The second Limerick volume, however, contained MacCarthy's version of events at Dromkeen, written from his vantage as O'Hannigan's adjutant.[11] *Limerick's Fighting Story* was evidently geared towards securing Limerick's claim to a prime position on the republican pantheon. This entailed grappling with problematic themes, not least the failure of the city and county Volunteers to rise in 1916 and the anomalous experience of a city 'soviet' in 1919.

The Limerick Volunteers were expected to play their part in the Easter Rising, 1916. Two were directly involved in the doomed attempt to liaise with the *Aud* conveying vital firearms and ammunition from Germany to the coast of Kerry. The decision to scuttle the cargo produced the countermanding order from Eoin MacNeill that paralysed Limerick and other sectors when the leadership adhering to Tom Clarke, Pádraig Pearse, *et al*, forged on regardless on 24 April. After much internal wrangling the decision of Volunteer Commandant Michael Colivet to surrender part of the city's armament to Mayor Stephen Quin of Limerick, a suspected unionist, confirmed that the local units would not rise. If ultimately vindicated by the executive of the Irish Volunteers, the inactivity of the sector cast a long shadow.[12] The slow deterioration in relations between what the British regarded as the lawful authority and that recognised by many Irish people was exemplified by the general strike of 14–25 April 1919. The 'Limerick Soviet', as it became known, evoked the successful Bolshevik bid for power in Russia in 1917, although this was clearly not attempted in Ireland. The incident was triggered by the unwise decision of the Brigadier-General C.J. Griffin to impose intolerable conditions on the freedom of movement of city workers and residents. The draconian Defence of the Realm Act (DORA) was used to designate Limerick as a 'special military area' but the army held back from direct confrontation.[13]

The catalyst for popular unrest was the death of IRA officer and union activist Robert 'Bobby' Byrne. He had been jailed on arms charges in January 1919 and as O/C of the IRA prisoners in Limerick jail embarked on a hunger strike to secure better conditions of confinement. On being moved to the Limerick Workhouse (aka Union Infirmary), an IRA squad led by Michael Stack attempted a rescue on 6 April. One RIC (Royal Irish Constabulary) member was mortally wounded, as was Byrne, who expired that night near Meelick, County Clare. Martial law was declared in the city on 9 April to prevent Byrne's funeral degenerating into a riot and on 14 April the Limerick Trades and Labour Council ordered a general strike. Up to 15,000 men effectively took over the city which was then cordoned off by the military. Defusing the situation required the intercession of the Catholic Bishop of Limerick, Denis Hallinan, and the Sinn Féin Lord Mayor, Alphonsus O'Mara. The strikers issued paper currency endorsed 'The workers of Limerick … against British militarism' and printed a newssheet.[14]

The bulk of *Limerick's Fighting Story* concerns the War of Independence which commenced near Soloheadbeg, Tipperary, on 21 January 1919. This coincided with the inaugural session of the First Dáil in the Mansion House, Dublin, which was dominated by Sinn Féin following their triumph in the December 1918 general election. The small IRA detachment in Tipperary shot and killed two members of an RIC patrol whom they had targeted over a number of days. The purpose of this unilateral action was evidently to press Sinn Féin to utilise its electoral mandate in pursuance of the Republic and to follow its declaration of sovereignty in Dublin with an endorsement of an IRA offensive.[15] The groundswell of unrest gained strength in Limerick city. On 1 February 1920 a British soldier was shot and wounded on O'Connell Avenue and an RIC sergeant was seriously injured three weeks later on William Street. Constable Murphy of the RIC was wounded in Thomas Street on 10 March, as was Sergeant Conroy the following week. The RIC were further provoked by the IRA's seizure of the mails on Davis Street on 9 March. Such activities were calculated to disrupt official administration, pressurise the police and gain intelligence. Low-level operations provided practical experience to the Volunteers and helped test unit security, command and capacity.

The RIC's inability to maintain a semblance of law and order in much of rural Ireland was addressed by the formation of the 'Black and Tans' in January 1920 and 'Auxiliaries' in July. Many of these ex-soldiers engaged in casual murder, assault and theft and succeeded in driving many nationalists towards tacit or active support for the IRA. Well-founded accounts of military depredations disconcerted British liberals and may have boosted London's interest in a negotiated settlement in 1920–21. *Limerick's Fighting Story* recounted numerous claims of military brutality and indiscriminate violence, instances which served to contextualise if not also justify the vigorous prosecution of revolutionary warfare by the IRA. The counter-insurgency strategy managed from Dublin Castle did not spare prominent republicans. On 20 March 1920 an RIC death squad led by District Inspector (DI) Oswald Swanzy smashed their way into the Cork home of Tomás MacCurtain and shot him dead. He was the Sinn Féin lord mayor of Cork and an IRA brigade commander. Similar events in Limerick the following year proved that the assassination in Cork was no aberration.[16] By April 1920 the RIC had ceded so much social and moral control that over five hundred bases had to be abandoned. The vacuum was filled by the robust counter-authority of Dáil Éireann, the Dáil courts and the IRA. On 4 April 1920 republicans burned approximately three hundred vacated barracks to ensure the permanent destruction of the infrastructure of repression.

On the night of 3–4 April 1920 Davy Dundon led part of 'C' company, 2nd battalion, Mid-Limerick brigade on a raid of the O'Connell Street tax offices and seized valuable documents. Joe O'Brien led 'D' company into the tax offices on Rutland Street, which, like those attacked by Dundon, was saved by the fire brigade when torched. Welsh Fusiliers responded by running amok and shooting dead a publican in Roche's Street and an usherette in the Coliseum Cinema. If anything, the deaths of innocents spurred the IRA to greater exertions. Unoccupied RIC barracks at Kilmurry, Ballinacurra and Blackboy Pike were razed on 9 April, a level of arson which underlined the strength of the IRA in the communities in which they lived.[17] Driving the British out of Ireland, however, necessitated removing them from strategic complexes they were prepared to defend. On 27 April 1920 the East Limerick brigade, backed by the South Tipperary brigade, struck an impressive blow in this regard by capturing Ballylanders RIC barracks. Tom Malone commanded on the occasion. Francis Costello in *The Irish Revolution* pinpointed the importance of core IRB activists and suggests that their militancy was a significant factor in securing the hitherto unparalleled success.[18] Improved tactics ensured that Kilmallock RIC barracks fell on 28–9 May 1920 in an attack which aroused particular attention given that the IRA succeeded where the Fenian assault in 1867 had failed.[19] MacCarthy's account of Ballylanders avoided direct comment on the fact that the incident helped resolve a damaging dispute between groupings aligned to Liam Manahan and Donnchadh O'Hannigan. MacCarthy only references factionalism within the East Limerick brigade in terms of the inactivity it caused.[20]

Seán Wall, a key figure in Sinn Féin and the East Limerick brigade, played a critical role in the Kilmallock victory. Wall's maternal uncle had taken part in the Fenian attempt and his reprise hastened his rise to the chairmanship of Limerick County Council.[21] Wall died in disputed circumstances on 6 May 1921 when republicans alleged he was summarily executed by the RIC once separated from associates near Annacarty, Tipperary.[22] By then the Limerick man had garnered sufficient kudos to become the subject of one of MacCarthy's chapters in *Limerick's Fighting Story*. The fact that Malone did not receive a discrete biographical sketch is explained by his good fortune in surviving the conflict rather than his roots outside the county. Equally daring was the Limerick city ambush of a Black and Tan patrol on 20 June 1920. William Barrett led part of 'E' company, Mid-Limerick brigade, in an attack on Henry Street in which one Tan was shot dead and two others disarmed. It was not deemed necessary to kill all three as the procurement of weapons was deemed a priority. Two ex-soldiers were acquitted of the killing, one of whom, Patrick Blake, had a brother shot dead by an RIC death squad at Oola. The other accused man, Jimmy O'Neil, was separately accosted on his return journey and shot by the RIC.

In mid to late August 1920, a series of incidents in the city led to the death of another Black and Tan and two RIC sergeants in Mallow Street. An escaping IRA prisoner, Michael Scanlon of Galbally, was tracked to a house in Little Catherine Street and mortally wounded by an Auxiliary on 27 October 1920. The tri-colour was taken from his coffin in William Street en route for burial but replaced by another before interment. This event was in turn avenged on 20 November

1920 when General Prescott Dieces, an intelligence expert, narrowly survived an attack on O'Connell Avenue. Two senior staff officers were wounded despite being escorted by Crossley tenders. Ireland was becoming ungovernable by any normal standards.[23] The ebb and flow of the unprecedented guerrilla campaign, replete with local detail and personalities, is well documented in *Limerick's Fighting Story*.

The county was distinguished in the annals of the IRA by virtue of being the first to develop the 'flying column' tactic. Fenians had manoeuvred with surprising freedom around Dublin, Limerick and Cork in 1867, but much of the continuity of theory and practice was lost in the long decades running down to 1919. In June 1920 the East Limerick flying column was assembled in order to maximise the impact of a comparatively small number of well-armed Volunteers. Inspiration was evidently taken from the Boer 'Commandoes' extolled by Arthur Griffith's *United Irishman* newspaper in 1899–1902, but Irish conditions shaped the variant used in the War of Independence. The decision to move with firearms in daylight was politically significant as it exemplified IRA confidence of popular support and combat readiness.

Compact locally recruited guerrilla forces were well suited to move cross-country and initiate opportunist attacks. In cases where good intelligence was available, combined columns were used to mount major ambushes. Personnel were typically highly motivated, well led and equipped with the best quality weaponry at the disposal of brigade level quartermasters. The IRA's limited stock of war material was replenished by successful encounters with the British and, while ammunition remained scarce throughout the conflict, the columns received the lion's share. In June 1920 Donnchadh O'Hannigan and Paddy Clancy were instrumental in putting this ambitious proposition to the test. Columns of twenty to forty men quickly proved themselves the equal of any similarly sized body of enemy regulars. British forces were obliged to commit large numbers of troops to generally fruitless and demoralising sweeping operations. If contact was established with the IRA under such conditions, their quarry invariably broke through the periphery of the cordon. Initiative and surprise often determined which protagonist secured a favourable casualty ratio and the intelligence sources available to the British military did not yield major success in the course of the conflict. Limerick, Tipperary and Cork fared better than other parts of the country where circumstances were less favourable.[24]

The survival of Limerick IRA activists was in no small part due to the republican counter-intelligence capacity which was as effective and ruthless as the campaign demanded. Identified informers were shot without compunction, in some cases by ex-members of the British army. While IRA GHQ did not deem it necessary to seed rural brigades with specially tasked units such as the Dublin 'Squad', certain Limerick City Volunteers were to the fore in shooting informers on the Canal Bank near Park Street and at other locations.[25] The necessity of such drastic actions was illustrated by the fate of Tom Malone who underwent extreme interrogation when captured by Auxiliaries in Cork in December 1920. Malone very probably avoided immediate execution by virtue of an elaborate cover identity which kept him alive long enough to mount a jailbreak.[26]

The Dromkeen ambush of 3 February 1921 was one of the most decisive of its kind. Hard won experience encouraged diligent planning and IRA surveillance; tactics, field craft and execution were excellent. The chance to spring a major ambush on a small convoy of Black and Tans and RIC drew the East Limerick and Mid-Limerick flying columns together to provide the requisite balance of forces.[27] The infliction of eleven fatalities on the Tans and RIC for just one wounded republican was a major success in the wake of a series of reverses. A combination of the brutal conduct of the military in Limerick in preceding months and a directive from IRA GHQ sealed the fate of the two healthy combatants taken prisoner at Dromkeen. Tom Toomey has established that a former member of the British army shot the pair while two of their badly wounded comrades were being medically attended.[28] This was obscured in MacCarthy's Dromkeen chapter in *Limerick's Fighting Story* which did, however, note the 'determined fight against hopeless odds' by several defenders.[29]

On 7 March 1921 George Clancy and Michael O'Callaghan were shot dead in their homes. Both had served as Sinn Féin mayors in a corporation controlled by the party since January 1920. Joseph O'Donoghue was also killed during the night of the 'curfew murders'.[30] It transpired that Major George Nathan, a British intelligence officer based in Dublin Castle, had led the assassins in Limerick. Nathan was destined to die fighting with the 15th International Brigade in Spain in 1937 alongside a number IRA veterans of the Irish War of Independence in Munster.[31] His actions in 1921 did nothing to reconcile the population to the administration responsible for carrying them out.

The original readership of *Limerick's Fighting Story* were apprised that the last men from the county to be executed under British rule remained interred in Mountjoy prison, Dublin. Edward Foley and Patrick Maher were implicated in the Knocklong ambush of May 1919 yet held until 7 June 1921 when they were shot in Dublin. In October 2001 these final two of the 'Mountjoy Ten' were reburied in their native county.[32] As important political legacies of the revolutionary period inch towards closure, Mercier Press have reissued *Limerick's Fighting Story*. This new life of a classic of its genre will facilitate a fresh evaluation of its unique perspectives on the genesis of the modern Irish state.

1   *Limerick's Fighting Story 1916–21, Told By The Men Who Made It* (Tralee 1948).
2   Colonel J.M. MacCarthy (ed.), *Limerick's Fighting Story, from 1916 to the Truce with Britain*, 2nd revised edition (Tralee 1966). All citations refer to the MacCarthy edition.

3   Information of Tom Toomey, 26 March 2009. IRA veteran Tom Malone (aka 'Seán Forde') was irritated by Seán O'Riordan's pseudonymous attempt to minimise his major role in the Ballylanders and Kilmallock operations. This grievance was undoubtedly sharpened by rivalry emanating from the Civil War and subsequent party political allegiances.

4   Florence O'Donoghue, *No Other Law* (Dublin, 1954).

5   Three of MacCarthy's chapters and Béaslaí's generic introduction also appeared in *With the IRA in the Fight for Freedom, 1919 to the Truce, The Red Path of Glory* (Tralee, n. d.). The preface of the book outlined *The Kerryman*'s policy of producing a collection of 'in a cheap and handy form'. *Ibid.*, p. 2.

6   See image of title page on www.philcleary.com.au. (Accessed 20 March 2009). O'Hannigan died in Dublin in August 1962. See *Irish Times*, 27 August 1962.

7   For the Daly family in Limerick see Nora de hOir, *Laochra Luimnigh, Uí Dhálaigh Luimnigh agus Éirí Amach na Cásca 1916*, pamphlet, Dublin, 2001 and Piaras F. Mac Lochlainn, *Last words, Letters and Statements of the Leaders Executed after the Rising at Easter 1916* (Dublin, 1990), pp. 65–74. The Daly Papers are in the Special Collections of the University of Limerick Library.

8   Tom Barry, *Guerrilla Days in Ireland* (Dublin, 1962), p. 136. The book was completed by Barry in 1948 and first published by the *Irish Press* in 1949. The Corkman objected to Béaslaí's contention in *Michael Collins and the Making of a New Ireland* (New York, 1926) that Munster area IRA officers informed GHQ in 1921 of their incapacity to maintain the campaign (Barry, *Guerrilla Days*, p. 136).

9   The book was well if not extensively reviewed. See *Nenagh Guardian*, 6 and 13 August 1966.

10   *Limerick's Fighting Story*, p. 89.

11   *Ibid.*, p. 124. O'Hannigan also sided with the Free State in 1922 and was central to efforts to avoid a bloody conflict in Limerick city. See Liam Deasy, *Brother Against Brother* (Cork, 1998), pp. 65, 91.

12   See John O'Callaghan, 'The Limerick Volunteers and 1916', in Ruán O'Donnell (ed.) *The Impact of 1916, Among the Nations* (Dublin, 2008), pp. 1–23. See also Charles Townshend, *Easter 1916, The Irish Rebellion* (London, 2005), pp. 231–2

13   For the impact of the DORA see Brian P. Murphy, OSB, 'The Wind that shakes the Barley: Reflections on the writing of Irish history in the period of the Easter Rising and the Irish War of Independence' in O'Donnell (ed.) *Impact of 1916*, pp. 200–20.

14   See Liam Cahill, *Forgotten Revolution, Limerick Soviet 1919, A threat to British power in Ireland* (Dublin, 1990), p. 76.

15   Interview with Paddy Ryan, Dublin, 4 December 2004.

16 For Swanzy see Jim McDermott, *Northern Divisions, The Old IRA and the Belfast pogroms, 1920–22* (Belfast, 2001), p. 50.

17 *Limerick's Fighting Story*, p. 158.

18 Francis Costello, *The Irish Revolution and its Aftermath, 1916-1923* (Dublin, 2003), pp. 51–2.

19 *Limerick's Fighting Story*, p. 23.

20 See Tom Malone, *Alias Seán Forde, The Story of Commandant Thomas Malone, Vice O.C. East Limerick flying column, Irish Republican Army* (Dublin, 2000), p. 41.

21 *Limerick's Fighting Story*, pp. 52-3.

22 *Ibid.*, p. 55.

23 *Ibid.*, pp. 159-3.

24 See Joost Augusteijn, *From Public Defiance to Guerrilla Warfare, the Experience of Ordinary Volunteers in the Irish War of Independence, 1916-1921* (Dublin, 1996), Chapter Four.

25 Interview with John Moloney, New York, 5 October 2007.

26 Malone, *Alias Seán Forde*, pp. 72–6.

27 See [Tom Toomey], *The Dromkeen Ambush, 3rd February 1921*, pamphlet [2009].

28 [Toomey], *Dromkeen Ambush*, (n. p.).

29 *Limerick's Fighting Story*, p. 128.

30 Matthew Potter, *The Government and the People of Limerick, The History of Limerick Corporation/ City Council 1197–2006* (Limerick, 2006), pp. 376–81.

31 Seán Cronin, *Frank Ryan, The Search for the Republic* (Dublin, 1980), pp. 120-21.

32 *Limerick Leader*, 20 October 2001 and *Irish Times*, 13 October 2001. See also the National Graves Association pamphlet *Honouring the Mountjoy Martyrs (The Forgotten Ten)* (Dublin, 2001).

Dr Ruán O'Donnell

University of Limerick

March 2009

FOREWORD

ALMOST THIRTY YEARS ago a small body of men engaged in combat with the armed force of an empire. Militarily they were weak. Their strength lay in their faith in their cause and in the unflinching support of a civilian population which refused to be cowed by threats or by violence.

For almost two years these men successfully maintained the unequal struggle and finally compelled their powerful adversary to seek a truce. The battles in which they fought were neither large nor spectacular: they were the little clashes of guerrilla warfare – the sudden meeting, the flash of guns, a getaway, or the long wait of an ambush, then the explosive action, and death or a successful decision. And the stake at issue was the destiny of an ancient people.

Before the war years imposed a restriction upon newsprint, as upon other commodities, *The Kerryman*, in its various Christmas and other special numbers, told much of the story of these men, the men of the flying columns, the active service units of the Irish Republican Army. It now gathers these stories into book form together with others hitherto unpublished. First in the series was *Rebel Cork's Fighting Story*; *Kerry's Fighting Story* followed. Now *Limerick's Fighting Story* is presented.

All the stories in these *Fighting Series* booklets are either told by the men who took part in the actions described, or else they are written from the personal narrative of survivors. The booklets do not purport to be a detailed or chronological history of the fight for independence, but every effort has been made to obtain the fullest and most accurate information about the incidents described. The publishers are conscious, however, that in the collection of data about such a period errors and omissions can easily occur and so they will welcome the help of readers who may be able to throw more light upon the various episodes related in the series. Such additional information will be incorporated to the second edition of the booklets which the present rate of orders would seem to indicate will be called for in the future.

The Publishers believe that the younger generation who know about those times by hearsay only will find these survivors' tales of the fight of absorbing interest, while to the older generation they will recall vividly a memorable era and the men who made it. In short, they feel that *Fighting* series, the story of the Anglo-Irish War county by county, is a series that will be welcomed by Irish people everywhere. For that reason, so that the booklets may have the widest possible circulation, they are being sold at a price within the reach of everyone. To sell these booklets, with their lavish collection of illustrations of unique historical interest, at the very moderate price of two shillings, the publishers were content to reduce their own profit and to produce the booklet at little above the mere cost of production. They will be satisfied if the series serve to preserve in the hearts of the younger generation that love of country and devotion to its interests which distinguished the men whose doings are related therein.

The Editor

THE IRISH VOLUNTEERS IN LIMERICK CITY

by A.J. O'HALLORAN

On 14 December 1913, a conference was held in the council chamber, Town Hall, Limerick, to consider the advisability of inaugurating a corps of the Irish Volunteers in the city. It had been convened under the following circumstances. There were two organisations primarily interested in the project – the Irish Republican Brotherhood and the Ancient Order of Hibernians. The AOH, though but recently introduced locally, was numerically very strong, and was, for several reasons, regarded with jealous disfavour by many of the other societies. Realising this, the members felt that if they were to take the initiative, it would militate against the success of a movement which was intended to embrace all sections of the community, so patriotically they refrained from making the attempt. On the other hand, the IRB, comparatively weak in numbers, wielded disproportionate power, because working *sub rosa*, they exercised influence in many and unexpected quarters. They also felt that if their open organisation, the Wolfe Tone club, were to undertake the task, the Volunteers would come into existence with the brand of intransigence, and having regard to the timorous attitude of the people generally to anything that savoured of 'Fenianism', it was not considered politic to launch the movement under its auspices. However, liaison was established between the two bodies, and arrangements made for a meeting on the day stated.

Informal invitations were conveyed to all cultural, friendly, political and labour societies in the city, but it was intimated that no delegates need be appointed, and that everyone who attended would do so in his individual capacity. The meeting took place as arranged, and was characterised by the utmost harmony. Mr James Ledden presided, and Mr C.C. Cregan acted as secretary. Amongst those who attended as recorded in the original minutes in the possession of Mr Cregan were:

Messrs John Dalton, BC, High St; J.P. O'Connor, 17 Hartstonge St; Daniel Bourke, 47 Rosboro' Rd.; Denis Curtin, 1 Bowman St; Joseph Halpin, Garryowen; Edward Fitzgibbon, 41 O'Connell Street; Garret O'Hanlon, Green Hill; P. Whelan, 22 Mt Pleasant Avenue; Michael Brennan, Meelick Cross; J.J. O'Beirne, 15 Emmet Place; Thomas Ryan, 17 Patrick St; James Quigley, do.; J. Brouder, do.; James Gubbins, 17 Thomas St; Seán Ó Murthuile do.; William O'Sullivan, do.; Peter McMahon, do.; George Clancy, do.; Joseph Purcell, do.; John Wixted, do.; Thomas O'Donnell, 16 Arthur's Quay; W.J. Fitzgerald, 8 Crescent Avenue; A.J. Blake, King's Island; C. Thompson, 63 Catherine St; J. Foley, 7 Sandmall; M.J. O'Brien, 12 Rutland St; A.J. O'Halloran, 6 Sexton St; John Lehane, F. McNamara (City Technical Institute); Richard Hogan, 22 Bowman St; William Barton, 6 Lower Henry St; William Henry, 15 Emmet Place; Liam Forde, 2 Church St; David Benson, 19 Ellen St; Martin Fitzpatrick, 27 Charlotte Quay; John McCaull, 11 Caledonia Terrace; Patrick O'Mara, 2 Little Newenham St; James Ledden, Thomas St; B. Collins, 14 Caledonia Place; P. Killeen, 2 Myles St; John McMahon, 2 St Joseph's Terrace; George Benson, 19 Ellen St; Thomas Devanny, 35 Pennywell; Joseph Dalton, Rutland St, and C.C. Cregan, 40 Mill View Terrace.

It was unanimously decided to arrange for a public meeting at which the movement could be formally launched, and the following were appointed a provisional committee, with the power of co-option, to carry out the work: Messrs George Clancy, P. O'Halloran, J.P.

O'Connor, J. Brouder, F. McNamara, James Dalton, E. Fitzgibbon, A.J. O'Halloran, M. Fitzpatrick, P. Clarke, J. Quigley, P. Whelan, P. O'Sullivan, James Ledden, and C.C. Cregan. Curiously enough, representation on the committee was shared equally by the IRB and the AOH.

The first meeting was held on 17 December, 1913, when preliminary talks as to the proposed public meeting took place, and the following were co-opted members: Messrs M.P. Colivet, 2 Castle View Terrace; M. Moore, O'Connell Avenue; P. Kelly, Thomas Devanny, Pennywell; John McSweeney, Mungret St, and T. Ryan, 17 Patrick St. Quite informally, those present discussed scenes that had occurred on 14 December in Cork, when at a public meeting held to establish a Volunteer corps, the platform had been stormed by men stated in the press to be members of the AOH, and the chairman, Mr J.J. Walsh, and others were brutally assaulted. It was considered that this outbreak had origin in the hostility prevailing in the southern capital between the followers of William O'Brien and the adherents of the Irish Parliamentary Party under John Redmond, and holding no significance for Limerick.

The next meeting of the committee was held on 22 December, and at this the members associated with the AOH sprang a surprise by urging that having regard to the turmoil in Cork, it would be well to await further developments before making definite arrangements for a public meeting. This was strongly combated by other members, and eventually it was decided to adjourn consideration to the next meeting. This was held early in the New Year, and when the matter came up for discussion, two or three members of the AOH supported the proposal to go on with the arrangements, and so the meeting was held.

It was ascertained later that the attitude of the AOH was the outcome of a confidential circular which had been sent to all divisions of the order counselling them to a certain course of action with regard to the movement. This was a most unwise proceeding, foreshadowing the disastrous effect of the attempt made by John Redmond at a later stage to capture control of the Volunteer organisation. No fear of such a lamentable development crossed the mind of any one present in the Athenaeum Hall on Sunday evening, 25 January 1914, when the mayor, Alderman P. O'Donovan, presiding, a crowded audience cheered to the echo as Pádraig Pearse and Roger Casement appealed to them to enlist in the Irish Volunteers. Elaborate arrangements had been made to deal with a possible disturbance, but these were not necessary, because no more unanimous or enthusiastic meeting had ever been held in Limerick, and practically every man present 'joined up'. Thereafter, the work of organising proceeded apace. Offices were opened at No. 1 Hartstonge Street, where enrolments took place nightly. It had been decided to organise on a territorial basis, and the regiment was divided into eight companies corresponding to the eight wards into which the city was partitioned for the purpose of municipal government. Care was taken to file separately the application forms of those who had service in the British army, with a view to establishing a section of drill instructors. Mr John Holland, who had been a member of a cadet corps, being appointed in charge, with the title of lieutenant.

At first, company drill was taught in a number of more or less unsuitable premises in different parts of the city, but eventually the use of the Butter Market Hall, and the Corn Market was secured and proved ideal for the purposes of the regiment. There, every Sunday, and on one evening in each week, parades were held, and the utmost enthusiasm and earnestness were displayed. Co-option took place at almost every meeting of the committee, so that eventually it become rather an unwieldy body, but no attempt was ever made to 'pack' in the interests of any section. Yet, despite that fact, there was an undercurrent of dissatisfaction prevailing amongst the rank and file, though the committee had announced their intention of holding an election at an early date.

Almost from the beginning, the provisional committee had

appointed a sub-committee under the title of military committee, which, as its name denotes, was intended to deal with matters of a purely military nature, such as the procuring of equipment. The records of the committee's proceedings have been lost, but it became, in effect, an executive body, which would make decisions on matters of an urgent nature. The personnel were practically that of the original provisional committee.

The first conflict of opinion was manifested at a meeting of the provisional committee held on 26 May 1914, when some of the members commented strongly on the fact that no public parade of the regiment had been ordered for the previous day to celebrate the third passing of the Home Rule Bill in the House of Commons. A long discussion ensued, but ended amicably.

Elections for the different offices, and a board of management were held on 25 June, when the following were declared elected: president, James Ledden; commander, John Holland; recording secretary, R.P. O'Connor; financial secretary, Liam Forde; organising secretary, James Dalton; hon. treasurer, P. O'Halloran; trustees, E. O'Toole and William Ebrill; committee, George Clancy, John Lehane, Michael Hartigan, M.P. Colivet, John Grant and C.P. Close. It has been found impossible to ascertain the total number in the regiment at that time; estimates vary from 1,200 to 2,000, but it was probably about 1,400. Yet not even 500 exercised the franchise at that election. And still the fact remains, that although most of those elected had not hitherto identified themselves with any political party, and only four of them were members of the IRB, the hostility that had manifested itself against the provisional committee was to be transferred to the board of management almost immediately after the election. In the month of July, the election of company officers took place, it being arranged that the first three heading the poll in each company would be provisionally selected as captain, 1st and 2nd lieutenant, but would have to undergo one month's special training and probation before appointment. The results of this election are not available.

On 10 August, the board of management passed a resolution having reference to certain declaration made by Mr John Redmond, and ending: 'That we are intended for the rights and liberties of the people of Ireland, and not for the crown or for the empire and if the conditions of service are considered by us to offend our national honour, dignity or self-respect, as Irishmen to whom Ireland comes first, we shall decline to accept same.' It was ordered that this should be sent to the provisional committee, Dublin, with a request that the position would be clarified. Seemingly, no comment on, or even acknowledgement of, this resolution was ever received. On 26 August, Seán MacDermott was on a visit to Limerick, and being a member of the provisional committee, called to the Markets to witness the Volunteers on parade. The board of management took advantage of his presence to hold a special meeting in order to point out of him how the resolution had been ignored, but he stated that he could not throw any light on the matter, as he had been away from Dublin for some time. At the request of the board, Seán MacDermott consented to address the Volunteers at the finish of drill. Apart from complimenting the regiment on their smart turnout, and referring in glowing terms to the Volunteers who had received the guns at Howth, he said very little, but the fact that he was allowed to speak at the parade at all created umbrage amongst a certain section, because he was prominently identified with what was termed in ignorance – the Sinn Féin movement.

On 18 September, 1914, the Home Rule Bill received the Royal assent, but with the proviso that it was not to come into operation for a minimum period of twelve months, or until the war was ended, and at the parade at on Sunday 26 September, a manifesto from the drill instructors, who were then acting as company commanders, was handed in. It expressed dissatisfaction with the refusal of the board of management to order a public parade through the city in celebration of that event, and also made certain demands connected with the general administration of the board. At the parade held on

Wednesday 23 September matters moved to a climax. There was a regular *émeute*, and for a while things looked dangerous. Eventually the parade broke up in disorder, but without any violence being used. This was the parting of the ways. Those who believed in the wisdom of John Redmond's policy took one path; those who adhered to the original constitution of the Irish Volunteers, the other.

Of the 1,400 estimated members of the regiment, how many remained Irish Volunteers? At the first parade after the split, about two hundred and fifty mustered, but there were powerful factors at work against the organisation. The war fever had gripped Ireland through the cleverness of English propaganda, and probably more than 90 per cent of the population regarded anyone who was not 'pro-Ally' as a traitor. Hence, 'pressure' in business and employment circles was brought to bear on the so-called 'Sinn Féin Volunteers', with the result that the weak-kneed succumbed. From a regimental roll in the possession of Mr M.P. Colivet, commandant, it is obvious that there was an immediate falling off in numbers. At the first recorded parade which was held on 4 October 1914, two hundred and eight were present, and exactly the same number attended on Sunday 11 October; but never again, until the threat of conscription came to swell the ranks, were there as many Volunteers on parade. The average attendance was little more than one hundred. Of the board of management the following members served their connection with the Irish Volunteers: Messrs John Holland and C.P. Close, while for business reasons, Mr J. Lehane had to retire. Some time subsequently the following were co-opted members: Rev. Fr Hennessy, OSA, and Michael O'Callaghan.

Before the split, a number of guns had been secured and these, with some 20,000 rounds of .303 ammunition, had been entrusted to the keeping of people who had remained to faithful to the ideals of the Irish Volunteers. Arrangements were soon made to have them distributed amongst the rank and file. It is impossible to state now with exactitude how many were available but the total number was probably about one hundred and thirty, most of them being Lee-Enfields, including some twenty Mark IVs, about fifty Martinis and the remainder shotguns. Practically all the revolvers and automatic pistols carried by the officers were of small calibre. Mr M.P. Colivet, who had been adjutant of the regiment previous to the split, was appointed commandant, and thereafter the Volunteers took to the work of learning the soldier's trade with the greatest earnestness. While one night each week saw them muster at the 'barracks', which was now transferred to the Fianna Hall, off Barrington Street, to receive instruction in various branches of military knowledge, practically every Sunday was devoted to long route marches and field work. Then, at intervals, bivouacs or all-night marches were arranged.

With the exception of Mr William Lawlor, all the military instructors had remained with the dissident majority. Consequently, the Volunteers would have been somewhat handicapped were it not that Captain Robert Monteith of 'A' company, Dublin brigade, was deported from Dublin and on invitation took up his residence in Limerick, where he acted as instructor, and organiser, both in the city and county. Having had long service, including war experience in the British army, and having acted as instructor to the Dublin brigade, he was an invaluable asset to the Limerick Volunteers.

No incident worthy of special mention occurred in connection with battalion until Whit Sunday, 23 May 1915, when certain events took place in the city which, for several reasons, deserve to be put on record, but rather have been unaccountably ignored by writers dealing with this period. 'A' company of the Dublin brigade had arranged for a train excursion to Limerick on that day, when they proposed to parade in full equipment through the city. Naturally they pushed the sale of tickets amongst other companies of the brigade, with the result that the idea of an armed parade in the 'City of the Violated Treaty' caught the imagination not only of Volunteers in the metropolis, but of those in Cork and elsewhere, and so Cork and Tipperary were also represented on that occasion. No attempt whatever was made by headquarters to make it a general parade, and it was learned that Volunteer corps in other counties had felt aggrieved that no opportunity to participate had been afforded them. Two special trains carrying some six hundred Volunteers, with hundreds of sympathisers and others, arrived from Dublin. A special also ran from Cork with about two hundred and fifty men, while Tipperary was represented about one hundred and fifty, chiefly drawn from the famous Galtee regiment. It is significant that another special from Dublin brought a battalion of British soldiers to augment an already strong garrison.

The arrangements of the day were as follows: The parade was to start from Pery Square at 1 p.m., and after traversing the main arteries of Newtownpery, including O'Connell Street, O'Connell Avenue and Boherbuidhe, pass through the Irish town and English-town, touch on Thomondgate by way of the Treaty Stone, and so back to the starting point through Sarsfield and O'Connell Streets. Incidentally, this was the route followed by all great religious and political procession for almost a century. It was intended that on arrival at Pery Square, a review of the Volunteers would be held in the People's Park. Thereafter, it was arranged the visiting corps would proceed to the Fianna Hall, where, if they so desired, they could stack their arms. The mayor had given permission for the use of the park, but withdrew it subsequently, and for the first time in a generation the park gates were kept locked on a Sunday.

Having regard to the state of public feeling at the time, it is questionable as to whether it was prudent to include the Boherbuidhe and Irish town districts in the line of march, since a very large proportion of the inhabitants of both quarters were connected either by ties of blood or friendship with the men serving in the British army. To make matters worse, the arrangements for the day's proceedings had been advertised in the local press, thus affording certain interested parties an opportunity of laying their plans accordingly. Information to the effect that a hostile reception was being planned was furnished by the intelligence staff of the Limerick regiment, but it was not anticipated that it would assume a serious form. Indeed it is morally certain that, left to themselves, any manifestation of ill-feeling on the part of the citizens would have been merely of a vocal nature. At all events, it would not have been possible at such a late stage to alter the proposed route of the march without loss of prestige, and so it was decided to adhere to it. Later in Whitsun week, Limerick headquarters learned that from some mysterious source, large sums of money had materialised to provide the dregs of the population with intoxicating drink on the day of the parade. The object was patent. Take an unpopular cause, and a few score rowdies primed with liquor, and no one can foretell what serious consequences may ensue. The plot failed, but the plotters could not blame their dupes; it was the wonderful discipline of the Irish Volunteers that foiled it. Certain specific instances of how the hidden hand worked might be given, but since many of the dupes afterwards made noble amends, no useful purpose could be served by doing so.

Altogether, there were about 1,200 in the parade, which started according to schedule, and as, headed by the hand of the Limerick regiment, they passed through the streets of the city, they should have inspired the respect, if not the admiration, of the citizens. Yet – and it may be difficult for the present generation to realise the fact – they could not have been regarded with more hatred had they been to a man goal birds of the vilest type. This was fruit of propaganda. Many of the Volunteers wore broken boots and shabby attire, because their scanty earnings were devoted to paying for the guns they carried; but in the eyes of the populace, they were traitors whose pockets were lined with German gold. Amongst the men who marched on that day were Pádraig Pearse, Tom Clarke, Willie Pearse, Liam Mellows, Seán MacDermott, Ned Daly, Terence MacSwiney, George Clancy, Tomás MacCurtain and scores of others who were destined before long to make the supreme sacrifice for Ireland.

No incident of note occurred until the parade reached Wolfe Tone Street, and here was observed that the windows of the new (now Sarsfield) military barracks, overlooking that thoroughfare, were filled with British soldiers, who, in their own inimitable lingo, jeered at the Volunteers. In view of the meticulous care that the British military authorities invariably took to secure that the rank-and-file did not indulge in political manifestations, it seems significant that in this occasion they were permitted to do so unchecked.

The march along the Boherbuidhe district was through a barrage of abuse from thousands of excited females, who hurled at the Volunteers such taunts, jeers, and reproaches as only the fertile wit of womankind can coin; but the men marched on with scarce a glance to right or left. It was not until the head of the column reached Irish Town that signs of a more malignant hostility became apparent. Mungret Street, its chief thoroughfare, is one of the oldest streets in the city, and behind it, on either side, lays the slum areas of Watergate and Palmerstown, which were wont to furnish some of the finest fighting material of the famous Munster Fusiliers.

The inhabitants, whose banked masses on both sides of the street scarcely sufficed a passage for the marching men, were not content with verbal compliments, but brought bottles, stones, and other missiles to reinforce them. They had been told that these men had cheered and gloated over every disaster that befell the Munsters in the war which was then raging, and so their hearts were filled with bitter hatred, of the 'pro-German Sinn Féiners', as they called the Irish Volunteers. It was calculated by plotters that Mungret Street, that street from which the women of 1690 had helped to hurl back the storm troops of William of Orange, would be the scene of an incident that would start a general conflagration. Some intoxicated rowdy would break through the ranks, some Volunteer would lose his head, shots would be fired, a general melee would ensue, and the tragedy of Bachelor's Walk would be repeated on a large scale. Then, what more simple? Irish public opinion being what it was at the time would not only demand, but insist, that the Volunteers should be disarmed. One can only speculate as to what the ultimate result might have been. But the plotters failed to take into account one very important factor – the morale of the Volunteers – and so, as oblivious of missiles as of insults, the green-clad ranks swept through that hostile mob as if bouquets were being showered on them, and their lines remained unbroken.

The remainder of the parade passed to Pery Square without incident. Owing to the fact that the Park gates had been kept specially locked on that day, it was not found feasible to hold the projected review. The visitors marched to the Fianna Hall, and having stacked arms, proceeded to seek refreshments, and to indulge in sight-seeing. Now that the parade was over, it was considered that all danger of a disturbance had passed, and the Volunteers generally were inclined to take a humorous view of the day's proceedings. They felt convinced that time was on their side and that in a short space the people would be with them.

But indications were soon forthcoming that the plotters had not yet abandoned the hope of achieving their object. Bands of intoxicated rowdies of both sexes roamed through the city attacking and maltreating not only the Volunteers, but lady visitors many of whom had no special sympathy with the 'Sinn Féiners' but had simply taken advantage of the cheap rail excursions. Each of the four companies of the Limerick regiment had taken turn in mounting guard over the arms stacked at the Fianna Hall, and it was found necessary, in consequence of reports arriving there, to dispatch detachments of Volunteers to protect the visitors from violence. In this connection it should be recorded that an officer of the Dublin brigade, a Captain Éamon de Valera, on going to the assistance of some ladies who were attacked by a mob in Parnell Street, was compelled to take refuge with them in a nearby licensed premises, whence they were rescued by a squad of Limerick Volunteers. Let it also be recorded that it was not until the Volunteers had been ordered to fix bayonets and load rifles that the mob could be brought to see reason. And all this time a number of members of the RIC stood by, either unable or unwilling to intervene!

In the meantime the instigators of the disturbance took advantage of a trifling incident to inflame public feeling to fever heat. An inquisitive urchin had got into the line of fire, when an enthusiastic 'pro-Ally' hurled a bottle at a Volunteer, with the result that his head was badly gashed. Hundreds who had not witnessed the incident saw the boy covered with blood, being rushed to hospital, and the story spread like wildfire that he had been shot by the 'Sinn Féiners'. Before another hour had passed, that boy had been metamorphosed into a score of men, women and children shot down into cold blood. The result was that thousands of decent men who, under ordinary circumstances, would never have countenanced an attack on the Volunteers, were stirred to frenzy, vowed vengeance on the 'murderers', and thronged the approaches to the railway terminus with the idea of wreaking it on the departing visitors.

It was now realised by Commandant Colivet and the staff of the Limerick regiment that the great problem was to get the Dublin, Cork and Tipperary corps entrained without provoking a serious conflict. The tempers of the rank-and-file of the local Volunteers were sorely frayed, not on their own account, but that they bitterly resented the treatment meted out to their brothers-in-arms, and so perhaps an order to deal drastically with the perpetrators of the day's outrages would not have been unwelcome to them. For this reason it was considered prudent to keep them standing to arms at the Fianna Hall while the visiting troops were marched to the terminus. Soon a report arrived that owing to the attitude of the mob it would not be possible for them to entrain without resorting to violence. The Limerick Volunteers were rushed to the double towards the scene, and had almost reached their objective when a messenger from Pádraig Pearse intercepted them with word to the effect that all was well, and that their services would not be required.

What had actually happened was that several of the local clergy, being apprised of the danger, hurried to the terminus and used their influence to quell the passions of the mob. Chief amongst them was the Rev. Fr Mangan, CSSR, who was then director of the Arch-Confraternity of the Holy Family, and who, apart from the powerful influence he wielded by virtue of that position, was personally very popular with the people generally. Mounting on a sidecar, he appealed to such members of the Confraternity as were on the scene to help to secure the safe departure of the visitors. His appeal was successful, and they co-operated with the members of the RIC who were present, under District Inspector Craig, in forming a passage through which the Volunteers and their friends entered the terminus. But even then some of the hooligan element, enclosed behind the cordons, struck at and injured a number of the Volunteers and tore nine or ten rifles from their hands. These guns were subsequently recovered, through the influence, I think, of Fr Mangan, and were returned to their owners.

The press of that time pictured more than a thousand Irish Volunteers flying in wild disorder before the women of Limerick, and being saved from utter rout by the efforts of the Royal Irish Constabulary, as anyone who cares to consults the files of those journals may see. That is why I considered it advisable to tell the true story of the Whit Sunday riots, while some two score Limerick Volunteers who participated in that parade survive to bear testimony to the fact that I have strictly adhered to truth, and that if I have erred, it has been on the side of moderation. In the years to follow many of the men who paraded that day were to give evidence of their selfless love of country; of their courage and daring in the face of overwhelming odds. That day in Limerick they gave absolute proof that they were disciplined soldiers, whose conduct and bearing under very great provocation could not have been surpassed by any body of veteran troops in the world.

The *Irish Volunteer* of 22 April 1916, carried a series of 'Notes from Headquarters' dealing with the projected Easter manoeuvres in which it was stressed that all units, even the smallest, should engage. It was specially emphasised that all Volunteers should parade with 'full equipment' which meant, full arms, ammunition and marching kit. However the 'notes' were so couched that no one could deduce from them that anything serious was afoot; but the secret 'orders' sent to the different commands were that at 7 p.m. on Easter Sunday they were to proclaim the Irish Republic and to go into action against the British forces.

Commandant M.P. Colivet, of the Limerick command, had eight battalions in his area, viz., one in the city, three in the county of Limerick, the latter including portion of Tipperary, and four in County Clare. But this statement must be qualified. A battalion comprises at the minimum five hundred men, and the city battalion at its fullest strength never mustered more than two hundred and five. This applied more or less to the other seven battalions. With the exception of the city battalion, all the others were most indifferently armed.

At Easter Week the officers of the battalion were as follows: 1st battalion Limerick City regiment: honorary colonel, James Ledden; commandant, M.P. Colivet; vice-commandant, George Clancy; Major J. McInerney; staff-engineers, Captain John Grant, Lieutenant J. McNulty; quartermaster, Captain P. Walsh; ambulance, Lieutenant J. Kirby; bandmaster, Lieutenant T. Glynn. 'A' company: captain, S. Dineen; 1st lieutenant, J. Gubbins; 2nd lieutenant, J.E. Cashin. 'B' company: captain, J. O'Donnell; 1st lieutenant, P. Whelan; 2nd lieutenant, F. Fitzpatrick. 'C' company: captain, Liam Forde; 1st lieutenant, A. Johnson; 2nd lieutenant, J. McKeown. 'D' company: captain, A. Kivlehan; 1st lieutenant, A.J. O'Halloran; 2nd lieutenant, R. Slattery. Lieutenant J.L. Connaughton (unattached).

Previous to the Easter Week period, the plan of operation approved for this command was, briefly, to hold the line of the Shannon from the Clare side. Some three weeks before Easter, the O/C received orders to 'hustle' things, and on the Tuesday of Holy Week, Seán

Fitzgibbon arrived with orders from headquarters to the effect that arms were to be landed in Kerry in a week or less; that Commandant Colivet was to arrange to have them received at Abbeyfeale, take what he required for his command, and have the remainder railed to Galway. Meantime, the enemy positions in the city were to be attacked with a view to facilitating the transfer of the arms train onto the Clare line. Subsequent to this, the outlying battalions would converge on the city, and the attack on the enemy would be pressed home. If, and when, matters had been stabilised in his area, the O/C was to move east.

As these orders obviously clashed with previously approved plans, Fitzgibbon advised Commandant Colivet to contact headquarters personally. He according did so, and Pádraig Pearse confirmed the orders brought by Fitzgibbon. On his return to Limerick, the O/C, with the battalion staff, drew up the following plans for carrying them into effect: *Basic Plan prepared by Wednesday night's conference at George Clancy's house, 19 April 1916.*

The city battalion was to move to Killonan on Sunday morning at ten, on an apparent two-day scheme of manoeuvres, and at 7 p.m. attack was to be opened on police and military barracks in the city, after cutting all telephone and telegraph wires, and demolishing rail connection with Limerick Junction and Dublin at Killonan and other suitable points. The objective was to keep the garrisons confined to barracks, without pressing home the attack, so as to enable the arms train from Kerry to go around the southern perimeter of the city by means of the railway loop-line, and across the Longpavement railway bridge into Clare, without being noticed or interrupted by the enemy. Later, when we received the armed reinforcements, the attack was to be pressed home.

Meanwhile, Major McInerney would go to Newcastlewest on the next day, take charge of all available units in West Limerick (rather poorly armed); post one party at Abbeyfeale to take over the train from the Kerry command; another at Newcastlewest to attack the police barracks and ensure that the arms train got safely through; and the remainder to attack and disarm all police units likely to interfere with the plan. Newcastlewest was a terminus station where all trains, including the engines, had to be reversed when passing up or down. It was very necessary to ensure that the delay thus caused was not used by the enemy to upset our plans. No overt action was to take place before 7 p.m. on Sunday. This proviso applied to all the operation plans for that day. As the train made its way up to Limerick every available Volunteer was to be armed and placed aboard, and at all stations a look-out was to be kept for such reinforcements.

The Galtee battalion was to put Charleville railway junction out of action, attack and disarm all police units in their district, and then move in towards Limerick city to take part in the reduction of the enemy there.

The Tipperary Town company was to act similarly with the Limerick Junction and the local police units, and then move towards Limerick city as soon as possible.

The Doon and Castleconnell units were to secure the lines Castleconnell–Killaloe and all the river crossings, demolish Birdhill junction, and link up with the city battalion and the Clare units.

In Clare, Captain Michael Brennan was to take charge of all Mid-Clare and East Clare units, take possession of Ennis and all stations up to Crusheen, attack and disarm all police units and then converge on the northern side of the river at the city, so as completely to surround it, and force an enemy surrender. All necessary arms were to be got from the train at Longpavement or other suitable station, and the Galway share to be conveyed to that command at Crusheen. In West Clare, Captain Paddy Brennan was to take command, collect all available units at Kilrush or thereabouts on Sunday, and seize sufficient boats to get his party across the Shannon to Tarbert or Ballylongford, whence he was to make for Listowel, or other suitable station, and come with it to Limerick. A good-sized party would be required to get the train past Newcastlewest.

Lieutenant McGee, of the Castleconnell company, who was then stationmaster at Castleconnell, was not in 'open' service at the time, but was acting in the 'Auxiliary' service. He was deputed to make all necessary contacts and arrangements with railway men to ensure the successful journey of the arms train.

When all was secured locally, we would make for Dublin.

***

ON EASTER SATURDAY morning the *Cork Examiner* carried a report relative to the discovery of a collapsible boat, pistol, etc., at Banna Strand, County Kerry. Commandant Colivet dispatched Lieutenant Whelan to Tralee to glean fuller information, and Seán Fitzgibbon hurried to Dublin for instruction in view of this development. He arranged to send a code message to the O/C as to whether things were 'on' or 'off'. Lieutenant Whelan returned from Tralee with the news that Austin Stack and Con Collins had been arrested, and that a ship supposed to be carrying arms had been sunk. Commandant Colivet sent Captain Forde and Lieutenant Gubbins to Dublin with this information, and on Saturday night, not having received any further word from headquarters, dispatched orders to all outlying battalions, cancelling previous ones, but arranging for the giving of fresh orders later. On Sunday morning, The O'Rahilly arrived with written orders from Eoin MacNeill: 'Volunteers completely deceived. All arrangements for tomorrow, Sunday, cancelled.' The O'Rahilly informed Commandant Colivet that there was a serious cleavage of opinion at headquarters, mentioning the arrest of Bulmer Hobson, and that a meeting had taken place, and that it had been decided to cancel arrangements. The O/C had requested Seán Fitzgibbon to have some lorries sent to Limerick, and Lieutenant Gubbins returned on Sunday morning with two lorries, which had been sent by Seán MacDermott. After consultation with his staff, Commandant Colivet sent out orders to the other units in his command, cancelling arrangements, and took the city battalion to Killonan, as if for a routine bivouac.

At the parade on Holy Thursday evening, the O/C had addressed the Volunteers, giving them to understand that the time was fast approaching when they might be called on to make the supreme sacrifice in defence of their principles, and ordered that everyone of them should parade on Easter Sunday morning fully armed and equipped, and carrying two day's ration. Those who for one reason or another had hitherto been exempted from publicly identifying themselves with the battalion, were to parade with the others. He furthermore ordered that any Volunteer finding himself unable to parade should hand over his rifle to his company officer. Articles of field equipment, including First Aid outfits, were distributed. About one hundred and thirty Volunteers paraded at the Fianna Hall on that Sunday, and the march to Killonan took place. Towards evening, as it was understood that the projected insurrection had been definitely abandoned, and as the weather turned wet and chilly, some forty or fifty Volunteers were allowed to return to the city, with the result that only between eighty and ninety remained in camp. On Sunday afternoon a code message came from Fitzgibbon that things were 'off'.

At midnight on Sunday, Captain Liam Forde returned from Dublin with orders from Pearse cancelling all arrangements, but instructing the O/C to be ready to receive further orders.

On Monday morning, Lieutenant Whelan came from a second visit to Tralee, and reported that he had met Captain Monteith, who told him 'that no men were coming', 'that the arms sent for the Volunteers were gone', 'that the Germans were out for cheap Irish blood', and 'that the best thing to do was to try and bluff through'.

Between 1.30 and 2 p.m. on Monday, a message from Pearse delivered to Commandant Colivet by the Misses Agnes and Laura Daly, read: 'Dublin brigade goes into action at noon today (Monday). Carry out your orders.' Immediately on receipt of this, he called a meeting of all the available officers who, having considered the message in the light of all the information at their disposal, decided that since the orders to the Limerick command had been based on the arrival of the arms ship, these orders could not be carried out. Then, having regard to the contradictory orders and messages, it was premised that only the Citizen Army, and a small section of the Volunteers had gone to insurrection. It was also taken into account that all the outlying battalions had been demobilised, and that only about seventy-six of the city battalion remained in the camp. Having reviewed all these circumstances, it was unanimously decided by all the officers present that nothing could be done. The Volunteers were accordingly marched back to the city and dismissed. As no one could anticipate what action the British authorities might take, conditional absolution was given by Rev. Fr Hennessy, OSA, who had hurried to the camp on hearing of the outbreak in Dublin, and the full store of .303 ammunition was distributed amongst the men. However, the battalion marched back to the Fianna Hall through William and O'Connell Streets without incident, and having been dismissed, returned to their homes carrying the rifles and ammunition.

On Tuesday 25 April, Commandant Colivet convened a meeting of the board of management, the battalion staff company commanders, and all officers who had any knowledge of the previous events, and it was decided by a majority of ten to six, that nothing could be done.

During the week, the Mayor, Councillor James Quinn, sent for the O/C and conveyed to him a demand for the surrender of arms from Colonel Sir Anthony Weldon, commanding the British forces in the district. A meeting of the combined board and officers decided to refuse this demand, which was several times made through the mayor, and as often rejected. Eventually, it was learned that the British were about to raid for the arms, and with a view to averting a useless effusion of blood, it was unanimously decided by the board of management and officers to surrender their arms, but with this stipulation, that each Volunteer was to hand his gun to Commandant Colivet, who would then give it into the keeping of the mayor, thus signifying that the arms were being surrendered to the First Citizen of Limerick to save the city from terror and bloodshed. This was carried out in the council chamber, Town Hall, on Friday, 5 May 1916, the mayor occupying the mayoral chair during the proceedings.

At daybreak on Thursday 11 May, the following were arrested and removed to the ordnance barracks: John Dalton, BC; James Dalton, Joseph Dalton, Edward O'Toole, John E. Cashin, James Kirby, Alphonsus Kivlehan, John Hurley, Michael P. Colivet, James Ledden, Edward Fitzgibbon, Patrick Whelan, James McInerney, John Troy, Martin Stapleton, George Clancy, Liam Forde, M.F. Fitzpatrick, James Gubbins, R.P. O'Connor, BC; A.J. O'Halloran, James McNulty, James L. Connaughton, Patrick Walsh, James O'Donnell, Patrick O'Halloran, F.J. O'Shaughnessy.

Later in the day, Sir Anthony Weldon attended at the barracks, and as a result of an inquiry, discharged the following: John Troy, Martin Stapleton and Joseph Dalton. All the others were removed to the county jail that evening. On Friday, Edward O'Toole was released. On subsequent dates, A. Mackey, B. Laffan, D. Hennessy, S. Carroll, P.J. O'Farrell, P. O'Sullivan and P. Ryan, Doon and others were arrested, but with the exception of Seán Ó Murthuile and James L. Connaughton, all the prisoners were released unconditionally on 15 May, and the latter two on the following day.

Almost immediately after these releases, the battalion resumed activities, but under cover, groups meeting at isolated places in the country districts surrounding the city, where company training, including rifle practice, was carried out.

Armed squads were sent to about ten of the polling station at the East Clare election in 1917. Soon after, open parades were again held, and uniforms worn.

There was an unfortunate development about this time. In May 1917, the Roger Casement Sinn Féin club, in the Irish Town district desired to form a company from amongst their own members, and applied to the authorities of the battalion for a drill instructor. This request was refused on the ground that a company already existed in that territory, with the result that it was decided to form a unit independent of the 1st battalion. A little tact on both sides would have prevented the unhappy situation which then arose.

Within a very short space of time companies were organised in other districts, and linked up together under the designation of the 2nd battalion. It did not tend to improve matters that some of those who became prominent in this body had been bitter opponents of the 1st battalion since the split in the Volunteers, though indeed they were afterwards to give positive proof of their courage and their loyalty to the Republic. There had been a certain amount of dissatisfaction amongst some members of the 1st battalion because no action had been taken during Easter Week, and Lieutenant A. Johnson and a small number of the rank and file seceded and joined the new body. Thus, there were two independent battalions existing in the city, each claiming to be in control, and though there was no real friction between them, relations were not good, since the spirit of co-operation was lacking. Commandant Colivet and Captain Forde made repeated attempts to heal the breach, but without success.

Limerick was to play a distinguished part in the Anglo-Irish war, but it would probably have done much more, were it not for this unfortunate division.

Both battalions sent strong contingents to Waterford for the election in 1918, and both were active in preparing to meet the conscription menace.

In 1919, headquarters sent Mr Richard Mulcahy to hold an inquiry as to the situation which obtained in the city, and as a result of his report, the 1st battalion was suspended. Training, however, continued as usual. At intervals, members of both battalions were arrested, charge with various offences and imprisoned.

In May 1920, Captain Forde joined the staff of the 2nd battalion, and was subsequently appointed brigadier, Mid-Limerick brigade. In the autumn of that year, a flying column was started with which some of the officers and Volunteers of the 1st battalion joined up, and in March 1921, the two battalions united, and thereafter worked as a unit.

AUTHOR'S NOTE – I desire to acknowledge that my account of Easter Week, and of the decisions taken in Limerick, is based on a report submitted by Commandant M.P. Colivet to the Irish Volunteer headquarters on its reorganisation in 1917. I have also to thank him for copy of *Basic Plan*. With regard to the number of Volunteers who paraded on Easter Sunday, there may be some slight difference of opinion, but at meetings of the surviving officers of the regiment held in recent years, it was assumed that about one hundred and thirty attended on that occasion. For the account of the circumstances relative to the formation of the 2nd battalion, I have to express my indebtedness to Mr David Dundon.

A.J. O'Halloran

LIFE AND DEATH OF COMMANDANT EDWARD DALY

by DAN MULCAHY

THE EASTER RISING was over and Dublin was broken and bleeding. O'Connell Street, one of the finest thoroughfares in Europe, was in ruins and a dense cloud of smoke hung like a pall over the capital. Down in the provinces the people, bewildered and confused by a succession of rumours and counter-rumours, anxiously awaited news of the insurrection in the city that had been all but isolated for more than a week. And indeed the capital was isolated in every sense of the word. It was Saturday evening of 29 April 1916, truly the most tragic day of a week that was otherwise filled with the glory of brave men and boys who went out against the might of an empire to dare and die 'in bloody protest for a glorious thing' – liberty. The great protest was made and now, following the surrender, the leaders of the Rising were huddled together under the strictest British military guard in the grounds of the Rotunda Hospital. Amongst them was Commandant Edward Daly, the patriotic Limerick son of a patriotic Limerick father. Four days later, on 3 May, Commandant Daly was tried by court martial and sentenced to death for his part in the Rising as officer in command of the Four Courts area. On the following morning he made the supreme sacrifice for Ireland. In his last interview with his sisters before he died he said: 'Did I not think it was an honourable surrender I, for one, would never have surrendered.' Such was the indomitable spirit of Ned Daly, as he was affectionately known; such was the man who dedicated his life to noble service of the nation and who died before the firing squad in defence of the cause of liberty.

In order to paint in true perspective a picture of Commandant Edward Daly it is necessary to study for however brief a spell the generous sources from which he derived his patriotic fervour and love of Ireland. His father and namesake, Edward Daly, was imprisoned in 1865, at the age of seventeen, for his activity on behalf of the Irish Republican Brotherhood. Released early in 1866, he took part in the gallant but ill-fated Rising of 1867. The rigours of imprisonment in his boyhood left, as might be expected, a permanent injury to his health and constitution. While still a young man he developed acute heart trouble which proved fatal in 1890 at the age of forty-two. His only son, Edward, the subject of this story, was born some months after his father's death. And appropriately enough at this stage there looms up in the background to the picture one of the most outstanding figures in the history of the more recent struggle for Irish independence. He is John Daly, one of the greatest if not the greatest of all Fenians. Jack Daly it was who succeeded in keeping intact, with very meagre support, the connection between 1867 and 1882. For this, on a bogus charge, he was sentenced to penal servitude for life in 1884, and was released due to hunger strike, after twelve and a half years incarceration. This may be said to be the first instance of the hunger strike weapon by an Irish republican. Released to die, he astonished the medical practitioners by seemingly regaining his normal health. However, in 1910 the state of his health gave cause for grave anxiety, and a year later he became an invalid, never to regain the use of his limbs again. He died an unrepentant Fenian on 30 June 1916, having just survived to share in the news of the tragic yet triumphal epic of Easter Week. Of such a stock was Commandant Daly, officer commanding the 1916 Four Courts garrison. His mother was Catherine O'Mara, from the historic West Limerick district of Ballingarry. Born into such a rich and fertile nursery of patriotism and devotion to the old land, how could it be otherwise with this Limerick son of Fenianism? So much for the background; now for something of the man himself, the soldier.

Born in Frederick Street, Limerick, on February 25 1891, Edward Daly was the youngest of ten children. All the elders having been girls, the advent of a son was a great joy and consolation for the death of his father in the prime of life, a short time before. He was christened John Edward owing to a baptismal misunderstanding, but he was always known to his family and friends as Ned. As a young boy he attended the Presentation Convent School in Sexton Street in his native city. At the age of seven, he went on to the Christian Brothers seminary in Roxboro' Road. His educational development showed no particular bent. Indeed, it has been started with authority that he had at all times shown an aversion to school life in general. At the age of fifteen he went to Lemy's school to get a commercial training fitting him to take over his uncle's business. The professor in charge of the institution described him as a very brilliant boy, but said he had no aptitude for study. It might be as well to mention at this stage the uncle just mentioned carried on a very successful confectionery and bread business in William Street, where it still flourishes under the very capable management of Ned Daly's brother-in-law, Mr Éamonn T. Dore, himself a veteran of the rebellion, and to whom we are indebted for the material for this article. Indeed, at this stage Mr Dore takes over with the following account of the principal subsequent events in the life and death of his brother-in-law and comrade-in-arms:

> Ned's uncle wanted his nephew to learn the business as a workman-baker, the better to fit him for the management of the business he was to inherit; but the tradesmen would not under any circumstances allow him to enter their domain. This decision was based on the ruling of their society 'that only the sons of bakers had the right to the baker's trade'. John Daly was

forced to send his nephew to a Technical School in Glasgow. Thither Ned went in 1907, at the age of sixteen. He remained there until 1908 when he returns home in bad health. The doctors in that city stated that he was not constitutionally fit for work in such a heated atmosphere. He then went to Spaight's (Limerick), timber merchants, as a clerk, and remained there two years, leaving to help his uncle in his then very extensive business. Here he worked for twelve months. Thence began his real connection with the city he was afterwards instrumental in making famous. Edward, or John, to call him his rightful name, went to Dublin in 1912 and worked in the office of Brooks Thomas, building contractors, for three months, leaving to fill a much better position at May Roberts, wholesale chemists, in Westmoreland Street, of that city. He remained in this post until a few short weeks before Easter 1916, when he left under orders from Seán MacDermott to help in the military side of the active preparations for the Rising, then so close at hand.

At the inception of the Irish Volunteers in November 1913 Ned was one of the first to be enrolled. He was then living with his sister, Mrs Thomas J. Clarke. On arriving home on the night of his enrolment he said to her: 'I am at least what I was always wanted to be'. She asked what, and in reply got the answer which sums up the man: 'A soldier'. His promotion from the first night was rapid and due solely to his soldierly qualities, and his energy for all work pertaining to the soldier's trade. Early in the New Year 1914, he was appointed the Captain of B company, 1st battalion, Dublin brigade, which he organised. His company, which financially was the poorest in the city, was at all times a model for discipline and rigorous attention to all duties, no matter how arduous. The writer, being then a private in this, the pioneer company in the metropolis, can speak with full knowledge of the men and their youthful Captain. He was younger by years than the majority of the privates, yet I never knew an officer so loved by his men. His company was by far larger than full strength at the end of its inception year, numbering in all one hundred men. This speaks better than anything I might say of the ability of the leader.

Captain Daly was in charge of his men at the Howth gun-running on 26 July 1914, and for his coolness and masterful handling of his company, when confronted with the British military, or, as it were, on active service for the first time, he was particularly mentioned by the officers in command. The following week saw him at Kilcool where, in the landing of arms at this seaside village, he again distinguished himself. It was only natural after two episodes, so much in the public eye at the time, that promotion could not long be deferred. In the beginning of the year 1915, Captain Daly was gazetted commandant of the 1st battalion, Dublin brigade. Notwithstanding the volume of work his new position entailed, he never neglected his old company. The drill hall in 41 Parnell Square saw him every Monday night, the drill night, the first in the hall at 8 o'clock and the last to leave.

At the O'Donovan Rossa funeral in the summer of 1915, Captain Daly was in supreme command of the Dublin brigade, Commandant McDonagh being in control of the Irish Volunteer Army in the city on that memorable occasion. Between the above period and 1916 little of note took place in his life. Of course there were the rumour of intended arrests, seizure of arms and other war materials, and during all this time of nerve-racking suspense, Commandant Daly showed all the thorough soldier's example to his men, never shirking or avoiding his duty. He never asked anybody to do what he was afraid or ashamed to do himself, and was always ready to give his all in the service of that cause uppermost in his heart. This trait was his common heritage, bequeathed to him by his forebears and still surviving in his sisters. A more unselfish devotion to the cause for its own sake, irrespective of gain or notoriety, could not be possibly exceeded by any of Ireland's martyred families. During the few short years between his first entry into the Volunteers and the final consummation of his life's ideal at the hands of the firing squad, he developed a taste for study foreign to his earlier life. Everything of a military nature, he, as it were, devoured voraciously, and his retentive faculty for such was the wonder of his fellow brigade officers. One reminiscence of note will show how deeply he loved his work.

Meeting his mother, who was on holiday in Kingstown, he asked her to pray for his success in his examination. She, not having heard previously of this examination, was overjoyed at, as she thought, his ambition to get on materially in the world, a trait which she knew up to this to be foreign to his character. On asking what examination she got the reply: Captain of my company in the Irish Volunteers. Such was the devotion lavished by this youthful and so little mentioned soldier in his preparatory work for Irish independence.

As Pearse in his inimitable way put it: 'It is not sufficient to say "I believe" unless I also say "I serve"; so Edward Daly, never a preacher, but an ardent worker, saw his few years' toil bear fruit on that Monday morning, 24 April 1916. He, like others, had to bear the agony of a traitorous attempt by one-time comrades to undermine and destroy what undoubtedly would have been Ireland's greatest effort to overthrow British rule. He was to live to see officers, not to talk of men, failing at the critical moment. He was to live to hear – and that while marshalling his men in Blackhall Place – 'It was not for this I joined.' So said one of his company officers. Picture the self-control of the man who only replied: 'We two will meet again.'

At that final muster, on the morning which was to mark a new epoch in Irish history, less than half the 1st battalion were on parade. This was due not so much to the men as to the order signed by John [Eoin] McNeill calling of the manoeuvres for Easter. Despite all the obstacles, Commandant Daly led his men in what then looked a forlorn hope into their position at the Four Courts and adjacent streets. His plan, as originally drawn up by general headquarters, was complied on the assumption that at least 75 per cent of the Volunteers would answer the call to arms. To hold with 150 men an area large enough to absorb 500 was superhuman effort. Yet Commandant Daly not alone held it intact during the week, but made numerous incursions into enemy territory with very marked success. He attacked, captured and demolished by fire the Linen Hall barracks, a very extensive building, well garrisoned. After charge and counter-charge he drove the British military out of the Bridewell, a building abutting on his own headquarters at the Law Courts. It may be mentioned here that the most intensive fighting during Easter Week took place in Commandant Daly's area. Bayonet charges were of daily occurrence and every inch of the ground was contested. Considering the resources of the enemy, it does not require extensive military training to know that the fight waged under this youthful commander compares favourably with the battles of history. It was in King Street that the British military, as a reprisal for their great losses, wreaked vengeance on the civilian population. They massacred hundreds, according to reports afterwards compiled. On Saturday night under cover of darkness Commandant Daly, with twelve Volunteers, was to attack Wellington barracks. The surprise attack might have been successful but the surrender intervened.

Edward Daly capitulated with the survivors of his heroic battalion on Saturday evening, 29 April 1916. They marched under British military instruction to O'Connell Street, where they were lined up with the headquarters battalions from the General Post Office. At 8 o'clock the massed battalions were marched to the grounds of the Rotunda Hospital where they were detained under military guard. The officer in charge was Captain Lu Wilson, later shot in Gorey, County Wexford, as a police officer. A more inhuman brute never donned a soldier's uniform.

During the night I saw Commandant Daly singled out and taken to the extreme end of the hospital grounds. His clothes were torn off him, and he was put through the most cruel form of search I hope it will ever be my lot to witness. During it all his demeanour was that of a soldier, looking with scorn on his cowardly would-be conquerors. When they had performed their degrading task he was marched back to the main body and there remained until 8 o'clock in the morning when he, with the rest, proceeded through the city to the Richmond barracks. There, with the writer and others, he was placed in the gymnasium. I saw him again being sorted from the ranks by a detective of the G division, Dublin police, and placed separate from the remainder. About an hour later, I, and about eighty others, were marched on to the barrack square. While passing I got what was to be the last earthly glimpse of a beloved and dauntless officer. It would only be fitting here to mention that in the war bulletin issued from General Post Office headquarters during the Rising, Commandant-General Connolly, chief of the Dublin forces, particularly mentioned Edward Daly as one of the greatest soldiers in Irish history. This tribute will convey more than my poor pen could ever hope to do.

Commandant Edward Daly was tried by court martial on 3 May 1916, and sentenced to death; the sentence was carried out at dawn on 4 May. In his final interview with his sister he said: 'Did I not think it was an honourable surrender, I, for one, would never have surrendered.' He met his death, according to the chaplain and others, as a soldier, knowing he had fought in a just cause and firmly believing that out of what he considered his poor sacrifice Ireland would regain her national soul and rise, Phoenix-like, to snatch from her old oppressor and hold against all nations her long-sought freedom.

Commandant Daly is survived by six patriotic sisters: Miss Madge Daly, head of the well-known Limerick bakery firm, who now spends most of her time in Dublin owing to an indisposition; Mrs Tom Clarke, Dublin, widow of the illustrious Tom Clarke of 1916 fame, and herself a life-long fighter in the national cause; Mrs O'Toole, Limerick; Miss Úna Daly; Mrs O'Sullivan, Limerick; Miss Cary Daly; and Mrs Éamonn T. Dore, Limerick. Long may they be spared to the nation.

Éamonn T. Dore, Commandant Daly's brother-in-law and intimate friend of the great Seán MacDermott, now carries on a successful bakery and confectionery at 26 William Street. A quiet, unassuming, yet lovable gentleman, he lives in a delightful bungalow out in Limerick's suburban Ennis Road, where his home is a veritable museum of pictures and mementoes of days that were great and glorious for resurgent Ireland.

EDWARD DALY'S COMMAND DUBLIN, 1916

by PEARSE BEASLAÍ
(who was his second-in-command)

SOME OF THE fiercest fighting of the 1916 Rising took place in the area in which Limerick's Edward Daly commanded the 1st battalion. The battalion's original plan of campaign covered an extensive area, the intention being to hold a line running from the Four Courts to Cabra, thus linking up with the 5th battalion under Thomas Ashe. The Broadstone railway station was to have been occupied and headquarters established at the North Dublin Union. Volunteers, who lived through those thrilling six days of Easter Week, 1916, in the Church Street area, must have vivid recollections of certain scenes witnessed and sensations experienced, but to reduce the whole to a coherent story is not so easy. The small body of men engaged occupied an area so widely spread across the city and where, of necessity, so little in touch with any save their own small units – especially in the latter stages of the fighting, when positions were cut off from one another by enemy attacks – that a great many persons should be consulted in order to obtain a clear and comprehensive view of the whole sequence of events. Furthermore, to men who were practically without sleep for four or five days, and in a conditions of severe tension, the recollection of occurrences is liable, at this stage, to be a confused jumble of memories, in which some trivial things stand out vividly and events of major importance are almost forgotten. And many in perfectly good faith, make erroneous statements. The memory, after a lapse of other thirty years, is very fallible. I have heard extraordinary conflicts of testimony as to what happened on certain occasions by persons who were actually present, and have myself been told things by conscientious eye-witnesses which were entirely at variance with my own recollections. Another complication is the fact that the Church Street area of today is a very different place from the scene of the fighting of 1916. Revisiting the place where one had gone through such tense moments is a bewildering experience. A large area in Church Street which was then full of ruins, demolished buildings and waste ground, is now occupied by streets of houses, and the same is true of the site of the Linen Hall barracks in Lisburn Street. One's adventures of 1916 seem to belong to another century. I shall endeavour to give a summarised account of the main events which took place within the confines of Edward Daly's command during that memorable week, directing my attention particularly to the fighting of the last two days. But to elucidate this, it is necessary to start at the beginning of the week.

According to the plans of our leaders, the 1st battalion was to occupy a line running from the Four Courts on the north bank of the Liffey (beside the Mendicity Institution on the south side) to Cabra, where it was to link up with the 5th battalion (under the command of Thomas Ashe). The Broadstone station, then the railway terminus for the west of Ireland, was to be occupied, and the North Dublin Union was to be the battalion headquarters. Had the parade announced for Sunday 23 April, duly taken place, and the full strength of the battalion been available, this plan would have been carried out in every detail; but unforeseen circumstances compelled us to modify part of our plans. When the Sunday parade was called off (for reasons which are well known) many Volunteers believed the Parade to be postponed indefinitely, and the surprise mobilisation on Monday morning found them unprepared. When the 1st battalion left their headquarters in Blackhall Street at noon, it did not number one-third of its full strength. Many members joined up later, and we were also reinforced by men from other battalions, Fianna boys and by a number who had come from England specially for the fight. The majority of the Volunteers who assembled in Blackhall Street had no knowledge when summoned to parade that they would be asked to go out in insurrection, though I think a good many had a shrewd suspicion, for some time previously, that an attempt of the kind was in contemplation. The order to go out to fight for Irish independence must have come with startling unexpectedness to many of the small band assembled in the hall; yet none refused to obey the call.

No sooner had the men reached the Church Street area and commenced to take up their positions, than shots range out. I do not think any unit in the city found itself in contact with the enemy earlier than 'C' company, though the encounter was entirely accidental. To this company, under the command of Captain Frank Fahy (now ceann comhairle of the Dáil), and Lieutenant Joe McGuinness was deputed the task of occupying and holding the Four Courts. While engaged in this task, and erecting a barricade at the end of Church Street, a body of mounted Lancers, escorting an ammunition wagon, came along the quays, travelling in the direction of the Phoenix Park. The Volunteers, believing themselves attacked, fired on the Lancers, killing one. A second Lancer galloped up Church Street firing wildly, and was shot down after he had killed a child. The rest of the Lancers retreated to a building in Charles Street, on the eastern side of our position, where they remained prisoners throughout the week, afraid to venture out.

After one unsuccessful assault on the building, we did not think it necessary to attack them again, beyond a little sniping to intimidate them, as they were penned up and entirely harmless. Meanwhile 'D' company, under the command of Captain Seán Heuston, and Lieutenant Richard Balfe, occupied the Mendicity Institution on Usher's Quay, on the south side of the Liffey, where they were soon attacked and put up a gallant fight against heavy odds. They were separated from the rest of the battalion by the Liffey, but were later reinforced by some members of the 5th battalion from Fingal. The whole of Church Street and adjoining streets, as far as the North Dublin Union and Constitution Hill were occupied by our men, and barricades were erected and manned at various points in Church Street and the side streets running off it, such as May Lane (leading to Jameson's Distillery in Bow Street), Mary's Lane, North King Street and Brunswick Street. A number of houses in these last two streets were also occupied, and theses posts figured largely in the fierce fighting of the last two days of the Rising.

There exists a widespread impression, even among Volunteers, that the Four Courts building was a headquarters, but this is entirely incorrect. The Four Courts was one of the extremities of our position, and the battalion commandant, Ned Daly, required a more central spot for his headquarters. On the Monday he took up his quarters in St John's convent, in Brunswick Street, where he was received with enthusiasm by some patriotic Sisters of Charity, and there it was that he met the late Fr Albert, OSF, and Fr Augustine, OSF, both sympathisers. From Tuesday to the end of the week, the Father Matthew Hall was used as our headquarters, as well as for the tending of our wounded by members of Cumann na mBan. It was on Friday night, when we were compelled to abandon this position, that the Four Courts became our headquarters – not many hours before the order to surrender reached us.

The late Éamonn Duggan acted as adjutant and Éamonn Morkan as quartermaster to the battalion. The greater part of Church Street was occupied by 'F' company, under the command of Captain Fionán Lynch, now His Honour Judge Lynch and important posts were held by Lieutenants John Shouldice and Diarmuid Hegarty, John S. O'Connor, F.X. Coghlan, Liam Archer, Frank Shouldice and Mortimer O'Connell. Martin Conlon was in general charge of the Father Matthew Hall. 'A' company was officered by Captain

Denis O'Callaghan (a Kerryman, who was given several special commands during the week), and Lieutenant Liam Ó Cearbhaill, and 'G' company by Captain Nicholas Laffan. There were other important posts held, but I do not pretend to give a complete list of these. In actual practice, men from various companies, and even from other battalions, were mingled with one another in the various posts occupied. Owing to our small numbers when we set out on Monday, it seemed impossible to occupy the spacious Broadstone station effectively, and no attempt was made to do so. When, later, our numbers were reinforced, the station had been already strongly occupied by British military, and a daring attack, led by Denis O'Callaghan, was repulsed, one of our men being wounded. Another officer of the battalion, Captain Frank Daly, who acted as engineer for the whole brigade, had been engaged from early on Monday morning with various demolitions, such as the blowing up of railway bridges and the putting of the railway lines out of action. The battalion adjutant, Captain James O'Sullivan, occupied positions on the Cabra Road and North Circular Road.

On Tuesday evening these positions were attacked by strong forces of British troops; artillery was used against the barricades, and the defenders were compelled to evacuate them. Captain O'Sullivan then joined the General Post Office garrison. Immediately beside our position in Lisburn Street stood the Linen Hall barracks, occupied by British soldiers, and on Wednesday a body of our Volunteers, led by Denis O'Callaghan, seized this building. It proved an easy task as the soldiers surrendered immediately. The barracks were burned to the ground. I think our position was unique in one respect – that whereas, in other parts of the city, buildings only were held, our troops were actually out in the streets in an area where a large civilian population resided, and our military problems were added to by problems of civilian administration. A good many of the residents were at first suspicious and hostile; but after we had been in occupation for a couple of days, they were impressed by our discipline and friendly attitude, and became more favourable. We advised all who could, especially the women and children, to move from the area to some safer quarter; but the majority preferred to remain where they were, despite the danger. The fact that we occupied an important thoroughfare, made things more difficult. For the first few days a constant stream of persons, seeking to pass through our barricades for various motives, had to be held up and questioned. Inside our position in North King Street there was a bakery in which bread was being baked daily, and, as other bakeries were closed, people from other parts of Dublin flocked there seeking loaves. Despite the danger to ourselves, we admitted them, but had to form a 'food queue' and 'ration' them, limiting each person to two loaves. In the Church Street area most of the shops remained open for at least four days of the week, and there was not the least trace of an attempt at looting or any irregularity such as occurred in other parts of the city. The Volunteers preserved perfect order.

A number of minor actions occurred in the earlier part of the week in which the Volunteers sustained some casualties and inflicted a great deal more – notably an engagement with British forces at close quarters on Church Street Bridge, in which the late Peadar Clancy, then a lieutenant in 'C' company, played a daring part. Seán Heuston's gallant little band, cut off and surrounded by a large force, inflicted heavy losses on its attackers before being compelled to surrender. Despite the overwhelming superiority of the enemy, it was not until the Thursday that any attempt was made to encircle our whole position. A number of snipers took up posts on buildings in the neighbourhood of Capel Street, from which they kept our barricades under harassing fire. At this time, owing to the waste lands adjoining, a considerable portion of Church Street was exposed to the fire. By Thursday night we were practically cut off from general headquarters in the General Post Office with which, up to then, we had been in constant communication. On Thursday night considerable portion of O'Connell Street was in flames, and Church

Street was lit up by the fires, rendering the men at the barricades a target for snipers. We had also buildings on fire in our own area, and Volunteers had to work strenuously to prevent the spread of the flames, which originated from the burning of Linen Hall barracks. On Friday evening a fierce attack was launched on our position in North King Street from the direction of Bolton Street, supported by armoured cars. A handful of Volunteers, under the command of Lieutenant John Shouldice, occupied the house at the north-western corner of Church Street and North King Street – licensed premises which we afterwards nicknamed 'Reilly's Fort'. On these men fell the brunt of the attack, which lasted many hours.

North of this, at Brunswick Street, posts were held by Lieutenant Laffan and his men, who also put up a spirited fight and, when next day, they were cut off from the rest of the battalion, they were the last to surrender. But the main British attack was directed against North King Street. The British soldiers, under cover of an armoured car, first took up a position behind an unoccupied barricade on the side of North King Street opposite 'Reilly's Fort'; but they were met with such a withering fire from the defenders, that they retreated in confusion, leaving some dead behind. They fled down Beresford Street where they came under a cross-fire from Volunteers in posts on the east side of Church Street and were mown down. The men in 'Reilly's Fort' dashed out and sized the rifles which the soldiers had dropped, bringing them back triumphantly to the 'fort'. They found that their firing, which had inflicted such a heavy casualties on the attackers, had also put several of their rifles out of action. Later the attackers broke into houses in North King Street, from which they kept up a heavy fire for many hours at our positions, concentrating their attack on 'Reilly's Fort'. It was afterwards ascertained that these same soldiers murdered some young men whom they found in the buildings – men who were not connected in any way with the Volunteers. At an early stage of the fight one Volunteer, Patrick O'Flanagan, was killed while entering the 'fort'.

The Father Matthew Hall, where we had our headquarters, was only about eighty yards from the position in North King Street which was being attacked. It contained a number of our wounded men and the members of Cumann na mBan who were nursing them, and was not in a position to be defended. Commandant Daly decided to transfer his headquarters to the Four Courts, and Morkan and I proceeded to carry down the ammunition and explosives which were stored in the Father Matthew Hall. As we had no men to spare from the barricades, we had to do it all ourselves, and it involved a number of journeys up and down and climbing over half-a-dozen barricades while heavily laden. All this time the fight in North King Street raged with fury and the long street re-echoed with the sounds of the firing. The whole area was lit up as though it were daylight, by the fires in O'Connell Street, and every now and then the ping of a bullet showed that a sniper was on the job. All night long and next morning the fight raged in North King Street, and the men at the barricades below, between them and the Four Courts, having to keep their thin line intact, could not be spared to go to the assistance of those holding the position attacked.

At length having been about sixteen hours under constant fire, the men in 'Reilly's Fort', spent and exhausted, discovered their ammunition was practically finished. Seeing no prospect of relief, they decided to evacuate the building. They made a dash across the street under fire, fortunately without casualty, and retreated down Church Street, rejoining their comrades at the barricade near the Franciscan church. No sooner was the 'fort' in North King Street evacuated than the British soldiers occupied it, and proceeded to pour a heavy fire down Church Street at the barricades. The men at the upper barricades fell back on the barricade at the corner of Mary's Lane. However, they rallied quickly and returned to their formed positions. At this point, I would like to pay a tribute to the coolness and courage of the late Joe McGuinness, then a lieutenant of 'C' company, who, having arrived on the scene from the Four

Courts, where he had been on duty, assisted the other officers in rallying the men. By that time our line was considerably shortened, and the men on the far side of North King Street were definitely cut off from us and surrounded. They held out gallantly, and after Laffan was wounded his place was taken by Paddy Holohan, who only surrendered on the following day. Immediately after the unsuccessful charge up Church Street, Commandant Daly called a conference of officers at which it was decided to make a fresh sortie that evening, and endeavour to recapture our lost positions. A daring Volunteer, Tommy O'Connor, undertook an attempt to convey a message from us to general headquarters, which we still believed to be in the General Post Office. We were not then aware that the building had been evacuated. During our conference, one officer called attention to the strange silence that had come over the city and remarked that evidently the enemy had suspended his attack for the present. After our ears had been deafened, day and night, by the sound of constant firing, the silence seemed unusual. We were not aware that a 'Cease Fire' order had been issued.

Some time later a priest arrived with news of the surrender, and finally Pearse's signed order to surrender was conveyed to Commandant Daly. He showed it to me, and his eyes filled with tears. He had borne himself like a gallant soldier through the week of fighting. Again he rose to this fresh test of soldiership. He checked the murmurings of those who objected to surrender by an appeal to discipline. They must obey the orders of the commander-in-chief, however unwelcome. He impressed the English officers with his dignity. They permitted him to march at the head of his men as they brought us through the empty streets (where the few people we saw were those who cursed us) to where other bodies of prisoners were assembled in O'Connell Street. And when the English general asked one of his own officers: 'Who is in charge of these men?' Daly proudly answered: 'I am. At all events, I was', a remark which, he must have known, would sign his death-warrant.

CON COLBERT OF ATHEA HERO AND MARTYR

by MADGE DALY

LIKE HIS COMRADES-IN-ARMS, Edward Daly and Seán Heuston, Con Colbert was little more than a boy when he faced the British firing squad after the glorious epoch of the 1916 Rising. 'Worthy comrade of the great men with whom he died,' wrote Brian O'Higgins, 'was Conn a Colbard than whom not one of them all, not even Mac Piarais himself, was more high-minded, more spiritual in thought and feeling, more unselfishly devoted to the cause that had called him even as a boy among the pleasant green fields of his native Country Limerick.' Such was the noble spirit of that young Athea lad, inspired by a patriotic fervour richly inherited from both side of his parentage. An uncle was out with the Fenians, and his mother was one of the McDermott's of Coolacare, who were in the vanguard of the national effort since 1882.

Leaving the gently sloping hills of West Limerick, Con secured employment at Kennedy's Bakery, in Parnell Street, Dublin, and in the city he became a pioneer of the Fianna Éireann, a movement close to his heart. He gave it every moment of his spare time, and even during his summer holidays he would don his Fianna uniform and cycle from place to place getting a few boys together to start a new *sluagh*. With his earnestness and enthusiasm he proved a most successful recruiting agent. Con joined the Irish Volunteers at the inception of that movement and was one of the first drill instructors. He was quickly appointed captain of 'F' company, 4th battalion, a rank which he held until the Rising. He was also a member of the Irish Volunteer executive at the time John Redmond attempted to gain control of the movement, and when the motion that would literally have put the Volunteers at the disposal of the Irish Parliamentary Party came before the executive council, Con voted against it, notwithstanding the very great pressure, brought to bear on him by Bulmer Hobson and others. His clear thinking and definite mind could not be influenced easily. Despite his youthful years Con shortly became one of the inspirations of the new and vigorous resurgence movement and in due course he was appointed to Volunteer headquarter staff.

During the years which preceded the fateful Rising of 1916 Con Colbert devoted every moment of his spare time to the work of organising the men and boys who were to participate in that historic event, and what is more, although his wages at the time were particularly meagre, he spent every penny of his hard-earned money in the advancement of the movement to which he had given his everything but his very soul. When Pádraig Pearse visited us in Limerick in 1916, he spoke of Con lovingly and as a dear friend. He told us how he had asked him to come to St Enda's College as drill instructor to the boys and how Con agreed despite the many other national activities which made his an over-full life. But when it was suggested that Con's name should be put on the pay-sheet he became so indignant that Pearse had to apologise and drop the idea.

An incident which took place on Christmas Eve, 1915, adequately portrays Con's consideration for others. He had travelled from Dublin by the night mail and arrived in Limerick about 3 a.m. As he was not expected in Limerick, we did not wait up for him, but rather than disturb us, Con walked the streets during that cold winter's night and knocked only when he saw a light in one of the windows. The maids were then going to early Mass so he entered the kitchen, made

71

tea, loaded a tray and surprised us all with an early cup. Laughing and joking, he did not look the least like a man who had worked all through Christmas Eve, travelled until three o'clock in the morning and then walked the streets for another five hours. The incident was typical of Con's kind and unselfish nature. He was ever bright and cheerful and I can never recall seeing him out of humour.

Whenever he passed through Limerick on his way home to Athea he would call to visit my uncle, and sometimes stay with us a day or two, sometimes only for a few hours. Soon a deep friendship developed between these two, the old, crippled Fenian and the young one. Con's visits were a source of great pleasure to my uncle as he brought him the latest news of the Fianna, the Wolfe Tone clubs and the other national groups in Dublin. He wrote to him, too, whenever there was a little news. My uncle had known Con's Fenian uncle, about whom Con was ever anxious to hear. The pair were seldom short of a subject and they often talked until the small hours of the morning.

The last time I met Con Colbert was in O'Connell Street, Dublin, a week before the Rising. I had gone there to get the latest news for my uncle, from Tom Clarke. Without a word being exchanged about the Rising I knew instinctively that Con was aware of the coming test and we both felt that it might be our last meeting. He invited me to the DBC, ostensibly for a cup of tea, but really to talk. It was then I realised that he was entering the fight convinced that he was going to his death. Yet he was as calm and happy as ever, talking of the risks as part of the day's work in the cause for which he lived. He said that he believed they would all go down in the fight but that the sacrifice would be well worth while. I disagreed pointing out that Thomas Clarke was so full of hope and that he believed that if they had some initial success the youth of the country would flock to their standard. With the whole country up in arms intensive guerrilla warfare would probably develop, and England, so hard-pressed to find soldiers to maintain her armies at full strength for the war against the Central

Powers, would be unable to provide the additional forces necessary to quell a general Rising in Ireland. Con could not see it that way but he had no doubt about the righteousness of their effort to win freedom, nor about the effect of their sacrifices. He was in the highest spirits when he left me, glad of the opportunity to play his part in the struggle. When the great day came and the flag of freedom was proudly unfurled over the GPO, Con Colbert took his place with the courage and determination of the true soldier and fought with conspicuous bravery and ability. Later, when the sad day of reckoning arrived, a British court martial paid him the significant tribute of a felon's death.

Round the open hearth fires in the homes among his native hills and valleys of Athea they still speak of Con Colbert with love and reverence, and passing years have but helped to mellow the honour and respect with which his name is spoken. Wrote Brian O'Higgins: 'Tom Clarke held him in high esteem; Mac Piarais trusted him as a friend and comrade ever welcome at the Hermitage; Éamonn Ceannt loved him and was for ever singing his praises. So spiritual was he that he abstained from meat during the seven weeks of Lent, and, like Mellows he was always slipping quietly away to say the Coróin Mhuire in the shadows of some Dublin church.'

The soul of chivalry always, Con saved the life of his superior officer at the post where he served during the Rising and forfeited his own by assuming command when the surrender came. At the last he was as brave, as calm, as happy, as nobly edifying as he had been through all the days of his short life. So grand was his bearing that the British soldier who was ordered to pinion him asked the privilege of shaking his hand. Fr Augustine, the brown friar who was with him in that last hour has written:

While my left arm linked the prisoner's right, and while I was whispering something in his ear, the soldier approached to fix a piece of paper on his breast. While this was being done, he looked down, and then addressing the soldiers in a mild and perfectly natural way, said: 'Wouldn't it be better to put it up higher nearer the heart.' The soldier said something in reply, and then added: 'Give me your hand now.' The prisoner seemed confused and extended his left hand. 'Not that,' said the soldier, 'but the right.' The right hand was accordingly extended and having grasped and shaken it warmly, the kindly, human-hearted soldier proceeded to gently bind the prisoner's hands and afterwards blindfold him. Some minutes later, my arm still linked in his, and accompanied by another priest, we entered a dark corridor leading to a yard and, his lips moving in prayer, the brave lad went forth to die.

Such was the noble and dignified death of the brave young Volunteer from West Limerick who died as he lived, a soldier and a saint. Ever a devout Catholic and daily communicant, Con Colbert had his own definite opinion as to where his duty lay – to God and to his country. He went that way regardless of censure, no matter what the source, and so he lived and died happily. A few days after his execution my uncle had the following little note from him:

Kilmainham,
7th May, 1916.

My dear friend,
Just a line to wish you goodbye and to ask your prayers for my poor soul. God prosper you and yours. May He love Ireland. Goodbye.

Yours ever, Con.

Con Colbert is survived by two brothers, Mr Jim Colbert, ex-TD, who now resides in Dublin, and Mr Mack Colbert, the well-known horseman of Ballysten, Shanagolden, Country Limerick.

SEÁN HEUSTON'S LIFE AND DEATH FOR IRELAND

by MADGE DALY

I FIRST MET Seán Heuston after the formation of the Fianna Éireann in Limerick. He was then working as a railway clerk in the city and took a prominent part in the training of the boy's organisation which he had largely helped to found. Like his youthful comrade-in-arms of 1916, Con Colbert, he always dressed in his Fianna uniform when with the boys. Like Colbert, too, he was a member of the Irish Republican Brotherhood, though little more than twenty years of age at the time, and looking younger. In 1908, Seán Heuston took first place in all Ireland at the Great Southern and Western Railway Companies' examination, and was quickly appointed to a position in Limerick, where he began in earnest the work for Ireland's freedom that led to a wall before a British firing squad on 8 May 1916.

At first sight, Seán Heuston appeared a quiet, unassuming boy, but one soon realised that his was a mature, clear-thinking mind, educated to an exceptional degree in subjects relating to his country. He had an extraordinary memory, and could quote day and date for most important events in our history. With all he was most practical, and had the special quality for managing boys and getting the best from them. A fluent Irish speaker, Seán used his own language whenever possible. He was methodical, and planned each year's Fianna programme in advance, arranging classes, lectures, marches and examination for the boys, and persuading his friends to present prizes. He realised that the success of the Fianna movement depended on keeping the boys fully occupied and interested, and in that work he had the willing help of many adults. History lectures were given by the Rev. Fr Hackett; Joe Dalton had charge of physical culture, while others conducted language class, and Seán himself took charge of drill, signalling and general scout training. He spend all of his spare time with the boys, inspiring them with his lofty ideas.

In 1912, my uncle and some of his Fenian friends had a hall built for the use of the Fianna on a plot of ground situated behind our house in Barrington Street. A lovely little hall, capable of seating some hundreds, it had additional space for exercises and drill, and was noted as being a centre of sedition until burned down by Black and Tans in later years. It was opened with great ceremony in December, 1912, Bulmer Hobson coming specially from Dublin for the event. My uncle was there, too, carried in his invalid chair to make a fine speech – his last one. Later Tom Clarke wrote to my uncle: 'Bulmer gave me a great account of the fine shape you were in. It is grand to find that you have made the Fianna such a great success in Limerick. You are away ahead of anything else in Ireland. In Dublin, they have not yet got the length of even thinking about building a hall.'

Roger Casement also was keenly interested in the Limerick Fianna Éireann. He came specially to inspect the *sluagh* on several occasions, and was ever generous and helpful in every way he could. I well remember the first big Fianna route march in Limerick, which, as well as I can remember, took place in the spring of 1913. Behind their own pipers band marched several hundreds of the boys, most of them in uniform. At their head marched the kindly Roger Casement, Seán Heuston and other Fianna officers, with my brother Ned. It was a heart-stirring sight, the first display of its kind in Limerick and as the boys swung into O'Connell Street, they were wildly cheered by the crowd.

During the year 1913, Seán Heuston was recalled to Dublin to take up a position in the traffic manager's office at Kingsbridge. He was then transferred to the *sluagh* Emmet of the Dublin Fianna Éireann. In a short time he was elected captain, and later became O/C for North Dublin. When the Volunteers were started towards the close of the same year, Seán joined immediately. A most active and useful member, his training with the Fianna fitted him admirably for the position to which he was soon appointed – captain of 'D' company, 1st Dublin battalion – a rank which he held until the Rising. From that time onwards, Seán had but one thought – to work and prepare for the coming attempt to win freedom for his country.

Seán commanded a tiny group of men as the garrison in the Mendicity Institute on Usher's Island on Easter Monday 1916. Because of MacNeill's countermanding order, the Volunteer companies posted to all parts of the city were far below strength, particularly in the beginning. Shortly after noon on Easter Monday, Seán occupied the institute with about a dozen men. While the necessary indoor defences were being seen to, Seán, with three men, left the building and erected a barricade on the quayside. When he returned to the building, he minutely inspected the fortifications, and having assured himself that the defences were to his satisfaction, he ordered each man to his post. It was thought by those in a position to know, that the intention was to hold the institute only for a few hours and delay the enemy's approach while Commandant Edward Daly was making effective preparations for resistance in the extensive Four Courts building and the surrounding area. Seán Heuston and his men would then fall back upon the latter command. By evening, however, the institute was cut off from the Four Courts for upon the first debouch of military from the Royal barracks, a warm reception greeted them from 'Heuston's Fort'. The enemy scattered for cover and, being reinforced, sporadic firing was the order from all sides throughout the day. All through the night the fight went on, the British bringing up fresh men, while the little garrison in the Mendicity Institute had no relief and no hope of reinforcement.

At Tuesday's dawn, Seán visited each post and cheered his men with an unflagging spirit of determination. No one grumbled. All were imbued with the resolve of their youthful commander to fight to the death. As the day wore on, the enemy's fire became more intensive, machine-guns on Queen's Street bridge raking the building. In the evening, in answer to Seán's dispatch, Commandant-General James Connolly sent a detachment of Swords men to the relief of the garrison. These North County Dublin men successfully fought their way through the British lines. The garrison then numbered little more than twenty. Throughout the night, the British increased their pressure, and by Wednesday the Mendicity Institute was completely surrounded. A merciless fire was kept up from the northern quays by riflemen and machine-gunners. A bombing party went into position immediately in front of the building, and kept up an unceasing attack which played havoc with the defences. Inside, the men fought on gallantly despite the increasing shortage of ammunition. They gave back round for round until the position became untenable, and two of them lay dangerously wounded. Completely encircled and without hope of new stores or men, Seán Heuston was prevailed upon to surrender. After all, the task that was his had been accomplished. He had engaged the enemy for three days, and further resistance now could not be calculated to hamper their advanced on the Four Courts.

Out trooped the little garrison under the flag of truce, and as they did, Peter Wilson, of Swords, was shot dead. Heuston and twenty men laid down their arms and were taken to Arbour Hill. The code of military honour was later to be extended to Seán Heuston in the same degree as that which had been shown to Peter Wilson. Tried by court martial, he was sentenced to death. The late Fr Albert, OSFC, penned this beautiful picture of Seán Heuston's last hours:

On Sunday night, 7 May 1916, Fr Augustine and myself were notified that we would be required at Kilmainham jail the following morning, as four of the leaders in the Rising were to be executed. At 1.30 a.m. a military motor car came for us to Church Street, and on our arrival at Kilmainham we were brought to the wing of the jail in which our friends were confined. Fr Augustine went to Éamonn Kent's cell, and I to Commandant M. Mallin's. Having visited Con Colbert and Éamonn Kent, I went to Seán Heuston's cell at about 3.20 a.m. He was kneeling beside a table with his Rosary beads in his hand. On the table was a little piece of candle, and some letters which he had written to near relatives and friends. He wore his overcoat as the morning was extremely cold, and none of these men received those little comforts that are provided for even the greatest criminals while awaiting sentences of death.

During the last quarter-of-an-hour we knelt in the cell in complete darkness as the little piece of candle had burned out; but no word of complaint escaped his lips. His one thought was to prepare with all the fervour and earnestness of his soul to meet his Divine Saviour and His sweet Virgin Mother, to whom he was about to offer up his young life for the freedom and independence of his beloved country. He had been to Confession and had received Holy Communion early that morning, and was not afraid to die. He awaited the end not only with that calmness and fortitude which peace of mind bring to noble souls, but during the last quarter-of-an-hour he spoke of soon meeting again Pádraig Mac Piarais and the other leaders who had already gone before him.

We said together short Acts of Faith, Hope, Contrition and Love; we prayed together to St Patrick, St Brigid, St Columcille, and all the Saints of Ireland; we said many times that beautiful little ejaculatory prayer: 'Jesus, Mary and Joseph, I gave you my heart and soul,' etc., which appealed very much to him. But, though he prayed with such fervour for strength and courage in the ordeal that was at hand, Ireland and his friends were close to his soul. He loved his own unto the end. In his last letter to his sister – a Dominican nun – he wrote: 'Let there be no talk of foolish enterprises. I have no vain regrets. If you really love me, teach the children the history of their own land, and teach them that the cause of Caitlín Ní hUallacháin never dies. Ireland shall be free from the centre to the sea, as soon as the people of Ireland believe in the necessity of Ireland's freedom and are prepared to make the necessary sacrifices to obtain it.' In his last message to me he said: 'Remember me to the boys of the Fianna. Remember me to Michael Staines and his brothers, and to all the boys at Blackhall Street.'

At about 3.45 a.m. a British sentry knocked at the door of the cell and told us the time was up. We both walked out together, down to the end of the large open space from which a corridor runs to the jail yard;

here his hands were tied behind his back, a cloth placed over his eyes, and a small piece of white paper, about four inches or five inches square, pinned to his coat over his heart. Just then we saw Father Augustine with Commandant M. Mallin coming towards us from the cell where they had been. We were now told to be ready. I had a small cross in my hand, and, though blindfolded, Seán bent his head and kissed the crucifix; this was the last thing his lips touched in life. He then whispered to me: 'Father, sure you won't forget to anoint me?' I had told him in his cell that I would anoint him when he was shot.

We now proceeded towards the yard where the execution was to take place; my left arm was linked in his right, while the British soldier who had handcuffed and blindfolded him walked on his left. As we walked slowly along, we repeated most of the prayers that we had been saying in the cell. On our way we passed a group of soldiers; these I afterwards learned were awaiting Commandant Mallin, who was following us. Having reached a second yard, I saw there another group of military armed with rifles. Some of these were standing, and some sitting or kneeling. A solder directed Seán and myself to a corner of the yard, a short distance from the outer wall of the prison. Here, there was a box (seemingly a soap box), and Seán was told to sit down upon it.

He was perfectly calm, and said with me for the last time: 'My Jesus, Mercy.' I scarcely had moved away a few yards when a volley went off and this noble soldier of Irish freedom fell dead. I rushed over to anoint him; his whole face seemed transformed and lit up with a grandeur and brightness that I had never before noticed. Later on, his remains and those of three other were conveyed to Arbour Hill military detention barracks, where they were buried in the outer yard, in the trench which holds the mortal remains of Ireland's noblest and bravest sons. Never did I realise that men could fight so bravely, and die so beautifully, and so fearlessly as did the heroes of Easter Week. On the morning of Seán Heuston's death, I would have given the world to have been in his place – he died in such a noble and sacred cause, and went forth to meet his divine Saviour with such grand Christian sentiments of trust confidence and love.

BISHOP O'DWYER OF LIMERICK SETS THE NATION ON MARCH TO VICTORY

by A.J. O'HALLORAN

Dr O'Dwyer stirred the heart of Ireland until it leaped with love for the men who died, with love for the cause that called them, with pride in them, and in this new champion who had risen up to speak for Separatist Ireland in its hour of need.

Brian O'Higgins

EDWARD THOMAS O'DWYER was born in Cullen, Tipperary, in the year 1843, his father, John R. O'Dwyer, who was an inland revenue officer, deriving from a family of gentleman farmers in that parish, while his mother, Anne Quinlivan, was a member of a Limerick city family prominently identified with the milling industry. When but a young child his parents took up their residence in Edward Street, Limerick, so that thereafter he regarded himself as being a Limerick man. In his scholastic career from the time the began his studies at the Christian Brothers schools, until he was ordained at Maynooth, he gave evidence of that intellectual brilliance, and of the other great qualities which were to distinguish him both as a priest and bishop. It was written of a great Limerick priest: 'He had the courage to be different.' This might also be said of Bishop O'Dwyer, since independent thought was the keynote of his character, and distinguished all his action in his early manhood, as in his old age.

More than forty years ago he attended a meeting held in the county courthouse, Limerick, to advocate certain reforms in the drink traffic laws. There were present at it representatives of all creeds and class, including several dignitaries of the Protestant churches. In the course of his speech Bishop O'Dwyer explained why it was that he had become a total abstainer. As a curate in the parish of Saint Michael, he had oft-times been approached by some poor woman whose husband was addicted to drink, with a plea that he would use his influence to effect a reformation, and when he went to their poor dwelling, it was not an uncommon thing to find the man stretched on a pallet of straw, which lay on a damp earthen floor. Now at this period it was customary with the clergy, as indeed with the better classes generally, to partake of a glass of punch after dinner by way of digestive. And he put this question to himself. How could he, who had a carpet under his feet, a good dinner to eat, and a cheerful fire to sit at, consistently remonstrate with such poor creatures for over-indulging in alcoholic drink, when they lacked all the comforts he enjoyed, while he himself partook of it, even in the strictest moderation? Thereupon he became not alone a total abstainer, but a most zealous and successful advocate of temperance.

The skill of the photographer, the genius of the painter, have preserved for posterity the lineaments of the bishop, a face stamped with intelligence, courage, and determination, a typically Gaelic face, evidential of the attributes that inspired and maintained a people's resistance to tyranny for a period of seven centuries. For the rest, he was of middle height, and slight of build, but as he moved through the city streets, clad as became his high office, he looked a striking figure, for his personality was such that had he been clothed in the simplest lay attire, he would have commanded attention. A most impressive speaker, he was a wonderful pulpit orator, his voice rising and falling in chant-like tones, so that every word he uttered sank into the minds of his hearers.

As it might be considered that it was his outspoken defiance of Maxwell that raised him to a position of pre-eminence, it should be stated that his remarkable intellectual gifts, his great force of character, and his sterling quality of candour had made him an outstanding personality amongst the Irish hierarchy long before 1916, as the following instance will testify. Even in his early manhood he had suffered slightly from deafness, and this disability grew with the passing of the years, so that eventually he became extremely deaf. Like so many afflicted with the complaint, he was rather sensitive about it, never flaunting the fact. At a synod in Maynooth, he was particularly interested in one matter which was down for discussion. When this item was reached it was fully debated, but Dr O'Dwyer sat silent. Eventually the assembled prelates arrived at an unanimous conclusion concerning it. Then the president rang his bell for the next item on the agenda. To the surprise of all present, the bishop rose, and spoke to the item which had just been decided, and spoke to such effect, that the meeting unanimously reversed their previous decision!

It is significant of the impression he had made on his brother clergy that on the death of Bishop Butler in 1886 this curate of forty-three years was placed as *dignissimus* of the three recommended by them to the Holy See as his successor. Nor indeed were the citizens of Limerick less appreciative of his great worth. The night following his consecration was turned into day, every Catholic home in the city being illuminated, hundreds of bonfires blazed in the streets, and a torchlight procession headed by the city bands paraded through the town.

How his heart must have glowed within him at this manifestation of his people's love. And yet, scarcely had he ascended the episcopal throne, when the clouds of unpopularity were to gather around it, casting on it a dark shadow that was that only to be dispelled by the passing of the years.

In 1886 John Dillon and William O'Brien, acting without the authority of Parnell, urged on the people the adoption of the Plan of Campaign as the most certain means of defeating tyrannical landlordism, and was accepted by them in no uncertain manner. Dr O'Dwyer was the first and almost only prelate to voice a protest against it because, as he was to state a little later: 'I have condemned the Plan of Campaign and Boycotting. I believe them not only at variance with the very first elements of civilised life, but unjust, and boycotting in particular as essentially anti-Christian.'

The British government sought through the medium of an 'unofficial' diplomat to enlist the aid of the Vatican in defeating this new menace, and Pope Leo XIII sent a high ecclesiastic to investigate matters. After an extensive and painstaking examination the monsignor returned to Rome and presented his report. In April 1888, His Holiness issued a prescript in which Boycotting and the Plan of Campaign were formally and authoritatively condemned. Incidentally, it was assumed at the time, that this decree was based on Monsignor Persico's report, but many years later some of his private correspondence, published by Arthur Griffith in the *United Irishman*, vindicated him from this aspersion and proved him to have been in sympathy with the aspirations of the Irish people.

In 1900, the Plan of Campaign was adopted by the tenants on the Glensharrold Estate, near Ardagh, County Limerick. This estate had been mortgaged to a Scottish insurance company, and later had been placed by them in the court of chancery. Bishop O'Dwyer intervened to prevent the plan from being carried into effect, and endeavoured to make a settlement. In the course of a letter to the parish priest, which was published in the press, he set out to prove that the terms offered the tenants were reasonable, and should certainly be accepted in preference to the wholesale evictions which were threatened. In referring to the bishop's action, during the course of a debate in the House of Commons, John Dillon denounced him in extremely strong terms.

Dr O'Dwyer, in a letter to *The Freeman's Journal*, retorted in kind, and as a result Irish public opinion ranged itself against him. Though a motion condemning his attitude was defeated on a vote by the corporation of Limerick, a great demonstration of protest was held in the city on Sunday 24 August at which John Dillon and William O'Brien were the principal speakers, and the bishop was held up to public odium.

Seventeen years later, when he received the freedom of the city from the corporation, he made a pathetic allusion to that demonstration:

> I thank you very heartily for this great honour conferred on me, but I confess that I feel somewhat strange in these surroundings of public favour. Popularity is a novel experience to me, and I must be on guard against its fascination, not indeed, that I ever attached much importance to it, or sought it. We all know the fickleness of *Popularis aura,* and the man who relies on it will probably be marooned in the end. Some of you will remember the early years of my episcopate when the correct thing politically was to treat me as an enemy of my country, because I had the audacity to think and to say that the methods of political agitation were amenable to God's laws. I was heartily in sympathy with the farmers in their movement to emancipate themselves from the yoke of an intolerable landlordism, but I condemned as immoral the methods of the Plan of Campaign and Boycotting as intrinsically unjust, and the latter as essentially unchristian, and for that, and that alone, an attempt was made to hound me down, and silence me. A meeting was held here in my own city, under the shadow of my own Cathedral, and the full strength of a powerful organisation was exerted to discredit and defame me.

That eminent historian, the Very Rev. Myles Ronan, in alluding to Bishop O'Dwyer entering the lists as the champion of the people after Easter Week, pictures him as ascending from the depths of Toryism to the apotheosis of Irish nationalism. But this is not correct. The bishop was proud to recall that he stood on Isaac Butt's platform when the 'Father of Home Rule' sought, and was elected, to represent Limerick city in the British House of Commons, and this despite the fact that the then bishop had plainly intimated that he disapproved of his clergy taking any part in the election. It must also be borne in mind that this great demonstration of protest against his attitude was held on the very eve of the disastrous Parnell split, which was destined to drive the Parliamentary Party into impotent factions, and to reduce national sentiment to its lowest ebb. Apart from the fact that he publicly identified himself with other members of the hierarchy in their attitude towards the leadership of Parnell neither he nor the clergy of his diocese participated in the squalid struggle that followed the split. And although from time to time, after the warring factions had coalesced in 1900, he occasionally gave vent to criticism of some of their actions, it certainly cannot be said that he ever showed an anti-national spirit. From the tenor of his speech on receiving the freedom of Limerick, it may indeed be deduced that for a considerable time he had been convinced of the fatuity of parliamentary agitation, especially as a means to obtain self-government.

But it was not until 1915 that the bishop was destined to prove that the spirit of nationalism was inherent in him, and to give a much-needed lead to the people. Since the Great War began in August 1914, the youth of Ireland had been pestered by a score of different agencies to enlist in the British army, and thousands succumbed to the wiles of British propaganda; but it was considered that there were many more thousands who would be suitable cannon fodder to help the designs of British imperialism. There were rumours of conscription and possibly as a result the tempo of emigration to the USA was quickened. Early in November some six hundred and fifty Irish boys arrived in Liverpool from Holyhead, and having booked their passages in Ireland proceeded to the office of the Cunard company to obtain them. A hostile crowd gathered, taunted them with being cowards and traitors, and mobbed them. As a sequel the Cunard company refused to ship them, and returned their passage money.

On 10 November *The Munster News* published the following from the bishop:

Limerick, Wednesday.

Sir

The treatment which the poor Irish emigrant lads have received at Liverpool is enough to make any Irishman's blood boil with anger and indignation. What wrong have they done to deserve insults and outrage at the hands of a brutal English mob? They do not want to be forced into the English army, and sent to fight English battles in some part of the world. Is that within their right? They are supposed to be free men, but they are made to feel that they are prisoners, who may be compelled to lay down their lives for a cause that is not worth 'three rows of pins' to them.

It is very probable that these poor Connaught peasants know little or nothing of the meaning of war. Their blood is not stirred by the memories of Kossovo, and they have no burning desire to die for Serbia. They would much prefer to be allowed to till their own potato gardens in peace in Connemara. Small nationalities, and the wrongs of Belgium, and Rheims Cathedral, and all the other cosmopolitan considerations that rouse the enthusiasm of the Irish Party, but do not get enough of recruits in England are far too high-flying for uneducated peasants, and it seems a cruel wrong to attack them because they cannot rise to the level of the disinterested Imperialism of Mr T.P. O'Connor and the rest of the new brigade. But in all the shame and humiliation of this disgraceful episode what angers me most is that there is no one, not even one of their own countrymen, to stand up and defend them. Their crime is that they are not ready to die for England. Why should they? What have they or their forbears ever got from England that they should die for her? Mr Redmond will say a Home Rule Act is on the statute book. But any intelligent Irishman will say a *simulacrum* of Home Rule, with an express notice that it is never to come into operation. This war may be just or unjust but any fair minded man will admit that it is England's war, not Ireland's. When it is over, if England wins, she will hold a dominant power in this world, and her manufactures and her commerce will increase by leaps and bounds. Win or lose, Ireland will go on, in her round of misgovernment intensified by a grinding poverty which will make life intolerable. Yet the poor fellows who do not see the advantages of dying for such a cause are to be insulted as 'Shirkers' and 'Cowards' and the men whom they have raised to power and influence have not one word to say on their behalf.

If there is to be conscription, let it be enforced all round; but it seems to be the very intensity of injustice to leave English shirkers by the million go free and coerce the small remnant of the Irish race into a war which they do not understand, and which, whether it is right or wrong, has but a secondary and indirect interest for them.

I am, dear sir, your obedient servant,

Edward Thomas, Bishop of Limerick.
10 November 1915.

Need it be said that this outspoken letter created a great sensation, but while it had the effect of compelling all thinking Irishmen to consider the position into which insidious British propaganda, and the political blindness of their leaders, had led them, it had the effect of exasperating public opinion in England, which was fanned to a white heat by the press of that country. A choice contribution was made by a columnist in the *Daily Sketch* who, writing over the *nom-de-plume* of 'The Man in the Street', vilified the Bishop as a traitor and claimed that:

> The Catholic clergy of Ireland have done magnificent work in stirring up the Irish people to a realisation of what the Allies are fighting for, and it is they who will be the severest critics and most remorseless judges of the Bishop of Limerick ... 'The crime of the emigrants,' says Dr O'Dwyer, 'is that they are not ready to die for England.' That, my good lord bishop, is a lie. The Irish leaders are asking them to die for the good old cause, for which brave Irishmen have always been ready to die: the cause of freedom, the cause of the weak, oppressed and tortured by the strong.

The Kerryman of 20 November carried this strong editorial protest against the diatribe of 'The Man in the Street':

> In an article which appeared in the English *Daily Sketch* of Wednesday, the Catholic Bishop of Limerick, Most Rev. Dr O'Dwyer, is vilified for having had the hardihood to protest against the action of an English mob at Liverpool in heaving insult upon some of his countrymen who desired to emigrate to America. The would-be emigrants were taunted with showing the 'white feather' and were called 'cowards' and 'traitors' by a crowd of Englishmen who were, with the exception of one, we are informed, all of military age themselves. This 'Man in the Street' of the *Daily Sketch* would do well to put his own house in order before trying to besmirch the actions of brave Irishmen, whom, he says, it would be absurd to treat as if they were English. This article should call forth a protest from every Irishman worthy of the name.

It would be almost impossible for the present generation to realise the sensation caused by the insurrection of Easter Week. From August 1914 onwards, the overwhelming majority of the people of Ireland had been carried along in the current of 'pro-Ally' sympathy by subtle British propaganda. Only a handful of Irish Volunteers scattered through the country preserved their sanity, and amidst the hostile jeers of the populace had kept the flag of Irish nationality flying. Accordingly the first reaction of the people generally, on learning of the outbreak in Dublin, was one of dismay and indignation. But with the barbarous execution which followed, when the chivalrous English lashed the bullet-shattered body of James Connolly to a chair as a target for their marksmen, came a feeling of revulsion. Yet even then, public sentiment was confused and bewildered. Ireland stood at the crossroads. But she had not long to wait for a lead.

Flushed with his triumph over the men of Easter Week, the blood-stained tyrant Maxwell had the audacity to send a note to the bishop in which he virtually ordered him to remove two of his priests 'to such employment as will prevent them having intercourse with the people' because he, Maxwell, considered them 'a dangerous menace to the peace and safety of the Realm'.

One might have anticipated from his temperament that Dr O'Dwyer would have sent a curt refusal to this insolent demand. But instead he replied through his secretary that the action Maxwell requested him to take towards these two priests would be a very severe punishment, which he had no right to inflict on them except on a definite charge supported by evidence. He asked that the charges against them should be specified.

Maxwell fell into the trap and furnished the particulars required. One of the priests had been reported as speaking against conscription in his church in November 1915; was said to have attended a lecture by P.H. Pearse on the Irish Volunteers of '82, and to have blessed the colours of the Irish Volunteers. The other priest, explained Maxwell, had been active in organising the Irish Volunteers; had got printed leaflets appealing to the young men of the GAA to join the Irish Volunteers and had been present at a meeting when a certain John McDermott delivered inflammatory and seditious speeches.

This was the bishop's acknowledgment of that letter:

Ashford, Charleville,
17 May, 1916.

Sir,

I beg to acknowledge receipt of your letter of 12th instant, which has been forwarded to me here.

I have read carefully your allegations against Rev. — and Rev. —, but do not see in them any justification for disciplinary action on my part. They are both excellent priests, who hold strong national views, but I do not know that they have violated any law, civil or ecclesiastical.

In your letter of the 6th instant you appealed to me to help you in the furtherance of your work as military dictator of Ireland. Even if action of that kind was not outside my province, the events of the past few weeks would make it impossible for me to have any part in proceedings which I regard as wantonly cruel and oppressive.

You remember the Jameson raid, when a number of buccaneers invaded a friendly state, and fought the force of lawful government. If ever men deserved the supreme punishment it was they, but officially and unofficially, the influence of British government was used to save them and it succeeded. You took care that no plea for mercy should interpose on behalf of the poor young fellows who surrendered to you in Dublin. The first information which we got of their fate was the announcement that they had been shot in cold blood. Personally, I regard your action with horror, and I believe that it has outraged the conscience of the country. Then the deporting of hundreds and even thousands of poor fellows without a trial of any kind seems to me an abuse of power as fatuous as it is arbitrary, and altogether your regime has been one of the worst and blackest chapters in the history of the misgovernment of the country.

I have the honour to be, Sir, your obedient servant,

Edward Thomas, Bishop of Limerick.

To General Sir J.G. Maxwell,
Commander-in-Chief, the Force in Ireland.

Need it be said that this closed the correspondence. From all over the country came resolutions passed by public bodies, congratulating him on his devastating rejoinder to Maxwell. In acknowledging one such from the Tipperary Board of Guardians, he wrote:

The Palace, Corbally,
June 23rd, 1916.

Dear Sir,

I beg to thank the Guardians of the Tipperary Union for the resolution which they were so good to adopt in approval of my attitude towards that brute, Maxwell, who, in my opinion, is only one degree less objectionable than the government that screens itself behind him. But Ireland is not dead yet; while her young men are not afraid to die for her in open fight and, when defeated, stand proudly with their backs to the well as targets for English bullets, we need never despair of the old cause.

And your resolution will be a comfort to those who reverence the memory of Ireland's martyrs, and will assure them that our countrymen, in spite of all the corruption that is at work, distinguish between genuine patriotism and all the spurious stuff that has been distinguishing us of late.

Personally, I am particularly glad that your resolution has been proposed by a Cullen man, Mr Quinlan, to whom, and to his seconder, Mr M. Ryan, I send with my blessing, my sincere thanks.

I am, dear sir, yours very truly,

Edward Thomas, Bishop of Limerick.
To the Clerk of the Union, Tipperary.

The corporation of Limerick unanimously voted him the freedom of the city, and when it was formally presented to him in the council chamber, Town Hall, on 14 September, 1916, he availed of the occasion to deliver a masterly exposition of the Irish political situation, and when he ended by declaring amidst the enthusiastic plaudits of the assembled citizens: 'Sinn Féin is, in my judgment, the true principle.' Edward Thomas O'Dwyer, lord bishop of Limerick, had set the nation on the march to victory.

LIMERICK CHALLENGE TO BRITISH TYRANNY

by JAMES CASEY

ON 9 APRIL 1919, the British military authorities in Ireland proclaimed the city of Limerick a special military area. Barriers were erected around the city, and parties going to and from their daily occupation had to face the bayonets of foreign soldiery and the insolence of the police. In reply to this gross act of tyranny, the United Trades and Labour Council of Limerick replied with a general strike which led to one of the most momentous struggles fought against foreign domination in this country. The result was an overwhelming victory for Limerick Labour and nationalist Ireland.

The supposed reason for proclaiming the city a special military area was the death of a policeman at the Union Hospital on the occasion of the rescue of a Robert J. Byrne, a prominent member of the Trades and Labour Council, who had been arrested on a charge of having possession of firearms. He was sentenced to twelve months' imprisonment with hard labour. On 1 February, the feelings of his fellow-workers were expressed in the following leaflet circulated by the council:

> That we, the members of the Limerick Trades and Labour Council, assembled in conference, protest most emphatically against the treatment meted out to the political prisoners at present confined in Limerick County Jail, and view with grave alarm the inactivity of the

Visiting Justices and Medical Officer. Furthermore, we call on the public representatives to do their duty to their fellow-countrymen and take the necessary steps to have the prisoners receive what they are justly entitled to, namely, political treatment; that copies of this resolution be submitted to the local Press, Visiting Justices and Medical Officer.

During the discussion which took place at the meeting of the council, it was disclosed that on Saturday 1 February, Robert J. Byrne, of Town Wall Cottage, a well-known citizen and member of the Trades Council was sentenced to twelve months' imprisonment with hard labour, because a revolver was found at his mother's house. Naturally, he protested against the barbarous sentence. He was backed up by the political prisoners and then confined in Limerick jail. At first they resorted to constitutional methods, but finding those unavailing, they resorted to more vigorous procedure. A force of police was sent for.

When the police reached the prisoners' cells they deprived the men of their boots, handcuffed them, and in addition strapped many of them. In that shocking condition they were kept night and day. In the same jail was a man convicted of the manslaughter of a girl in circumstances of revolting brutality, and sentenced to twelve months' imprisonment in the first division by a judge lenient to his ilk. This man had nothing to do and was supplied with all comforts: a cot, books, newspapers, slippers, glasses, writing materials, in fact, everything that could be procured in a first-class hotel. Men who never committed a crime believed they were entitled to at least the treatment that the criminal was receiving. Those responsible for the administration of law in Ireland at that time treated him as a gentleman and tried to degrade the others, who held honour dearer than life, and who, while ready to suffer for their national principles, would never willingly submit to be branded as criminals. In that attitude they naturally expected the vigorous support of the people of Limerick.

Because of the barbarous treatment meted out to them, Byrne

and others went on hunger strike and had to be removed to the Workhouse Hospital, as their lives were in danger. Byrne was shot in his hospital bed by his guard when an attempt was made to rescue him, and he died on the same evening in a house to which he had been carried. During the attempted rescue the policeman who guarded him was shot also. The Proclamation of the City followed, and when it became known that barriers with military and police guards, tanks, and armoured cars were to be erected on all the roads and bridges, strong resentment was expressed by the workers towards the attempt to prevent them attending to their work. Permits to enter the city were supposed to be granted by the military, but in reality the people were at the mercy of the police. Those who asked for permits had to present themselves at an office where they were first vetted by the police. If the policeman thought the applicant a fit and proper person, whose loyalty was beyond doubt, he might recommend him to the military authorities who then recorded his height, weight, the colour of his hair, eyes, and other details. Those particulars were all recorded on a card duly stamped and dated. In some instances applicants for permits had to go through the ordeal every day, as the permits were only granted from day to day. It is easy to visualise how impossible it would have been for workers to carry on under such conditions.

Accordingly, on 13 April, the Limerick Trades and Labour Council, which was composed of the representatives of thirty-five trades unions, held a special general meeting for the purpose of considering what action should be taken to meet the hardships imposed on the workers by the military proclamation and the erection of barriers at which they would have to face the bayonets of foreign soldiery and the insolence of the police when going to or coming from work. After solid deliberation at that meeting, and also at the further meeting held the same evening, it was unanimously decided to order a complete general stoppage of work on the following morning, 14 April. A proclamation to that effect was issued by the strike committee, and the strike began at 3 a.m. on Monday. Every

worker obeyed the call loyally. The strike committee took charge
of the entire city, and committees were immediately appointed to
take care of propaganda, finance, permits, food, and vigilance. The
propaganda committee was one of the most efficient and important
of many committees set up. It was in the charge of a member of
the Clerical Worker's Union and a member of the Typographical
Society. One of its smartest bits of work was done the night the
strike was declared. The strike was finally decided upon at 11.30
p.m. on Sunday, when naturally all printing offices were closed; but
inside of two hours the whole city was covered with the following
proclamation:

LIMERICK UNITED TRADES AND LABOUR COUNCIL
PROCLAMATION

The Workers of Limerick, assembled in council, hereby DECLARE
CESSATION OF ALL WORK from five a.m. on MONDAY, FOUR-
TEENTH OF APRIL, 1919, as a protest against the DECISION OF
THE BRITISH GOVERNMENT IN COMPELLING THEM TO
PROCURE PERMITS IN ORDER TO EARN THEIR DAILY
BREAD.

By order of the Strike Committee,

Mechanical Institute.

Any information with reference to the above can be had from the Strike
Committee.

NEXT MORNING THE propaganda committee commandeered a
sympathetic printing works, and with the permission of the printers
associated, it was worked day and night. There was as much sedition
printed in one hour in this office during the strike as would normally
get the operators ten years' imprisonment. The propaganda committee
was also responsible for drafting and printing money, printing
permits, proclamations, lists of food prices and the citizens' news

sheet, *The Daily Bulletin*. It was also the duty of the committee to prepare each evening a report of the proceedings of the day, for the foreign press correspondents who were then in the city. These reports were issued only to correspondents who undertook to have them published verbatim. It was particularly fortunate that, at the time of the strike, there were in the city numbers of correspondents from many countries, in view of a proposed transatlantic fight by a Major Woods, who was supposed to land in Limerick for re-fuelling. Those press correspondents were used to the fullest advantage, notably Mr Morris of the Associated Press of America, whose agency served seven hundred and fifty newspapers circulating in that country; also Miss Ruth Russell, of the *Chicago Tribune*, and Mr Philmore, of the Paris *Matin*. Those representatives had direct communication through the American Cable at Valentia without interference from the British authorities. Consequently, within twenty-four hours the press of America and Europe rang with the news of the Limerick workers' answer to the British proclamation.

An amusing incident occurred regarding a paragraph which appeared in an English daily pictorial describing the situation as 'Limerick's Comic Opera Strike'. A picket immediately dispatched to the hotel where the correspondent of that paper was staying, went straight to his room, and in less than half-an-hour he was standing before the general strike committee. Pale and trembling, he explained that the paragraph was evidently the editor's comments on the notes he had sent, and that he could not be held responsible. A warning that if anything further appeared in his paper detrimental to the interests of the strike committee, light, food and water would be immediately cut off from his hotel, had the desired effect. Like any organised government, the Limerick Soviet issued and controlled its own finance. A sub-committee attached to the propaganda committee was responsible for the printing and issuing of the famous paper money, specimens of which were later on exhibition in Limerick, Cork, Dublin, New York and San Francisco. This sub-committee was mainly composed of workers from the accounts departments of such big city firms as Messrs Cleeves, bacon factories, flour mills and corporation offices. A monetary scheme was devised by which it was possible to alleviate all immediate distress and to purchase food. This money was issued in denominations of 10/– and 5/– and 1/– notes, and to the tune of some thousands of pounds. The money was accepted by numbers of shopkeepers on the promise of redemption by the Trades Council. Ultimately the notes were redeemed and left a surplus from a fund that had been subscribed by sympathisers in all parts of Ireland.

The permit committee was in charge of four city councillors, men who had a thorough knowledge of the needs of people. Permits were issued to merchants to save perishable goods, to obtain and carry such commodities as coal, butter and flour from the railway station to traders. The necessary labour to maintain plant was provided in the gas and electricity works and in factories. Every effort was made to prevent inconvenience. Permits were also issued to doctor's chauffeurs and car drivers when necessary. Applications from American, Continental and British journalists were also granted to interview Major Woods on his proposed Atlantic flight. Sir Stephen Quinn obtained a permit to remove from the city the petrol necessary for Major Woods' machine, on the condition that Sir Stephen would tell the Major that it was through the permission of the strike committee that the flight was taking place. Another American journalist in need of a change of linen, made an eloquent appeal to the committee for permission to buy a shirt. The chairman, not convinced of the urgency of the request, brought him before the general strike committee. That committee being busy at the time, one of its members suggested that the applicant should get a short shirt. It is not recorded whether our American friend availed of the suggestion.

The food committee was divided into two sections, one for the reception of food and one for distribution. In connection with the reception of foodstuffs, the farmers of the surrounding districts rose nobly to the occasion and sent in tons of food. Rev. Fr Kennedy of Ennis, did trojan work among the farmers of Clare in getting food for the besieged inhabitants of Limerick. Through his efforts, ably assisted by the Dalcassians, the food problem was eased. The committee established four food distribution depots which supplied the ordinary traders at prices fixed by the committee. Any trader found not carrying out instructions was immediately closed by the picket and his supplies stopped. A vigilance committee watched the distribution of foodstuffs and saw that no profiteering or unequal distribution was engaged in, and that the prices, as published by the food committee, were strictly adhered to. Shopkeepers were required to use direction in rationing supplies and to see that no undue quantities of foodstuffs were given to individuals. Equality of sacrifice was for all classes.

The pickets, which were numerous, paid particular attention to the opening and closing of shops at the prescribed hours, for the sale of necessary food, regulated queues outside provision shops, and controlled traffic. In fact, it was generally admitted that the city was never guarded or policed so well previously. The people for once were doing their own work, and doing it properly. Public houses were not allowed to open during the strike. Neither soldiers nor mis-named police were in evidence. There was no looting, and not a single case came up for hearing at the Petty Sessions.

The only vehicles that appeared on the streets were owned by those who had appeared in person before the permits' committee and obtained the necessary permission to ply. Any car that appeared without displaying the notice: 'Working under authority of the strike committee', was immediately ordered off the streets by the citizen police. An officer of the United States army arrived by train and obtained the necessary military permit to enter the city. It was his intention to visit relatives in the country, but he could not induce any of the hackney men to drive him to his destination. In time he appeared before the appropriate committee and received a permit to proceed. He delivered a spirited address, promising to expose British rule in Ireland when he returned to the States. 'I guess,' he concluded, 'it is some puzzle to know who rules in these parts. One has to get a military permit to get in; and be brought before the soviet to get a permit to leave.'

A typewritten notice posted up by the military in the streets disclaimed responsibility for the inconveniences caused to the people, and placed the blame for such upon 'certain irresponsible individuals'. To this the strike committee replied:

> Fellow citizens, as it has come to our notice that the military authorities are endeavouring to spread the falsehood that it is we, rather than they, who are trying to starve you, we hereby disclaim any such intentions, as we have already made every arrangement whereby foodstuffs will be distributed to our fellow citizens. Our fight is not against our own people but against the inhuman and tyrannical imposition of martial law by the British government which is solely responsible. As peaceful workers, we only desire that we should be left alone to exercise the right of free men in our own country. What is happening in Limerick now, what may happen thereafter, will be laid at the door of the British government, and in our fight for freedom we disclaimed responsibility for the doings of the said government. We confidently appeal to our fellow citizens of Limerick to aid us in preserving the order of our city and to cooperate with us in every way in making the strike effective. Should any suffering or inconvenience be occasioned, we rely on the men and women of Limerick, inspired as they are by old and proud traditions, to suffer them patiently, as our forefathers did before us in the glorious cause of freedom. Limerick has proud and noble traditions to uphold, and now in our hour of trial, we confidently rely on Limerick to fight gallantly in this glorious cause in which we shall soon have millions of supporters from all over the world.

And from the bishop and clergy of the city came the following manifesto:

> 1. That we consider the Proclamation of the City of Limerick in existing circumstances as quite unwarrantable without investigation of any kind. The citizens of Limerick are being penalised for the commentable incidents at the Limerick Workhouse.
> 2. That the military arrangements of the funeral of the late Mr Robert

Byrne were unnecessarily aggressive and provocative. The presence of armoured cars on the route and the hovering of aeroplanes over the city during the funeral procession were quite an uncalled for display, in the circumstances, of military power, and calculated to fill every right minded person with feelings of disgust and abhorrence.

3. That in fixing the boundaries of the military area, the responsible authorities have shown a lamentable want of consideration for the convenience of the citizens at large and especially for the working classes.

(Signed): DENIS HALLINAN,
Bishop of Limerick;

David Canon O'Driscoll, PP, VG, St Munchin's; David Canon Keane, St Munchin's College; Michael Murphy, PP, St Patrick's; P.A. O'Connor, PP, St Mary's; B.J. Connelly, Adm., St John's; Fr Bonaventure, OFM, Guardian, Henry Street; P. Hennessy, Prior, OSA; S.M. Fahy, OP, Prior; L.B. Potter, SJ Rector; J.F. Kelly, CSSR, Director of the Men's Confraternity.

At a special meeting of the Limerick chamber of commerce held on 19 April, a resolution couched in strongest terms was passed, and sent to Mr Bonar Law, the British statesman, demanding that material law be removed. Martial law was removed, and on 26 April the strike committee ordered all back to work, having demonstrated to the world that the people of Ireland united were competent to manage their own affairs without interference, whatever the pretext. During the whole two weeks of Limerick's protest there was not a single case of looting or disorder of any kind.

The women of Limerick, true to their grand traditions, played a noble part in the general strike, and the spirit of the very poorest was inspiring. Sarsfield himself would have been proud of such defenders of his city. From 1690 to 1919 was a long stretch, but the spirit of Limerick was as strong, proud and defiant at the time of the great general strike as when William battered its walls in vain. The city had sustained two memorable sieges in the past, and the third proved as big a stumbling block to British tyranny as any of its predecessors.

Whilst the Trades Council and strike committees controlled all activities inside Limerick city, during the general strike, the Irish Republican Army was busy without. Supplies of much needed food for the beleaguered population were systematically collected from neighbouring towns and villages. After nightfall, relays of boats with muffled oars were successfully used to run the food and other supplies through the blockade, and to maintain communication with the citizens. Numerous stratagems were employed to elude the military cordons, and funeral hearses from the Union Hospital and other districts outside the city, did not always have a corpse in the coffin.

DARING RESCUE OF SEÁN HOGAN AT KNOCKLONG

by DESMOND RYAN

ON TUESDAY, 13 May 1919, the name Knocklong became famous. A small County Limerick station on the main Dublin–Cork railway line, won overnight a fame henceforward memorable and evocative. The events which gave Knocklong its new fame began at a dance in a Tipperary farmhouse and were rounded off by a song which swept through Ireland. That summer many a ballad singer drew his crowd with the lines:

> Now rise up, Mother Érin, and always be of cheer,
> You'll never die while at your side there stand such Volunteers.
> From Dingle Bay to Garryowen, the cheers will echo long
> Of the rescue of Seán Hogan at the Station of Knocklong.

Seán Hogan had been arrested early on the morning of Monday 12 May, at Meagher's of Annfield, near Thurles.* On the previous

---

* Seán Hogan, with Seán Treacy, Dan Breen and Seamus Robinson of the 3rd Tipperary brigade, and others, were much wanted by the British following the ambush at Soloheadbeg, three miles from Tipperary town, on 21 January 1919, when a consignment comprising 160 lbs of gelignite and thirty electric detonators was captured, and two policemen who guarded it were killed. The British offered a reward of £10,000 for information leading to the capture the four men named.

Saturday, Seán Treacy, Seamus Robinson, Dan Breen and Seán Hogan arrived in Rossmore, after a tour of the Clonmel district. They were persuaded to remain over the weekend and attend a dance on the Sunday night at Éamonn O'Dwyer's of Ballagh. The dance lasted into the small hours of the morning, and the four men waited until it was nearly over. Dan Breen was the first to leave with some friends for Rossmore, having arranged to meet the other three at O'Keeffe's of Glenough, where they were to sleep. Con O'Keeffe and Seán Hogan stayed behind after Treacy and Robinson left to make their way to Glenough, across the fields by Rossmore. They found Breen there before them. Exhausted by their wanderings during the previous weeks, and the long and merry dance, they went to bed at once and fell into a deep sleep, without worrying very much at Hogan's absence. It is true that Treacy had been at first disturbed when Michael Davern told him as he passed through Rossmore, that Hogan had decided to go on to Meagher's of Annfield. But he knew that Hogan was armed and, in ordinary circumstances, well able to care of himself. It seems that Con O'Keeffe and Seán Hogan had heard, as the dance broke up, that Miss Brigid O'Keeffe was going over to see her cousin, the Meaghers, at Annfield, and have breakfast there. They decided to go with her.

Although Seán Hogan was armed with a revolver, his visit to Annfield was to justify Seán Treacy's presentiment of danger. Unfortunately, Hogan had not a good knowledge of the house and the fields around Annfield, and he was also worn out with his night's dancing and the many sleepless nights and hardship of the weeks before. Hogan was so tired that he began to doze over the breakfast table. He finished his meal, however, laid his revolver and belt aside, and was soon sound asleep on a sofa. The work of the Meagher household went on. Mr Meagher and his two daughters, May and Brigid, were busy in the farmyard with preparation to send milk to the creamery. They had a clear view of the road, and saw a raiding party of six constables approaching.

In particular, they recognised one very officious constable from Roskeen whose presence in itself was warning. One of the daughters rushed in and shouted to Seán Hogan, who could easily have escaped if he had known the ground better. He buckled on his belt, and dashed for the field beside the house, a long field above the level of the road, screened by hedges, which, he thought, gave the quickest exist to the road. Behind him lay the wide stretch of land northwards, with ample cover where he might have eluded his pursuers, but unfortunately this was unknown to him. Hogan also mistakingly thought that the raiders were already entering Meagher's gate. In fact, they had seen him running down the field and were waiting for him when he dashed through the hedge right into their arms. Hogan, thus surprised, could make no fight for it, because his revolver was in his belt. He was at once overpowered and handcuffed.

The Royal Irish Constabulary had no suspicion of Seán Hogan's identity. He refused to give his name or any information whatever. Sergeant Wallace, Constables Ring, Reilly, Batt O'Shea and the rest were very puzzled by their prisoner. All they could discover before they marched him down to Roskeen barracks was that his Christian name was 'Seán'. Miss O'Keeffe had come up as they were leading him away and said, 'Good-bye, Seán!' If the raiders had recognised her, and raided O'Keeffe's of Glenough, they would have found, besides a very hot reception, Treacy, Robinson and Breen. But they had no idea that one of the wanted Soloheadbeg men was in their custody. Indeed beyond the fact that they had captured and armed man with some seditious documents in his possession, the police were not very excited by the results of their morning's work. Wallace, Reilly, Ring and O'Shea marched away. But the Meaghers had not seen the last of Sergeant Wallace.

They glowered at the retreating sergeant and his men tramping off to their barracks in Roskeen with Seán Hogan handcuffed in their midst. The police were hardly out of sight before Miss B. Meagher was on her way to warn Patrick Kinnane, who lived between Annfield and Glenough, of the arrest. Kinnane at once rushed down to O'Keeffe's. He had guarded these men on sleepless nights after Soloheadbeg, and now one of them was in the hands of the enemy. It could be only a matter of hours before Hogan was identified. Kinnane found the three men sound asleep. 'One of your follows is arrested,' he cried, 'the young fellow, I forget the name.' With his first words Treacy, Breen and Robinson were wide awake, and, in spite of their broken sleep, full of the resolution to rescue Seán Hogan, or go down fighting in the attempt. At that moment their information of Hogan's fate was very scanty, apart from the fact of his arrest. They did not know then that he had been taken to Roskeen, nor the circumstances of his arrest, nor that Wallace had sent a message to Thurles with news of the capture of an unknown armed man, nor that Hogan had been removed almost immediately to Thurles by police van, and there identified as one of the much-wanted Soloheadbeg men.

Whilst Treacy and the others debated and sent out messengers to gather any available news, Hogan was already under lock and key – and persistent interrogation – in Thurles, where he was to be detained until Tuesday evening. The police exhausted every effort to make him give information against his companions, from flattery to threat of violence; they insinuated that Breen and Treacy had turned informers and were on their way to London with a free pardon and a handsome reward; they offered Hogan money and a safe-conduct if he could give away the secrets and plans of the Volunteers. Seán Hogan laughed at the threats and bribes, and said nothing in reply. About 6.40 p.m. on Thursday evening he was led out from Thurles barracks. His escort consisted of Sergeant Peter Wallace and Constables Reilly, Ring and Enright, the first three from Roskeen and the last from Thurles. The journey to Limerick Junction was uneventful. At Limerick Junction, Sergeant Wallace produced the tickets he had bought for the party at Thurles, and said significantly: 'Four returns, *and one single*!' The sergeant himself had been the victim of hard and prophetic words earlier in the day when he had been present at raid at Annfield in company with Inspector Hunt of Thurles, which had lasted from one to five o'clock without result. As Sergeant Wallace had come down a steep ladder from a loft to the kitchen he said jocosely: 'This is like the descent into Hell!' The Meagher girls snapped tartly in reply: 'You will be there quick enough!'

Between Hogan's removal from Thurles and the news of his arrest having reached Treacy thirty-six hours before, much had happened. In the very loft in Annfield which Wallace had searched, Philip Meagher had heard the night before from Patrick MacCormack not only the whole story of Soloheadbeg, but the plans – or rather the first plans – for Hogan's rescue at, not Knocklong, but Emly. Miss B. Meagher, as soon as the news of Hogan's detention in Thurles reached her, boldly visited the barracks several times and asked a detective named Fox on what train Hogan was travelling. Fox knew Miss Meagher quite well, received her courteously, but evaded her questions. He laughed, shook his head, and said finally, 'Oh, well, I suppose he's your young man, but I can't tell you.' After the Knocklong rescue, Fox kept the incident of her visits and questions to himself. Seán Treacy remembered this to Fox's credit, and later intervened from Dublin and stopped a proposal to shoot the detective. Treacy could not forget Fox's kindliness and his silence about the inquiries, which might very well, especially in view of the Meaghers' record, have implicated Miss Meagher in the rescue plans.

When Treacy learned that Hogan was in Thurles, he knew at once that Hogan would be taken to Cork, the usual destination for all men arrested under DORA in Munster, and he knew, too, that Hogan would be removed there by train. An attempt at rescue en route was at once decided upon. Emly was first discussed as suitable as it was near the borders of Cork, Limerick and Tipperary, with the police barracks a mile from the station, and no military garrison nearby. Moreover, Treacy, Robinson and Breen had the trusted

'Galtee battalion' of Galbally at hand, if the need arose. The plans were several times, of necessity, changed; eventually Emly was dropped in favour of Knocklong at the last minute, and adjustments in detail were necessary. The last minute alteration was responsible later for the misunderstanding which occurred about a message sent to Con Maloney, acting commandant of the 3rd Tipperary brigade, which informed him indeed of the intended rescue, but contained no demand for immediate help or reinforcements. This first message of Treacy's reached Con Maloney safely, but no further message was received by him or by Dinny Lacey in Tipperary town on the critical date. A persistent belief arose after the Knocklong rescue, however, that Treacy, at some stage sent an appeal for help to the Tipperary men which miscarried. Exhaustive inquiries failed to trace any such message, although Con Maloney, Dinny Lacey, Seán Fitzpatrick and the other officers in Tipperary made every effort to do so. There was resentment among the Tipperary men at any suggestion that they would have left Treacy or the others in the lurch.

Con Maloney himself confirmed that the misunderstanding arose from the sudden change of plan. And this becomes clearer when the movements of Treacy, Robinson and Breen are considered. They rode by a circuitous route from Rossmore, having satisfied themselves that any attempt to attack the barracks at Thurles was impossible – at eleven o'clock on the morning of 12 May 1919 – and in the small hours of the following day reached Maloney's of Lackelly, in the neighbourhood of Emly. It was between 3.30 and 4 a.m. They came by Donohill, Oola and Ballyneety, and had been obliged to avoid the main roads. They knocked up the Maloney household and were warmly welcomed. Mai Maloney was impressed with the extreme agitation of Seán Treacy. He was, she declared, 'nearly off his head thinking'. And when he asked a question aloud, it was about trains and timetables, about this station and that station. In those tense small hours of 13 May, around the breakfast table, the Knocklong rescue was planned. As the three men sat there it was very evident that they had reached a decision. Knocklong it was to be. The countryside there was quiet and deserted on one side of the station, and the two nearest barracks were at least three miles away.

Seán Treacy was disturbed when he could not discover definitely whether Hogan would be moved or not. He asked Mai Maloney to go to Thurles and make inquiries, and when she agreed, declared that he would look after the house in her absence and do all the work. (She was very amused on her return to find that he had more than kept his word.) Before she left, the final rescue plans had been fixed. By now, all idea of summoning the Tipperary men, some seven miles away, had been abandoned. Nor would it have been possible to summon them. Four messengers only were available. In Lackelly, Mai Maloney, who had gone to Thurles; Jerry Callaghan, who left for Galbally with an urgent message for Éamonn O'Brien from Treacy; Joe Taylor and Bill Fitzpatrick. None of these was, in fact, sent to Tipperary. Seán Treacy instructed Fitzpatrick to inform David Bourke, who was in charge of the area, to tell Thomas Shanahan of the Knocklong Coal Store to be on the lookout for code telegrams which would be sent to him. These telegrams would deal with Hogan's movements and should be brought to Treacy at Knocklong station. Hogan would be referred to as 'the greyhound'. If Hogan left by any train, the telegram was to state that the greyhound was travelling by that train; if Hogan was detained in Thurles, the telegram would read: 'greyhound still in Thurles'.

Mai Maloney had arranged with Michael O'Connell who had public house in Main Street, Thurles, and his friend, Joe McLoughney, to send these wires to Shanahan. Unfortunately, David Bourke was unable to get in touch with Shanahan, who was, therefore, very bewildered when he received a telegram in the early afternoon. This telegram had been dispatched from Thurles 1.45 p.m. and read: 'Greyhound in Thurles still. Michael O'Connell.' The 9.15 a.m. train from Dublin had reached Knocklong at 1.29 p.m. and left three minutes later (just at the time when Sergeant Wallace was busy raiding Annfield). The three men met this train at Emly. Seeing that Hogan was not on board, they returned to Maloney's, and prepared to meet the next train at Knocklong, which was due there about 8 p.m. On their return to Lackelly, Jerry Callaghan was sent, as before mentioned, with a short dispatch to Éamonn O'Brien informing him, to quote the actual word of the message: 'Will operate in Knocklong, 7 p.m. Meet Maloney's, Lackelly, and bring help.' Éamonn O'Brien knew at what this short dispatch meant, and what Treacy wanted him for. He knew that Hogan had been arrested and guessed that it was a last desperate attempt to save Hogan from the hangman. The result of any trial of Hogan was a foregone conclusion, and Éamonn O'Brien understood quite well that Treacy, Robinson and Breen would stick at nothing, not even this desperate venture of intercepting the train and snatching their young comrade from his well-armed guards. Nor was Éamonn O'Brien a man to count the cost. He and his brother John Joe, had two revolvers between them, but he knew quite well that he had no arms to give the men whom he immediately summoned: Jim Scanlon, Edward Foley and Seán Lynch. He told his brother: 'I'll be away this evening. If anything happens, and I don't come back, keep an eye on my wife and child.' But when John Joe heard what dangerous work was afoot, he at once said that he, too, was coming to share the risks.

The five Galbally men set out for Maloney's at Lackelly where they met Treacy, Breen and Robinson. Treacy came to the point at once and explained the revised plan. Four of the Galbally men, John Joe O'Brien, Foley, Lynch and Scanlon were to cycle to Emly, board the train, find out if Hogan was on board, and signal to Treacy, O'Brien and the others at Knocklong station. Word had been sent to Thurles that a local Volunteer was to watch and board any train by which Hogan might travel, and to wave a white handkerchief from the window as a signal that Hogan was on the train. This man, 'Goorty' MacCarthy, did in fact travel on the train. His presence aroused no suspicion, but he had no opportunity to give his signal as things moved much too fast. It is very probable, however, that it was he who gave Seán Hogan the first inking that something was in the air. Hogan was unable to shake off the vigilance of the Royal Irish Constabulary escort. Several times he asked to be taken down the corridor, but he was always under strict guard. He noticed a man, vaguely familiar in appearance, who persisted in hanging round the corridor, and who edged near him as if to whisper. The incident set him thinking as he sat in the carriage. He knew that Treacy, Robinson and Breen were capable of the most reckless and determined efforts to save him, and in some way this hovering figure was a message of hope. Hogan was seated with his back to the engine, still handcuffed, between Sergeant Wallace and Constable Enright, both of whom were armed with revolvers. Opposite him were Constables Reilly and Ring, both armed with loaded carbines. He looked past Wallace into the corridor through the sliding door of the carriage.

Already the party at Maloney's in Lackelly had broken up. The four Galbally men had set out for Emly. Robinson and Breen cycled straight into Knocklong. Treacy and O'Brien went down to Knocklong station by the chapel, and arrived about 7.45 p.m. They still had some twenty minutes to spare. As David Bourke's message had failed to reach Thomas Shanahan, he was still a bewildered man. O'Connell's telegram about the greyhound was in his pocket, and, by a coincidence, it might very well have concerned his own private business. He had not connected with Seán Treacy or Volunteer affairs in spite of Michael O'Connell's name. The day before he had sent a greyhound bitch to Mr Twamley, of Rathcoole, County Kildare, by the morning train, and wired to Twamley that it had been sent.

The telegram from Thurles puzzled him, but he connected it naturally enough with the previous day's business. After some discussion with the stationmaster, Thomas Canty, he wired to Michael O'Connell to send back the greyhound; and then, still a worried man, went across the road from the coal store for a drink. Shortly afterwards Treacy and O'Brien arrived in Knocklong. Treacy had expected that a messenger would meet him at the station. He sent Éamonn O'Brien in search of Shanahan, and gave him a close description of the man, as O'Brien did not know him. O'Brien was directed to the public house, where he looked round, and at once saw a man who resembled the description that Treacy had so minutely given. He called the man aside, asked him his name. It was Thomas Shanahan, who looked very relived when O'Brien next asked him whether he had any message. Shanahan knew then that the telegram was a code, and that he could stop worrying about his greyhound in Kildare. He handed O'Brien the telegram which read: 'Greyhound in Thurles still'. As O'Brien hastened back to Treacy, he thought that there would be no rescue that evening. Treacy heard the message without comment, or giving any sign of his feelings. He decided to wait for the Galbally men coming in the train from Emly. At that moment there was a warning of the grave risks the rescue party was taking. As a rule, the evening trains from Cork and Dublin arrived simultaneously at Knocklong, and very often there were police or military on both. The Dublin-bound train came in first. Treacy and O'Brien stepped back into the shadow of the platform shelter. There was a party of armed soldiers in one compartment of the train, and in another some Galbally policemen, who descended and made their way out of the station. The train moved out towards Dublin. Treacy and O'Brien stepped out onto the platform, much relieved. They wanted no sideshows until Hogan was rescued, if indeed he ever was rescued. Seán Treacy, as a much-wanted man, could afford no risk of recognition until he had done the work upon which he was staking his life. Éamonn O'Brien was glad that he had escaped the eyes of the Galbally policemen, who knew enough about him to keep a constant watch on his movements. Away down the line came the welcome sight of the Cork-bound train, and the whirl of smoke from its funnel as it swept rapidly under the bridge. Just then, Thomas

Shanahan came through the door and handed a second telegram to Éamonn O'Brien, which he was to never read. He found it in his pocket the following day, and tore it into small pieces. But Shanahan had read it, and the code was plain enough this time, although there was a new signature to the message, which ran: 'Sending Wednesday evening, by 6.30. Bridget Fitzpatrick.' The time for codes was past, however. There was to be a very full quarter of an hour at Knocklong station. As the train stopped, and before it quite came to a standstill, John Joe O'Brien, who was standing at the window of a carriage, opened the door and jumped on the platform without waiting to use the footboard of the train. Behind him, as he jumped, another of the Galbally men pointed to a compartment near the engine. John Joe said quickly to his brother: 'They are there. Hogan's on the train.' Seán Treacy had half-turned towards the station exit as the train stopped. He thought the evening's work was over. As Éamonn O'Brien turned and told him what John Joe's message was, Seán Treacy took off his glasses, placed them in the case, shoved the case in his side pocket, with the words: 'Is that so? Come on then!'

Treacy was first into the corridor, his revolver drawn, with Éamonn O'Brien close behind him, his revolver ready, too. The two men passed down the corridor, the startled passengers gaping at them as they went. They threw back the sliding door of the carriage where Seán Hogan was sitting, with a sharp cry of command: 'Hands up! Come on, Seán, out!' The challenge took the police by surprise, and for a moment it appeared that the rescue would be a bloodless one. Sergeant Wallace and the three constables half rose, half raised their hands. Then Seán Hogan felt the cold muzzle of Enright's revolver on his neck as the constable crouched behind him suddenly, using Hogan as a shield. Treacy and O'Brien promptly opened fire with their revolvers. Enright clutched Seán Hogan's shoulder tightly and fell back dead, with a bullet through his heart. Afterwards, Treacy and O'Brien could scarcely remember why they fired, but they agreed that they would not have done so if Enright had not menaced Hogan. They resented the police evidence at the inquest later, and the ban on any questions which might have shown that the Knocklong rescuers had repeatedly asked Wallace and the rest of the guard to surrender, or that there had been any intention of shooting, except in a fair fight. That Treacy and O'Brien should fire in these circumstances was very understandable, in view of a rumoured order that all prisoners were to be shot incase of an attempted rescue. O'Brien himself, in describing the opening shots, said that the action of Treacy and himself had been spontaneous. 'We certainly,' he said, with emphasis and feeling to the writer, 'would never have fired if Enright had not made a move to attack Hogan.' As will be seen, too, in their subsequent prolonged duel with the determined Wallace, they made repeated appeals to him to surrender. Hogan wrenched himself free, and crashed his manacled hands in the face of his nearest captor. Treacy and Sergeant Wallace were locked in a death-grip. Enright's body thudded on the floor as Hogan hurled himself on Ring. Reilly had leaped on O'Brien's back after the first shots were fired, and now these two men wrestled fiercely together. The other Galbally men rushed in – unarmed with the exception of a dagger and a small revolver, both ineffective and futile weapons as it proved – Jim Scanlon, John Joe O'Brien, Seán Lynch and Edward Foley. They wrenched Reilly's carbine from his grasp, crashed it on his head, and he collapsed apparently unconscious on the floor. Even at the height of the struggle, Seán Treacy was determined that Hogan, handcuffed though he was, should escape. Lynch was ordered to take Hogan away. At first, even if Hogan had been willing to go, it would have been impossible because the struggle between Treacy and Wallace barred the exit as they hurtled to and fro, from carriage to corridor. Finally, Hogan and Lynch got into the corridor, but they did not descend onto the platform until the fight was over.

Fierce and thorough as the Knocklong fight was, it was a comparatively short one. The actual rescue in all lasted under fifteen minutes, between the arrivals of the train at 8.13 to its departure at

8.27, according to the statement of the stationmaster subsequently. The tussle between Treacy and Wallace – the central episode of it all – was finished in less than five minutes, although to the participants, every second was packed with effort and danger. Seán Treacy remained cool and silent, not a word escaping from him in the heat of it all, except his appeals to Wallace to surrender. He admired Wallace's courage, but his own was unbreakable as the two wrestled stubbornly for life and death. Panic reigned in the neighbourhood of the compartment, crowded with struggling men. Ring, dazed with the blow that Hogan had dealt him, and the reports of the revolvers ringing out in the narrow space of the carriage, jumped, or was thrown, out of the window. Wallace was deaf to every appeal: his great physical strength defied the combined onslaught of Treacy and O'Brien. Ever after they spoke with deep respect of his courageous and stubborn stand. Wallace and Treacy battled for the possession of the sergeant's revolver, a short Webley. Seán's own weapon had fallen from his hand, and was lost in the scurry of the struggling mass, hurtling and heaving together, cramped and constricted. Treacy gripped the sergeant's hand tightly; he stuck his thumb between the trigger and cap, and held on. None of the others could help him very much. John Joe O'Brien drew his revolver, a small .32, and fired at Wallace point blank, but the weapon missed fire. He asked Jim Scanlon to give him Reilly's carbine which Scanlon was vainly trying to use as a bludgeon, hampered by the proximity of his companions.

With the carbine John Joe O'Brien would have opened fire and finished the fight, and averted an approaching danger that was soon to threaten disaster to the rescue. But Jim Scanlon, who had come unarmed into the fight, obstinately refused to surrender the carbine. At last, seizing a favourable opportunity, Éamonn O'Brien closed with Wallace from behind and shouted at him for the last time to give up the struggle. Wallace was twisting his revolver towards Treacy's head; O'Brien tried to throw the sergeant to the floor, but Wallace, with a powerful effort, shook himself free. A shot rang out, and a sharp pain seared Treacy's throat. For a moment Seán believed that he was dying. With a violent concentration of all his will and strength, he wrenched the gun from his enemy's hand and fired twice. In that last stand against Treacy and O'Brien, Wallace's resistance had at last snapped, and now he collapsed on the floor, unconscious and fatally wounded. As the party turned to leave the train, a carbine cracked sharply twice outside on the platform, and O'Brien and Scanlon were wounded, although not seriously. Wallace had already wounded Treacy, who was feeling himself grow weaker and weaker, though no word of this escaped him. 'I thought I was a dead man,' he told Brian Shanahan afterwards. 'I had to hold my head up with both hands, but I knew I could walk, and I could jump off a ditch.' It was Constable Reilly who was firing the carbine. According to his own story later, he had lain senseless on the floor – or shamming insensibility, as Jim Scanlon always contended. At all events, Reilly recovered either his senses or his nerve towards the end of the struggle, and noticed Ring's carbine which he knew was loaded, under one of the seats. He secured it and wormed his way out unnoticed while the last stage of the fight raged. His own story was the Wallace and two men were in the corridor struggling, and the sergeant was on the point of collapse. Reilly gave one look round the carriage, empty except for Enright lying on the floor, dashed onto the platform and fired through the window at the two men, and saw blood immediately on the face of the man who was holding Wallace from behind. He saw no more of the two men who then, according to his story, disappeared. But he certainly became very busy with his carbine.

The *Tipperary Star* report of the rescue somewhat acidly commented that Reilly 'when he recovered from the staggering jab he had received in the affray, dashed out firing shots like a man entirely out of his senses. The stationmaster, among others, had a narrow shave from random bullets.' At this critical moment, the reports of the revolver and rifle fire brought Dan Breen and Seamus

Robinson hurrying down the crowded platform thronged with excited passengers. The last phase of the Knocklong rescue was a fast and furious exchange of shots between Reilly and Breen. Just as Reilly had fired into the carriage, Breen rushed up, and distracted his attention by a fierce and determined fusillade of revolver shots. Reilly fell back, still firing his rifle, and turned his attention to other targets. Breen had saved a very ugly situation, because his comrades were half-exhausted, some wounded – Treacy, as we have seen, almost fatally – and they had lost nearly all their weapons in the struggle. Breen however, himself was shot through one of his lungs and right arm. His revolver dropped from his hand. Half-blinded with blood and dizzy with pain, he picked up his revolver with his left hand and stood his ground. Robinson and Breen had been on guard outside the station, and both had been misled by a message sent out to them earlier that Hogan was not on the train, that is, when O'Brien had read the first telegram, 'Greyhound in Thurles still'. Robinson had also been surprised by the suddenness with which the fight started.

During the discussion of the plans, he had more than once impressed upon the party not to open fire without orders, and, as he heard the revolver and rifle fire as he entered the station, he first feared that a premature shot had ruined the rescue. Panic still reigned, and it was some minutes before Robinson could discover the actual position. He saw, however, that the worst had not happened. He prepared to intervene as soon as he could with effect. A thought flashed into his mind, a curious oversight in the plans. There had been no provision against any attempt to start the train. Robinson hurried quickly to a spot where he could keep his eye, and his gun, on the engine driver. The next minute he saw Treacy, Breen and Hogan, and knew the rescue had indeed succeeded. Hogan had been snatched from an armed guard and death, but at a heavy cost. It was the merest chance that Seán Treacy left the station alive. Dan Breen was semi-delirious with pain, and on the edge of collapse from loss of blood. He had a vague memory of being helped from the station into the roadway by an Irish soldier in khaki who had previously cheered for the Irish Republic while the fight raged. The rescuers hurried from the scene. Seán Hogan was taken into a neighbouring shop and his handcuffs broken with the aid of a butcher's cleaver and a heavy weight.

At the first blow, the handcuffs flew open, and Hogan hurried forward to rejoin the others. Seamus Robinson was the last to leave the station. The party pressed on quickly to Michael Shanahan's near Knocklong, where Dr Hennessy of Ballylanders (later a member of the Dáil) attended to Breen and Treacy. Breen's condition was so serious that morphine was administrated at once, and both the doctor and a priest, who arrived soon afterwards, were certain that he would not survive his wounds. Treacy, on the other hand, kept on his feet, remained cool and silent, and apparently had recovered from the shock of the encounter. Breen and Treacy were soon afterwards removed to Clancy's of Cush. In the meantime, Volunteer guards had been posted at all approaches to the house, and preparations pushed forward to place the rescuers beyond pursuit. Treacy and Breen had been driven from Shanahan's to Clancy's in a pony and trap. They arrived early in the morning and stayed there a day.

Dr Fitzgerald, of Cush townland (afterwards of Ardpatrick) was summoned to Clancy's soon after the two men arrived. He found Breen lying in a deep and drugged sleep. Seán Treacy was walking about, very calm and self possessed. When the doctor examined him, Treacy merely complained of a loose upper tooth, caused by a blow during the struggle. Dr Fitzgerald removed it with a forceps, and Treacy said no more. Ever after, the doctor judged Treacy by that request. He had the narrowest of escapes, said Dr Fitzgerald, and it was the merest luck that he ever left Knocklong alive after the throat wound inflicted on him, because the slightest deviation of the bullet to the right or left would have been fatal. The big blood vessels had just been missed. In its way, the wound was serious enough: it was very near the jugular vein and carotid arteries. 'Seán Treacy,' said Dr Fitzgerald to the writer, 'was not complaining about the big and painful wound in his throat. Most men, myself included, would not have bothered about anything else. Yet, all that worried Treacy was the loosened tooth. Treacy was the coolest man there, far cooler than I was. That was Seán Treacy!'

Until the removal of the Knocklong party, the Kilfinane Volunteers remained on guard with their scouts vigilant, while Seán Finn completed the arrangements to remove Treacy, Robinson, Breen and Hogan as quickly as possible. Between eleven o'clock and midnight two cars arrived at Clancy's in charge of Garrett McAuliffe. Breen, still very weak and semi-conscious, was carried to one car which was left in darkness, and Seán Hogan accompanied Breen. The first car went ahead with lights full on, as a pilot car, or decoy. The cars rushed along at a high speed right through the town of Kilmallock, where the bodies of Wallace and Enright had already been brought to the local barracks for an inquest, and eventually reached their destination, Keane's of West Limerick, between Newcastlewest and Dromcollogher, safely.

Éamonn O'Dwyer was raided at about one in the morning of 12 May. The raid lasted some hours, and as the military and police departed, a Limerick Volunteer arrived outside on a motor-cycle from Keane's with a dispatch from Seán Treacy giving full details of the affray, with a request for all available funds to be sent for the care of the wounded. He sent reassuring message to his mother, to Mrs Breen, Mrs Hogan, and a number of other friends. Éamonn O'Dwyer sent back some eighty pounds which, however, was returned to the Volunteer funds, because there was plenty of free and willing medical help available. Éamonn O'Brien and Jim Scanlon were taken charge of by friendly Volunteers, and after some narrow escapes from capture reached County Cork in safety, where Seán Treacy sent them a copy of the *Hue and Cry* with unflattering descriptions of themselves. Jim Scanlon was amused by the words: 'Jim Scanlon Wanted for Murder … in appearance remarkably like a Jew!' The Knocklong fight left its mark on Jim Scanlon until the day he died in the autumn of 1939.

He was closely connected with Treacy's fights and fortunes. He met Treacy and all the outstanding Volunteer organisers and leaders – Monteith, Ernest Blythe and Seán MacDermott among the number, in the beginnings of the movement in 1913; he marched with the Galbally company (of which he was an active officer and organiser and gun-runner into the bargain) to the projected attack on Ballylanders in Easter Week, and there met Treacy when he arrived with the news of the collapse of the Rising in the south. Scanlon and O'Brien were not to meet Seán Treacy and his three companions again until the autumn, when the Big Four formed their guard to the SS *Killiney* en route to the United States with dispatches from Breen and Treacy for their friends in America. During the summer of 1919 the Big Four spent a wandering life in the south. In West Limerick, they stayed in turn with the Long's, Sheehan's, Keane's, Duffy's and Kennedy's, then with friends in Kerry, Clare and North Tipperary, Seán Treacy spent some of the time on an island off the Clare coast with Seán Carroll and Joe Herbert of Castleconnell. Among their friends in North Tipperary were Frank McGrath, brigade commandant of the area, and a prominent GAA man, and 'Widger' Meagher, also a famous athlete. When Treacy, Breen and Hogan had been restored to health, they determined in consultation with Seamus Robinson, to discuss the whole position with the Dublin headquarters. Treacy and Breen cycled to Dublin and after an interview with Michael Collins, then adjutant-general of the Irish Volunteers, it was decided that the four men should go to Dublin. By the autumn of 1919 they all arrived there safely.

TRIALS AND EXECUTIONS OF EDMOND FOLEY AND PATRICK MAHER OF GALBALLY

by LINDISFARNAN

EAST LIMERICK WAS well represented in the rescue of Seán Hogan at Knocklong Station, for participating in that daring episode with the Tipperary men, Seán Treacy, Dan Breen and Seamus Robinson, were Ned Foley, Seán Lynch, Jim Scanlon and John Joe O'Brien, all from the parish of Galbally. When the rescue was successfully effected, the four wounded IRA men were carried across fields by their comrades to Shanahan's of Glenbrohane. There the party divided, as, whilst Treacy and Breen remained some time at Shanahan's, Scanlon and O'Brien were quickly taken by trap, first to Crowley's of Ballylanders, and later to P. Maguire's of Glenahoglisha, Ballylanders. Guided by T. Crowley of Ballylanders, and other local Volunteers, Dr Hennessy of Galbally, attended the wounded men. After some time, Scanlon and O'Brien moved on to Anglesboro, where they were sheltered under the friendly roofs of Ned Quane and Hanna Cleary.

When the wounded had been safely sheltered and given medical attention, Ned Foley, Seán Lynch and John Joe O'Brien returned to their homes. Immediately after the rescue, there was great police and military activity, which was conducted vigorously and over a wide area for some months. Ultimately, the British operations gradually eased off, and as Foley, O'Brien and Lynch did not appear to be under suspicion, they decided to remain at home. On the morning of 23 September 1919, however, the British swooped again and arrested Patrick Maher, Michael Murphy and Michael Scanlon who were taken under heavy escort to William Street barracks, Limerick. Charged with the murder of Sergeant Wallace and Constable Enright, who were killed in the Knocklong rescue, they were paraded with others for identification, and were picked out by crown witnesses as having participated in the rescue of Seán Hogan. For about three months subsequently they were remanded in custody from week to week, and during that time the British also arrested Thomas Shanahan, brother to Michael, and Michael O'Connell. With the exception of O'Connell, a Thurles man, all men held in custody were natives of Knocklong or Galbally. By that time, too, Seán Lynch and John Joe O'Brien had gone 'on the run' to avoid arrest.

The prisoners were returned for trial to the Belfast Assizes, where J.J. Power, solicitor, Kilmallock, with P. Lynch, KC; R. Best, KC, and Joseph O'Connor acted on their behalf. Mr Lynch and his colleagues made application to the High Court to have the trial changed to Dublin, but instead of granting that request, the high court fixed the hearing for Armagh Assizes, in July 1920. Shortly before the trial was due to commence, there was a hunger strike of the prisoners in Mountjoy, as a result of which one of the accused men was released. On the eve of the trial, Sergeant Reilly, who had been with the RIC at Knocklong as a constable, was kidnapped, and an application by counsel for defence for adjournment to the next Assizes, because of the absence of the Sergeant Reilly, was granted. The Grand Jury returned 'true bills' against three of the accused, Foley, Maher and Murphy, who were accordingly put back again for trial. The Shanahan brothers were acquitted. In the meanwhile, trial by court martial of all political prisoners superseded trial by jury, and the three accused were removed to Dublin and trial by court martial in the City Hall. Their trial, which began on 15 March 1921, lasted for five days, and at the end of the fifth day, Patrick Maher and Ned Foley were found guilty and sentenced to death. M. Murphy was acquitted. Maher had nothing whatever to do with the Knocklong rescue, and was sentenced to death with Ned Foley, so that the British could extract full vengeance for the death of the two policemen killed in fair fight. Foley was unarmed at Knocklong, as were in all three of the rescuers.

During the concluding stages of the trial, Mr Best, who closed the case for the accused, said that the broad issue before the court was whether they were satisfied with the identification of the two accused by three of the crown witnesses who had given evidence. To decide against the accused, the court should hold that the crown case had been proved beyond reasonable doubt. Counsel having contended that the evidence of crown witnesses was unreliable, referred to different descriptions given by them, and to a disagreement between two of the witnesses as to whether the man identified as Patrick Maher had or had not an overcoat at the scene of the rescue. It was also said that the man was injured, but Maher, who was at work next morning, had no more scratches on him than counsel had at that moment. Regarding the descriptions of the men wanted, which were compiled after the rescue at Knocklong, counsel said that it was fair to infer that they were prepared from reports given to superior officers by constables and soldiers who had been on the train. He asked the court to consider these descriptions, and said that he was absolutely confident that neither Maher nor Foley answered them, in whole or in part. When sentence had been passed, Mr P. Lynch declared that it was a terrible thing that these two Catholic peasants were brought up North to be tried by orange jurors in Armagh, and were again brought to Dublin and tried by military court.

Ten weeks had elapsed from the time of their conviction before the date for the executions of Ned Foley and Patrick Maher was fixed – Tuesday, 7 June 1921.

At six o'clock on the morning of the executions, the outer gates of the prison were opened, and from that time onwards groups of people wended their way towards Mountjoy. Between the inner railing and the prison door, a strong military guard taken up positions, whilst the armoured car stood facing the crowd. A large crucifix, surrounded by lighted candles, was placed on the railings which separated the military from the gathering of citizens who knelt in fervent prayer. Shortly after six o'clock, Mr and Mrs William Foley, parents of Ned Foley, and their second son and two daughters, accompanied by a number of relatives, arrived at the prison. They showed no traces of emotion, and quietly related to some friends an extraordinary occurrence which had taken place during the night at the Four Courts Hotel where they were staying.

At midnight the hotel was entered by crown forces who enquired for all male relatives and friends of the condemned men. In addition to the father and brother of Ned Foley, there were seven male relatives present, all of whom were picked out and removed in custody. They included Timothy Keogh and William O'Brien, uncles; John Sheehy, David Condon, Michael O'Brien, Michael Hayes and Michael Walsh, cousins. This news was received with great indignation by the crowd gathered outside the prison. Mrs Maher and her daughter then arrived, and soon relatives of both men joined the crowd in prayer. Hymns alternated the prayers, and the entire proceeding, which took place in brilliant sunshine, were deeply impressive and inspiring. Soldiers, who were on guard on the roof of the prison, as well as those who occupied positions outside the prison gate, looked on in silent wonderment and awe. Prayers for the dying were recited as the clock struck seven, and soon afterwards there was a deathly silence.

Meanwhile, inside the prison the condemned men, who had slept for three or four hours, were quite cheerful when awakened, and happy in the cause for which they were about to give their lives. Very Rev. Canon Waters, prison chaplain, accompanied by Rev. Fr McMahon, assistant chaplain, entered the prison shortly before six o'clock and proceeded at once to the condemned cell. Canon Waters celebrated Mass in the cell at six o'clock, and imparted Holy Viaticum, after which the condemned men received the Papal Benediction. A second Mass was celebrated by Fr McMahon at 6.30. During the masses, and up to last moment, both men prayed incessantly and with great fervour. Members of the Auxiliary division were present as guards at the last religious ceremonies, there being nine persons in the cell during the celebration of the masses. A few minutes before seven o'clock the executioner and his assistant entered and pinioned the hands of both men behind their backs. Then began the procession to the gallows. In front walked one of the executioners, followed by Canon Waters, reciting the prayers. Beside the canon walked Patrick Maher, who responded in a firm voice. Fr McMahon followed with Foley, who prayed fervently, and whose demeanour was calm and collected. The second executioner brought up the rear. On entering the execution chamber, the condemned men stood side by side on the trap beneath the scaffold beam.

Both stood under the ropes on the platform; the white caps were placed over their heads, and the ropes adjusted and tightened. The bolt was pulled, and both men gave their young lives for Ireland. Death was instantaneous, and the young Irish boys had faced it bravely and with fortitude and resignation. The two priests rushed forward, Canon Waters reciting the last prayers, whilst Fr McMahon anointed the bodies. Immediately prior to the executions, one of the Auxiliaries gave Ned Foley a pair of scapulars which came from Lourdes and which were worn by himself during the war. The scapulars were subsequently removed from the body and returned to the Auxiliary.

At 8.15, a typewritten notice, which announced that the death sentence on Patrick Maher and Edward Foley had been carried out, was affixed to the main gate at Mountjoy prison. Another copy of the notice, brought to the outer gate, was immediately seized by the people and carried off before the prison officials had time to post it up. Subsequently, possession of the notice at the main gate of the prison was obtained, and it was also taken away by somebody amongst the large crowd which had assembled in the vicinity.

Both Ned Foley and Patrick Maher had spent the last two years of their lives in Mountjoy jail, and had received Holy Communion, every morning for the last ten weeks of their lives. They were buried in one grave inside the prison walls, both chaplains performing the last rites. Theirs were the last executions before the Truce, and on the day before they faced the scaffold, they addressed the following last message 'to all the boys':

Fight on, struggle on, for the honour, glory and freedom of dear old Ireland. Our hearts go out to all our dear old friends. Our souls go to God at seven o'clock in the morning, and our bodies, when Ireland is free, shall go to Galbally. Our blood shall not be shed in vain for Ireland, and we have a strong presentiment, going to our God, that Ireland will soon be free, and we gladly give our lives that a smile may brighten the face of our 'Dear Dark Rosaleen'. Farewell! Farewell! Farewell!

WHEN THE IRA HELD NEWCASTLEWEST TOWN

by SEÁN

DURING THE YEAR 1919 and in the early part of 1920 the Irish Republican Army in Newcastlewest was faced with a particularly dangerous internal problem. Large numbers of ex-British soldiers, demobilised after the close of the first Great War, had returned home to the town. Many of these men were decent, upright Irishmen, and subsequently more than a few of them gave staunch support to the independence movement. There was amongst them also, however, and especially amongst the younger men who had been through the war, an element whose attitude to the national forces constituted a menace to the local success of the national cause. Prominent IRA, men and members of the Sinn Féin organisation were insulted and assaulted in the public streets; acts of lawlessness by ex-servicemen were frequent occurrences and highway robberies took place on roads leading to the town. For a time people from the country districts were afraid to go into Newcastlewest because of the reign of terror which was gradually being created there. The IRA had good reason to believe that this dangerous local situation was strongly encouraged by the British forces in the town. The climax was reached following the municipal elections of 1920. These took place in the month of January and the new council comprised IRA men, prominent members of Sinn Féin and of Cumann na mBan, with an agreed Labour representation. It was a revolutionary change in the constitution of the town commissioners as the outgoing body had included several justices of peace, and its chairman was an ex-captain of the British army and Irish land agent to an English earl.

At their first public meeting the newly elected commissioners of Newcastlewest renounced the English local government department and proclaimed their allegiance to the First Dáil Éireann as the lawful government of the Irish Republic. Whilst the meeting was in progress in the courthouse a strange scene was taking place in the streets outside. By the fitful light of the sparse street lamps, the townspeople observed a formidable company of British ex-servicemen march towards the courthouse in military formation and led by a hefty professional pugilist, stripped to the waist. The ex-soldiers were obviously bent on trouble-making, and a sinister background was imparted to the scene by a large patrol of RIC who appeared in open formation and with rifles at the ready. Amongst the shadows a small number of IRA men watched and awaited developments. The business of the town commissioners having been concluded three of the members, Michael Dore, Seán Brouder, and Gearóid McAuliffe, local IRA commander, left the building to attend a meeting at the Carnegie Library, then used as the headquarters of the local IRA company and of all national organisations. (It was later burned to the ground by the Black and Tans.)

The three men had barely entered the building when the ex-servicemen's battalion halted outside and threatened to wreck the library. The commissioners decided to go out into the street again and to contact IRA men in the vicinity with a view to calling up the entire IRA company with all possible speed. They had scarcely reached the centre of the street when they were surrounded and set-upon by the overwhelming crowd outside. Quickly though this attack developed it was no more swift than the counter measures of the few IRA men in the vicinity. These included Dan Enright, Johnny Brouder, Jim Meagher and Neddy Cregan, who were instantly in the middle of the fray, fighting grimly back-to-back. The attackers with their big advantage in numbers concentrated upon disarming Gearóid McAuliffe. They gathered round him on every side endeavouring to pinion his arms whilst they sought the automatic pistol which he carried. But Gearóid, having managed to free his right hand, got a finger to the trigger of the gun he carried and fired through his coat. The bullet lodged in the arm of one of his assailants who cried out that he had been wounded and ran to the RIC barracks. Thereupon the other attackers also loosen their hold and joined in the run for the shelter of the barracks.

Whilst the mêlée had been in progress Paddy Nunan, faithful IRA scout, had commandeered a bicycle and dashed for help. In response to his urgent summons IRA men rushed at the double towards the scene of the conflict. They came from every street in the town and from the outlying districts and as they concentrated in the square the Royal Irish Constabulary patrol also ran for their barracks. The big front door was slammed shut, chained and barred and the police took up positions behind the steel shutters then fitted to all police barracks. The IRA, of course, was an outlawed organisation compelled to meet and drill in secluded fields outside the town. That night, as a gesture of defiance, they came quickly into military formation right in front of the most strongly garrisoned Royal Irish Constabulary barracks in Country Limerick, and in a matter of minutes they had cleared the town of all who opposed them. They next placed patrols of their men on every street and peace and order, such as the town had not known for a long time, prevailed.

In the early hours of the morning a young lady employed at the local post office approached one of the IRA officers and warned that the police had sent an urgent message to military headquarters in Limerick city stating that the town of Newcastlewest was occupied by the IRA; that the police were powerless and were in fact besieged in their own barracks. Information was immediately sent out to the various patrols in the town advising the officers to prepare for the arrival of the military. A short time afterwards a fleet of Crossley tenders filled with soldiers and accompanied by an armoured car dashed into the town at high speed and pulled up in the square. Troops in full war kit jumped onto the road and, having lined up, a bayonet charge was immediately ordered in the direction of the Protestant church at the south of the square. The military had advanced but a few yards when the street lamps went out, plunging the town into darkness. The charging soldiers ran right up against the stone wall of the Protestant church, the IRA patrol in the square having easily eluded them in the darkness which fell so suddenly. It afterwards transpired that the officer commanding the IRA had previously arranged with the workers in the power house that the lights would be cut out at a pre-arranged signal. The troops then withdrew to the barracks. At daybreak they carried out raid for arms in the houses of Gearóid McAuliffe, Michael Dore, Jim Kelly and Seán Brouder. They searched Charles Davis, Paddy Nunan and Dick Kenny whom they encountered whilst raiding one of the houses.

A few nights subsequently British forces swooped upon the town again and this time they arrested Michael Dore, Seán Brouder, Eoin McAuliffe, Jim Liston, Neddy Cregan, John J. Brouder. Jim Kelly, Dan Enright and Jim Nunan. Gearóid McAuliffe and M.J. O'Gorman escaped the round-up. Escorted by a big detachment of soldiers in Crossley tenders and accompanied by the inevitable armoured car, the prisoners were conveyed to Limerick jail in a military lorry. Every possible attempt to humiliate them was made. They were handcuffed and kept in solitary confinement whilst nobody was permitted to visit them until the saintly and patriotic Bishop of Limerick, Most Rev. Dr Hallinan, visited each in his prison cell. Dublin Castle was at its wits end for a serious criminal charge to bring against the prisoners. Ultimately, it was considered a good idea to indict them jointly on a charge of attempted murder. This pretty scheme was upset by Brigade Commandant Seán Finn. Although 'on the run' for many months he and some of his Rathkeale boys marched into the town of Newcastlewest shortly after the arrests and his presence there had such a salutary effect on those who swore the depositions that there was no witness for the crown when the prisoners were ultimately brought to trial before two resident magistrates at Adare courthouse. The case, accordingly, collapsed and Arthur Griffith, regarding it as one of great importance from the propaganda point of view, sent down the late Louis J. Walsh, a patriotic Derry man and litterateur, to interview the released prisoners. Mr Walsh, who later became District Justice Walsh, was at the time acting as Irish solicitor in a case in connection with a state trial in London of a newspaper which had attacked Lord French's military administration in Ireland. He was then collecting information to be used in defence of the English journal which had the temerity to challenge the wisdom of French's jackboot rule.

FORMATION OF THE EAST LIMERICK BRIGADE
ITS FIRST COMMANDER

by LIEUT-COLONEL J.M. MacCARTHY

This article, from the pen of Seán Wall's intimate friend and brigade adjutant, is written out of the experience of close personal contact with this well-known East Limerick leader and the events of his active career in the IRA. Lieut-Col MacCarthy was associated with the Volunteer organisation from its inception, and was one of the original organisers, and at a critical period O/C of the famous Galtee battalion. Later he became vice-O/C, and adjutant of the East Limerick brigade, and as an officer of the brigade's active service unit took a prominent part in the many actions in which the unit was engaged. When the 4th southern division was formed Lieut-Col MacCarthy was appointed deputy divisional commander and divisional adjutant. He has filled many important posts in the army, and graduated with distinction from the command and staff school.

IT HAS BEEN said that Irishmen, with their highly developed sense of individuality and independence, besides making difficult subjects to command successfully, tend to produce more than the normal quota of leaders and aspirants to leadership. If this saying be true – and our history, as well as the record of Irish unit in other armies, appears to support it – a standard of leadership above the ordinary is necessary if Irishmen are to give their best as soldiers.

So it was, at any rate, on the eve of the Black and Tan campaign in East Limerick in 1918, as the then loosely linked Irish Volunteer organisation in that area strove to weld its component parts into a compact and unified brigade formation in preparation for the coming conflict.

The obstacle in the way of achieving this closely knit organisation was not a lack of leaders. On the contrary, it largely consisted of a multiplicity of talent and candidates for leadership. At this time the Volunteer movement in East Limerick was composed of a number of independent battalions. All of these could reasonably aspire to provide the leader of the proposed brigade in the person of their own commandants, nearly all of whom were of proven capacity with strong claim for selection. Indeed, more than one candidate was forthcoming, or in prospect, from some units. One battalion in particular was a prolific source of potential leaders. This was the Galtee battalion, a unit which calls for special mention here, not only on the grounds of its relevance to the story, but because it held an unique place in the Irish Volunteer and IRA organisations.

Originally embracing that corner of Limerick County between the Tipperary and Cork borders (Galbally, Ballylanders, Kilfinane, Knocklong, Ardpatrick and adjoining townlands), the unit was one of the earliest and most active formations in the movement. Because of its status and strength, its area was selected in 1915 as the location for one of the first Volunteer training camps organised by GHQ and in charge of the late Colonel J.J. O'Connell. But its proudest claim to fame rests on having originated the idea of the flying column or active service unit, the battalion flying column composed of Volunteers giving wholetime service as a unit, having been the first of its kind in IRA organisation.[†] As is now so well known, the active service unit system, once it became widespread,

---

† For a tribute in this connection see Ernie O'Malley's book *On Another Man's Wound*.

was the spearhead of the IRA operations, and the chief medium of the military successes of the Volunteers from 1918 to 1921.

It was the affairs of the Galtee battalion that gave rise to the circumstance leading to the formal establishment of the East Limerick brigade, and the appointment of its first brigadier in the early summer of 1918. Deciding to investigate questions arising out of a conflict of personalities within the battalion, GHQ detailed a staff officer to visit the area, and to examine the situation on the spot.‡ The GHQ representative, after preliminary investigations, ordered a formal court of inquiry at which he presided. With Lord French's proclamation issued just then – purporting to outlaw the Irish Volunteers – to give a little added solemnity to the proceedings, this court held protracted sittings at Knocklong. As the outcome, the GHQ delegate decided upon the unprecedented step of selecting and, in effect, appointing a brigade commander. This step was not, of course, in conformity with the procedure then governing such appointments, these normally being made by-election. That the assembled unit commanders did not seek to have this election system adopted – the right to which they were perfectly aware they could enforce under the constitution of the Irish Volunteers – was of itself evidence of their *bona fides*, and of the genuineness of their difficulties in choosing a leader in the circumstance already mentioned. This attitude, by the way, tends to refute the charges of mere factionism to which are sometimes ascribed the features of the Irish character exhibiting a lack of the sheep-like quality of being easily led and which in reality, as previously suggested, arise from a deeply seated sense of individuality and independence.

The choice of the GHQ representative had fallen on Seán Wall, an officer of the Bruff battalion, or as it subsequently became in the brigaded organisation, the 3rd battalion East Limerick. It is of

‡ M.W. O'Reilly, FCII, the present managing director, Irish National Insurance company, whose help in recalling relevant facts is acknowledged.

interest to record the general reasons for the selection of this officer –
until then acting as a company commander – in the GHQ delegate's
own words:

> From all the investigations I had made I was satisfied that I was justified
> in taking this action and subsequent events fully confirmed the stability
> of his character, strength of purpose and determination and qualities of
> leadership which Seán Wall possessed, and in a higher degree than might
> be ordinarily required. He not alone possessed those qualities but he
> also exercised them in the handling of that very delicate situation which
> existed before my arrival in the area, and perhaps to a greater extent
> immediately afterwards. He had been as it were planted in authority and
> others had been dispossessed of even the right to attain that authority,
> and yet despite these obvious disadvantages, Seán Wall rose above them
> all and had [made] his brigade one of the best fighting units in Volunteer
> organisation up to the time of his heroic death in action.

Born in 1888, near Bruff, of farmer stock, the newly appointed
brigadier was of more mature age than the great majority of those
he was now to command. For long a prominent and very energetic
worker in the Sinn Féin, Gaelic League and Volunteer movements,
and coming of a family closely identified with the national cause,
he was well known either personally or by repute throughout the
country. His brother, Fr Tom Wall,[§] was one of the two curates of
the Limerick diocese round whom had centred in 1917 the famous
controversy between the then bishop of Limerick (the late Most Rev.
Dr O'Dwyer) and General Maxwell, the British C.-in-C. The latter
had thought to induce the bishop to intervene against the two priests
in connection with their national outlook and activities, especially
their encouragement of, and association with, the Volunteers. Dr
O'Dwyer's stand in face of this demand, his rejection of General
Maxwell's proposals, and his comments on the foreign, political and

---

§ Now the Very Rev. T. Canon Wall, PP, Ballingarry.

military regime, were so caustic and uncompromising as to receive nationwide – one might say worldwide – publicity. Coming from such an eminent, respected, and for many an unexpected source, the support thus given was invaluable to the national cause at a time when the Volunteer organisation was but slowly recovering from the aftermath of the Easter Week Rising, and when the people in general were but beginning to feel the fresh surge in the nation's life-blood which followed the insurrection.

From an early age Seán Wall had given evidence of processing resource, determination and self-confidence – characteristics which figure prominently among the basic qualities required for leadership. The death of his father and mother within a few months of each other had terminated his secondary education at St Munchin's College, Limerick, leaving him at the age of sixteen to assume his parents' place in charge of the family affairs. Developing the means at his disposal, he quickly launched out into many fields of activity, displaying an inventive and progressive outlook in all he undertook. He became an expert building contractor, founding the firm of Wall and Forde which extended his contracting business throughout County Limerick, and was responsible for the erection of some of the principal creameries in that home of the dairying industry. The name of this firm, by the way, was to prove a stumbling block for the hostile intelligence at the height of the Black and Tan struggle. By then a 'much-wanted' man in the Limerick area was Thomas Malone, whose *nom-de-guerre* was Seán Forde. For long the latter was believed by the opposition to be the firm's junior partner who had no actual connection with the revolutionary movement. The many false trails thus followed and the waste of time and effort involved, amounted to a 'dispersal of force' by no means to be despised in the circumstances then prevailing.

On the inventive side, Seán Wall devised new cheese-making machinery in co-operation with a young engineer from the same locality, Nicholas O'Dwyer, who has since attained eminence in his profession. Another project of this combine was the manufacture of milk-power, concerning which they entered into negotiations with the authorities in Dublin. As a further instance of his progressive mind and his receptiveness of new ideas – both very desirable attributes in a leader – it may be recalled that he acquired a large steam threshing mill in the early days of its development, and shortly after he was to be found advocating and demonstrating the value of the newly-designed mechanical milking apparatus, being responsible for the introduction of this machinery to County Limerick. While thus busily occupied with many-sided activities, the things of the mind were not neglected. He was an enthusiastic member of the Gaelic League, the organiser of the local feis and regular attendant at the local Irish language classes where his mentor was George Clancy, who later as Alderman Clancy and mayor of Limerick was to be one of the two murdered holders of Limerick's mayoralty. In his spare time, which was little, nothing pleased him more than trips on his motor-cycle to visit places associated with the patriot dead, such as the scene of O'Neill-Crowley's last stand at Kilclooney Wood, and the grave of Fr Nicholas Sheehy at Clogheen.

Like so many others of his generation who gave to the Volunteer movement allegiance and devoted service, his national outlook was largely fashioned by a lifelong adherence to the Fenian tradition. A maternal uncle of his had taken part in the attack on Kilmallock barracks in the Rising of '67, being instrumental in recovering on that occasion the body of the single fatal Fenian casualty – a mysterious stranger whose identity was never fully established, and to whose memory as 'Unknown Fenian' a stately monument now stands in Sheares Street, Kilmallock.

With this background and trend of mind, Seán Wall's membership of the Volunteers from their inception in 1913 could be taken for granted. So too could be assumed his subsequent refusal to take the false turning into which so many of the Volunteers were diverted temporarily in the following year by the then dominant political party through its policy of enticing Ireland's manhood to action in the 'far foreign field' of the First World War.

Thenceforth, despite the claims of a now greatly expanded business, much of his time was given to political organising in the interests of Sinn Féin, and on the military side, his efforts were directed towards repairing the damage done by 'The Split' in the ranks of the Volunteers. He gradually revived the Bruff Volunteer company of which he became commander, though, as in most areas, this revival, as well as the propagation of the Sinn Féin policy, was uphill work until the nation's reaction to the 1916 Rising, followed by the conscription crisis of 1918, came to the aid of the faithful few, and began to convert the bulk of the people to an uncompromising national policy.

The occasion of the Roscommon and Waterford by-elections in 1917 found him specially active in raising funds in aid of Sinn Féin candidates, and in dispatching to the election area parties of Volunteers to act as election workers. And with the advent of the general election in 1918 he became one of the leading organisers who ensured that his own constituency of East Limerick shared in the general triumph of Sinn Féin by returning Dr Richard Hayes with an overwhelming majority.

That year also saw Seán Wall appointed brigadier in the circumstances already set out. Setting himself to the task of equipping and developing the organisation of his new command, he soon had its five battalions – previously of so independent and self-sufficient an outlook – functioning in full co-operation, and imbued with a strong pride of unit as brigade components. It would be tedious to list here the wide range of military engagements and activities to the credit of that brigade. It suffices to say that by common consent the record has entitled it rank among the premier fighting units of the IRA. One operation in which Seán Wall personally participated and organised may, however, be singled out for mention as possessing some points of general interest, and as an event which had a special appeal for him because of historical and family associations. This was the attack on Kilmallock RIC barracks in May 1920.

In that attack the Volunteers were attempting a task bristling with difficulties that seem insurmountable, but they had the satisfaction of successfully concluding an effort which had proved too much for their predecessors in 1867. As in the '67 Rising, the attackers on this occasion also suffered one fatal casualty. Curiously enough, the parallel was further continued in that the Volunteer killed, Liam Scully, like 'The Unknown Fenian' of '67, was a stranger in the locality, being a native of County Kerry who, but a short time previously, had taken up a Gaelic League teachership in the neighbourhood, and was but little known locally.

Looking over old papers dealing with the Rising of '67, another notable circumstance comes to light. The roll of the participants in the Kilmallock attack in '67, who were tried and sentenced to transportation or imprisoned for – as the charge had it – 'most wickedly, maliciously and traitorously making open war against our said Lady the Queen', was repeated almost name for name, and in many cases, in blood relationship, by the attackers of 1920.

New expedients, some of which had their origin in the inventive mind of the brigadier, were used by the Volunteers to overcome the difficult obstacles in the way of this attack. One was the improvisation of what would now be called Molotov cocktails, and to these missiles the destruction of the barracks was largely due. Their use ensured that a fire, started by an incendiary bomb in a wing of the building, was steadily expanded to embrace the whole barracks and defeat all effort by the garrison to extinguish the blaze.

If Seán Wall had nothing else to his credit as a commander, his ready appreciation of the value of the idea of a whole-time active service unit when this was initiated by the Galtee battalion, and the official backing he gave the unit's first O/C Donnachadh O'Hannigan (now lands officer at the department of defence), would alone entitle him to a place among the outstanding leaders of the Volunteers. If his attitude on this matter now appears merely as the acceptance and support of an obvious and logical development of the Volunteers' operational system, it should be realised that at the time the new scheme was a revolutionary proposal cutting across the accepted framework and lines of action of the organisation. Indeed, when first formed, the active service unit – then somewhat derisively known as 'the Circus' – had to contend against such obstacles arising from the existing system of control, especially the sole responsibility of the local commander for operations in his own area, that it could have made no headway had these difficulties not been smoothed out by the tact, authority, and zeal of the brigade commander.

The latter was soon called on to add another office to that of his military command. Elected unopposed to the county council, he was appointed chairman of that body. It is here worthy of remark how, without any formal policy or pre-determined design to unite military and civic functions in one individual, such unification did in fact take place in very many counties and boroughs at this period. It was an early instance of the now fully demonstrated fact that the successful waging of a war, big or little, requires not only effective military action, but the close and efficient co-operation of the economic and administrative machinery of a nation.

As chairman of Limerick's first republican county council he found a fresh outlet for his organising abilities and progressive mind, as well as further scope for his abundant energy and determination. The newly elected council, in common with most other such bodies throughout the country, declared its allegiance to Dáil Éireann. This entailed a complete upheaval in local administration and brought to a head a very critical phase of the national struggle. It is sometimes overlooked that the 1918–21 fight for independence was conducted chiefly by three agencies – military combat, secret service and local administration – and that the latter was by no means the least important of these. Indeed, the fight on the administrative plane is an aspect to which justice has not been done, and which merits to be fully chronicled if the events of the period are to be seen in their proper perspective. The revenues of local bodies were subjected to such severe demands under British legislation – specially enacted at the time – coupled with the withdrawing of grants and power to seize rate monies, that chaos in local administration would have resulted if special steps had not been devised to meet the situation. Had this chaos eventuated or had the people in general succumbed to the very strong temptation not to pay their rates to what were virtually illegal bodies, the whole political position would have been undermined and even the military fight would have been fatally compromised. It was in this sphere more than any other – except only that of the shelter freely given the members of the various active units – that the loyal support of the general public made the 1918–21 struggle a really national one, and imparted to it the stamina which brought eventual success.

Under the chairman's guidance and driving force Limerick county council was second to none in the way the serious threat to the national policy of a paralysed local administration was countered, much needed reforms introduced, and the civic tasks assigned by the Dáil authorities effectively executed. Here the tact of the chairman, and his pleasing personality were particularly valuable in securing the willing co-operation of those executive and administrative officials of the council whose services might otherwise have only reluctantly, or not at all, been forthcoming under the new regime, co-operation with which for many of them carried numerous risks, financial as well as physical. Among the projects undertaken by the new council at the chairman's instance was a survey of the Shannon, and the taking of levels of the river, thus anticipating by some years the preliminary work of the Shannon Scheme.

To add still further to his many-sided activities, Seán Wall was intimately associated with the organisation and working of the Dáil courts and in the drive for the republican loan. It was in no small measure due to his energy in the latter connection that a record subscription to the loan, some £30,000, was credited to the East Limerick constituency.

Had Seán Wall been spared, he possessed all the attributes necessary to have brought him far in a military career, though his gifts as an administrator might well have called him to other fields of endeavour and confirmed him in high office and responsibilities. But his allotted span was short. It drew to a close in May 1921. On 6 May, while on the way to a divisional council meeting, he and his staff were attacked by a police raiding party in a house near Annacarty, County Tipperary. In the ensuing fight along the approaches to the house, he was cut off from his companions, his dead body being subsequently found on the roadside beside that of one of the raiding party. The exact circumstances of his death were never known, beyond the fact that the fatal wound appeared to have been inflicted by a shotgun fired at close quarters.

Beannacht Dé lena n-anamacha go léir.

DESTRUCTION OF BALLYLANDERS POLICE BARRACKS

by S.R.

FOLLOWING EVENTS OF Easter week, 1916, in the southern part of East Limerick, there developed in the area a bitter internal dispute in which former officers and rank-and-file took opposite sides. The dispute increased in intensity until general headquarters in Dublin was compelled to take action, and in May 1918, Michael W. O'Reilly was sent to hold an inquiry. The inquiry was held in the house of Danny Moloney, Bridge House, Knocklong, and resulted in the suspension of many officers and men whose names subsequently figured prominently in the war for independence. It also resulted in the disbandment of the Old Galtee brigade which had operated since the formation of the Irish Volunteer organisation. It was replaced in the scheme of organisation by the East Limerick brigade which continued to act during the reminder of the fight against the British forces in Ireland. In order to preserve the historic name of the Galtee brigade, however, three battalions of the newly-formed East Limerick brigade were named the 1st, 2nd and 3rd Galtee battalions. The 1st Galtee battalion comprised the area covered by the former Galtee brigade, with the addition of a previously independent small battalion area surrounding Kilmallock. Later the East Limerick brigade was divided into six battalion areas and the word 'Galtee' was completely dropped.

The Ballylanders company area was the hub of the dispute referred to, and despite the general headquarters inquiry and several other efforts to eliminate it, the bitterness continued to increase. As a further effort to bring the situation under control, following the inquiry at Knocklong, general headquarters appointed Seán Wall of Bruff as brigade O/C of the newly-formed East Limerick brigade; and Seán T. O'Riordan of Kilmallock as battalion commandant of the first Galtee battalion. As both officers had no connection with the dispute it was thought that their election might eliminate it. In spite of the move, however, partisanship entered into the election of practically all the other company and battalion officers in the 1st battalion. Thus, the dispute continued to persist, to the detriment of the work of organisation.

In these circumstances the battalion council of the 1st Galtee battalion decided to attack the Royal Irish Constabulary barracks at Ballylanders which was in the centre of the disaffected area. It was hoped that the engagement would bring the two factions together in an operation which would make them forget their differences. It was further decided that the operation should be particularly a battalion one, but as a test of efficiency all Volunteer companies between Limerick city and Mitchelstown, and between Tipperary and Mallow, were brought out on the night of the attack, to block roads and cut communications. Accordingly, what was a local battalion operation took on the appearance of widespread activity inside the points mentioned. In fact, evidence given later at the court martial of Michael Gamell and Seán T. O'Riordan of Kilmallock, suggested that over three hundred men were engaged in the attack. In point of fact those who took part in the actual fighting and for whom arms were available at the time, numbered only twenty-nine men. Seán T. O'Riordan of Kilmallock was in command of the operation and the assault party on the roof of the barracks was in the charge of Tomás

Malone who was on the run in the locality and who assumed the name 'Seán Forde' to hide his identity from the enemy.

The plans for the attack on Ballylanders barracks were drawn up at the house of Ned Tobin, of Ballinalackin, about two miles from Ballylanders. Amongst the officers present on the occasion were Seán T. O'Riordan; Seán McCarthy, brigade ordnance officer; Tomás Malone, operations officer, and Ned Tobin himself, brigade quartermaster. A dispatch from brigade O/C Seán Wall advised Ned Tobin to be on the alert for a consignment of rifles and bombs on their way from Doon to Ballylanders. These arrived shortly afterwards, due largely to the courageous work of Bertie Burke. Martin O'Dwyer of Herbertstown also lent special aid. Bombs were manufactured at Tobin's forge, Ballinalackin, and at David Clancy's, Cush, Kilfinane. The plan of operation, adopted for the first time, prescribed that the attack should be chiefly directed against the roof of the barracks, whilst at the same time the building should be covered by fire from all side in order to keep the garrison of about six Royal Irish Constabulary fully occupied. The building itself was a most formidable one and, commanding the street of Ballylanders, was easily suited to defence. Its walls were of solid stone, and there were stout steel-lined doors, steel-shuttered windows and loopholes placed at strategic points. The four particular points from which the attack was launched were: Number One position, the dispensary which adjoined the barracks, with 'Seán Forde' in charge; Number Two position, Ellen Burke's house, with Seán Lynch, Galbally, in charge; Number Three position, Denis O'Grady's house, with Seán McCarthy in charge; Number Four position, Christopher Upton's house, with Paddy Hannigan in charge. There were sniping posts in the houses of David Condon and Jack Walsh, and in Upton's stables at the rare of the building.

The party in the dispensary post under 'Seán Forde' got on the roof of their building, and from it they reached the roof of the Royal Irish Constabulary barracks. Some hours earlier the attackers had mustered quietly at Ballylanders bridge, about a mile below the village. There they were issued with firearms, bombs and ammunition, and detailed to their various posts.

At eleven o'clock it was ascertained that two of the constables were in bed and that the sergeant and the remaining constables were in different parts of the building. At exactly 11.20 'Seán Forde' flashed the 'open fire' signal from the roof of Number One position, and there was an immediate volley of rifle fire and a shower of grenades, to which the garrison replied intensively. Immediately that the attacked had commenced the assault party on the roof set about breaking a gaping hole into the building. This was effected by the use of sledgehammers, and bombs and incendiaries were immediately thrown in to set the building on fire. After some while a lighted torch soaked in paraffin and tar set fire to a bed which, in turn, fired a wooden partition. In a few minutes the entire building was blazing furiously, and the barracks had become a raging furnace. In the meantime, however, the party on the roof had many narrow escapes from the rifle fire of the garrison, some of whom blazed away through the hole in the roof of their barracks. Hot exchanges were also in progress between others of the garrison and the IRA sections which occupied the different positions surrounding the doomed building. After fifteen minutes fighting Seán Meade, Ballintubber (now of Crecora), was shot through the left lung by a rifle bullet. He was one of the party in the post at Mrs Fanny Burke's house, directly opposite the front windows of the barracks, and it was thought that he exposed himself to fire whilst endeavouring to free his rifle which had jammed. All the while the countryside was continually lit up by Verey lights from the barracks, signalling for assistance from other enemy posts in the locality.

After about half-an-hour's fighting the blazing building had become untenable, and the sergeant in charge hoisted the white flag of surrender which was attached to a rifle and waved through one of the windows. Following their surrender the Royal Irish Constabulary were lined up outside their barracks and marched under armed escort down the main street to the home Constable Stafford. They were treated with the utmost courtesy by their captors. All arms and ammunition, and many of the explosives belonging to the garrison, were secured at great risk by the attackers. Official books, papers and correspondence kept in the barracks were also seized, and were taken in charge by Liam Scully. The mills bombs captured were afterwards used in the attack on Kilmallock Royal Irish Constabulary barracks; in fact, all war material captured following the surrender of Ballylanders barracks played an important part in the subsequent operations by the East Limerick brigade. The captured documents gave valuable information about enemy communications, the activities of the Royal Irish Constabulary, and their instructions.

Seán Meade was the only IRA casualty, but his wound was serious. He was immediately taken to Hannie Crawford's First-Aid station where he was given medical attention by Doctor William Hennessy, and where Fr O'Brien, CC, attended to him spiritually. Fr O'Brien, a great friend of the brigade was uncle to the patriotic Dolan family of Ardpatrick. When his wound was temporarily dressed, Meade was driven by Jack Crowley to Sheedy's at Ballingaddy, and thence to Con Ryan's off the Ardpatrick road. Later, the sorely wounded Meade was taken to still safer shelter at Mrs Burke's of Laurencetown, Kilmallock, far removed from enemy activity and from prying eyes. Owing to its location Burke's home was known as 'The Dardanelles' amongst the men of the column. There Meade was attended by Dr Fitzgerald, Mortalstown, Kilfinane, who immediately directed that he should be remove to hospital for an operation if his life were to be saved. He ultimately reached the County Infirmary at Limerick, where he was admitted under an assumed name and entered as a pneumonia patient. There he was given every attention and nursed back to health and vigour.

The attack and capture of Ballylanders police barracks had a far more reaching effect than was thought at time by those engaged in the operation. It was an audacious enterprise, carried out within easy reach of enemy forces, at Tipperary, Fermoy and Ballyvonaire. The road-blocking operations carried out by the companies of IRA between these places and Ballylanders was so effective that no assistance could be sent to the beleaguered garrison.

When the attack was all over the captured arms, together with arms used by the attackers, were taken to Ballingarry Cross and there handed over to Jim Fogarty, Tom Howard and Bill O'Sullivan, who found them a clever and almost inaccessible hiding-place in Glenbrohane.

The following IRA men were in the attacking party at the destruction of the Ballylanders barracks: Seán T. O'Riordan, Tomás Malone ('Seán Forde'), Ned Tobin, David Clancy, Con Kearney, Michael Gamell, Pat Carroll, Seáinín Murphy, John Lynch (Kilmallock); John Lynch (Galbally); John Joe Crawford, Jack McCarthy, Donnachadh O'Hannigan, Paddy Hannigan, Seán Crowley, Michael Crowley, John Crowley, Mick Keeffe, David Cremmins, Willie Purcell, J. Clarkson, Paddy Power, Mick Scanlon, Peter Crowley, M. Quirke (Moore Abbey); Jack O'Brien (Holy John); David Clancy, Tony Barrett, Dan Breen, Jimmie Mortell, Tim Keane, Jerry O'Callaghan, Peter Steepe, Danny Moloney. Amongst the girls at the First-Aid station were Hannie Crawford, Annie Murphy, Julia Connery, Lena Crawford, Kattie Crawford, Molly Joe Powell, Debbie Scanlon, Bride Crowley, Lizzie Cotter and Magennis.

DESTRUCTION OF KILMALLOCK RIC BARRACKS

by FENIAN

FOLLOWING THE DESTRUCTION of Ballylanders Royal Irish Constabulary barracks the British authorities distributed the men who comprised the garrison over various police posts in neighbouring towns. Kilmallock received Constables Strafford and Roberts, both of whom, in common with their comrades, were given courteous treatment by their captors following the surrender at Ballylanders. They signalled their arrival at their new posts by immediately identifying Seán T. O'Riordan, Kilmallock, as having led the Ballylanders attack; and Michael Gamell, also of Kilmallock, as being one of the attacking party. On 12 May, 1920, police and military participated in the arrest of Seán T. O'Riordan, who was conveyed to Limerick jail. The following day was a church holiday, on which two hurling matches were arranged for Kilmallock. When news of the arrest of battalion Commandant Seán T. O'Riordan reached Ballylanders, a party of the IRA immediately got together, and plans were made to proceed to Kilmallock next day under cover of the crowd attending the hurling games, and attack the Royal Irish Constabulary barracks to avenge O'Riordan's arrest. The party was under the command of Tom Crawford of Ballylanders. Immediately on the arrest of Seán T. O'Riordan, however, Commandant Michael Scanlon, Kilmallock (brother of James Scanlon, wounded in the Knocklong train rescue), assumed command of the 1st Galtee battalion. Having learned of the intention of the Ballylanders IRA party, he left Kilmallock and met the men at Mack's Cross, about a mile, outside the town. There he endeavoured to dissuade them from carrying out the proposed open attack on the RIC. Tempers became frayed, and for a long time the Ballylanders party obstinately refused to heed orders or listen to entreaties. Ultimately, a compromise was arrived at, whereby Commandant Scanlon agreed that Kilmallock Royal Irish Constabulary barracks would be the object of the next attack, which would take precedence over an attack already planned against Bruff barracks. The men were thereby given an opportunity to avenge the arrest of their battalion commandant, and thus originated the decision to single out Kilmallock barracks for immediate attack in preference to any other RIC post in the brigade area. But for this sequel to the arrest of Battalion Commandant Seán T. O'Riordan, there was an important reason why Kilmallock barracks should not have been interfered with at that time. In fact, had O'Riordan been permitted to remain at liberty, it is possible that the attack might never have taken place, or at least not for a long time, as the garrison had been unwittingly providing IRA intelligence with important information affecting a wide territory.

Following the inquiry at Knocklong and the direct appointment by GHQ of Seán Wall, of Bruff, as brigadier of the newly constituted East Limerick brigade, and of Seán T. O'Riordan as commandant of the 1st Galtee battalion, both brigade and battalion headquarters operated from the offices of John J. Power, solicitor, Kilmallock. There a telephone line between Power's office and the Kilmallock post office was tapped, and every enemy message passing through was intercepted. Thus, all message passing between the county inspector's office in Limerick and the district inspector's office in Bruff, and between Bruff and all Royal Irish Constabulary barracks in the network covered by the Kilmallock post office exchange, were in the hands of the IRA, even before they reached the police or military for whom they were intended. Morgan O'Carroll, of Kilfinane, was in daily attendance in the vicinity of Power's office, in readiness to rush urgent intelligence to Kilfinane, or to any eastern part of the county. A number of local Volunteers were always available to cover other districts. Many coups brought off by the local IRA and innumerable fruitless enemy searches, carried out over a wide area and after the most strict and apparently secret preparation, may be attributed to that unique intelligence system which also enabled so many members of the IRA 'on the run' from many areas to be sheltered and safely housed at any point in a great part of East Limerick.

The sequel to the arrest of Seán T. O'Riordan, already described, spelled the end of that extraordinary intelligence service, as it also became the immediate reason for the attack on Kilmallock barracks which took place on the morning of 28 May 1920. Plans for the ambitious project were hurriedly prepared, and assistance was sought from West Limerick, East Clare and South Tipperary. Volunteer leaders from all over the south were eager to assist, as it was against the Kilmallock barracks that the '67 men launched their unsuccessful attack when the unknown Fenian fell. Although it would certainly end an important IRA source of intelligence, it was realised that the destruction of Kilmallock barracks would constitute an important blow against the morale and effectiveness of the local Royal Irish Constabulary, who regarded their barracks as impregnable; who boasted that in the days of the Fenians and Land Leaguers it overawed the people, and that it would continue to keep the unruly and seditious in their proper places in 1920. Amongst other things, the boasting rankled in the minds of the East Limerick IRA, and partly inspired one of the fiercest of all barracks' attacks in the War of Independence.

Kilmallock barracks was a substantial fortress, strongly protected by steel shutters and sand-bagged defence works. IRA intelligence had learned that whilst the normal strength of the garrison was two sergeants and eighteen constables, this varied almost nightly, as individual RIC men on special plain clothes duty came and departed, sometimes by train and sometimes by Crossley tender. Accordingly, it was never possible to estimate accurately what the strength of the post might be, and on the night of the attack it consisted of twenty-two men, well armed with carbines, rifle grenades and Mills bombs, in addition to a plentiful supply of ammunition. In short, the police were in the position of an exceptionally strong military force with every prospect of holding out for days against even overwhelming numbers. In marked contrast to the arms and equipment of the police, service rifles were few in the East Limerick brigade area, and the greatest difficulty was experienced in getting together thirty for the attack which it was decided would take place on the night of 27 May 1920.

These rifles, some ammunition and all available shotguns were dumped on the western side of Kilmallock, having previously, been repaired and attended to by Michael Gamell and Seán Murphy, of Kilmallock. The greater portion of the ammunition, bombs and explosives was dumped in the eastern side of the town. A large quantity of ammunition and explosives for use in the attack were brought by train from Dublin by Brigadier Seán Wall personally, and another IRA man. These materials were taken off the train at Emly station, County Tipperary, and conveyed to the cottage of John O'Brien at Ballycullane, Kilmallock. They were guarded there until required on the night of the attack. Explosives and ammunition used in the Ballylanders attack had previously been stored in the same place. The explosives and ammunition earmarked for the attack on Kilmallock barracks were supplied to Seán Wall by Michael Collins in Dublin, and comprised grenades, Mills bombs and rifle ammunition.

Following the successful reduction of Ballylanders police barracks by attacking the roof, the East Limerick brigade staff decided to employ similar tactics in the Kilmallock operation. The post, a rather low squat, strongly built structure, situated in the main street, was overlooked by other buildings which the attackers could seize and in particular by Clery's Hotel. It was obvious that provided the attackers could successfully occupy these buildings, they would secure a dominant position over those in the barracks. It was apparent, too, that such a strong position could not be carried by a short, sharp attack, and that it would have to be besieged. The time in which the barracks could be reduced constituted a vital factor, as a protracted fight would certainly permit time for reinforcements to come to the relief of the garrison, and the attacking force was too small and poorly equipped for that risk to be lightly regarded.

All available help was mobilised in the locality by nine o'clock on the night of the attack, and all main roads, by-roads, and railway tracks for a radius of about fifteen miles round the town were rendered impassable to every form of traffic. These operations involved a tremendous amount of work, but it was cheerfully and effectively carried out, and it was well that it was so done for the barracks proved a far tougher proposition than had been calculated. The preliminaries having been completed, the men from the various battalions participating in the attack concentrated upon Kilmallock, and by 10.30 p.m. the different detachments had linked up. The main body which assembled to the west of Kilmallock was under the direct command of Seán Wall. Progress towards the town had been slow because of the thoroughness of the obstructions placed over the roads. About thirty men specially recommended by their local commanders, and armed with the best of the rifles and a fair supply of ammunition, were then detailed for the direct attack on the barracks. The remaining men, who numbered about forty, armed with shotguns and all sorts of miniature weapons, were detailed to guard entrances and exits. The thirty men selected for the direct attack were then divided into five sections and, each having chosen its own leader, was given detailed instructions concerning the buildings surrounding the barracks which were to be occupied and fortified. Clery's Hotel stood directly in front of the barracks, and being about twice its height, afforded an excellent commanding position. IRA intelligence having reported on the previous day that it could not be entered very late at night either by front or rear, the following plan was adopted in order to make certain of gaining admission. An IRA man arrived in the town by the evening train and, posing as a commercial traveller, booked a room in the hotel for the night. This man having successfully got inside had prepared a report of the occupants and drawn up a plan of the interior before the attackers took up their positions.

The simple plan worked splendidly, and when the leader of the section detailed to occupy the hotel tapped gently on the door, the IRA man inside lay down the book which he had been reading, and gave entry to his comrades who quickly and quietly occupied the building. The proprietors, guests and staff were immediately evacuated to a place of comparative safety. About the same time the premises of the Provincial Bank of Ireland (now the offices of Messrs Bennett & Walsh, solicitors) adjoining Clery's Hotel, were quietly entered through the fanlight of the private door and occupied by the IRA.

Neither Mr Andrews, the bank manager, nor his wife was aware that anything out of the ordinary was taking place, until a member of the IRA knocked on their bedroom door and ordered them both to dress. They were later removed to safety in the Central Hotel. Although his sympathies were with the British forces, with the officers of which he frequently associated during the subsequent military occupation of Kilmallock, Mr Andrews paid tribute to the manner in which his wife and himself were treated by the IRA on the night of the attack. He also referred to the scrupulous manner in which the attackers sought to protect the bank's property, apart from the military necessity of occupying the premises for the purpose of the attack.

Another house taken over by the IRA was that of Con Herlihy, grocer, situated on the other end of Clery's Hotel, and now the offices and showroom of Messrs Harris Brothers, garage proprietors. There the IRA were admitted personally by Con Herlihy, an ardent

Gaelic Leaguer, who was well aware of what was about to take place. It was from these three high buildings that the main frontal fire of the IRA was maintained during the attack. Windows in the houses were immediately barricaded, but, needless to say, the material available was not altogether ideal for that purpose, and a poor substitute for the steel-shuttered windows opposite. Nevertheless, a high spirit of confidence animated the IRA men, and after midnight all were in readiness at their posts with rifles loaded, patiently awaiting the signal to commence the attack. All civilians had been removed from the streets earlier and, with others found on the country roads around the town, had been held for some hours previously in selected places, either for their personal safety or as a security measure by the IRA.

About six paces from the gable-end of the barracks, and towering over it, Willie Carroll's house faced south-west. Its roof had been bored through earlier, as it had been planned that from that vantage point the roof of the barracks would be breached and fired. The signal to open the attack was three lamp flashes given by the leader of the section on the roof of the Carroll's, and as zero hour approached, all eyes strained towards that point. Three was no sign of life or activity within the barracks, and the IRA seemed to have completed their dispositions without arousing suspicion. Suddenly from Carroll's rooftop three flashes winked in the night, and instantly there was a roar from thirty rifles. At the same moment 'Seán Forde' sent a fifty-six-pound weight crashing through the slates of the barrack's roof, and two more, slung by members of his section, followed in quick succession, their crashing noise passing almost unnoticed in the bedlam of cracking rifles and bursting bombs. The post was thus effectively breached in the roof, and through the opening bottle after bottle of petrol was hurled by 'Seán Forde', Edmond Tobin, Ballinalackin, Ballylanders; his brother, David Tobin, who was killed on active service at Ballinalackin in January 1921; P. O'Donnell, Cush, and Liam Scully, Glenbeigh, County Kerry. Bombs were then thrown into the breach, but, whilst they burst with terrific force and caused terrific damage, they failed completely to set the roof on fire. Meanwhile, the fight raged fiercely all round the barracks with the large garrison manning every loop-hole and returning the IRA attack by hot fire. It looked for the moment as though the IRA could not succeed in forcing the police either to surrender or to evacuate, as the firing of the petrol soaked roof, upon which great hopes had been set, did not appear to be working out. Eventually a Mills bomb thrown by 'Seán Forde' sent it into a blaze. The stream of paraffin was still played upon it, with the result that in a few minutes the roof became a veritable sea of flames. The battle had then raged without intermission for approximately two hours, after which period 'Seán Forde' sent out a ceasefire signal from Carroll's rooftop.

It was obeyed instantaneously, and there remained only the sound of the cracking flames and the intermittent fire of the defenders. It was a weird sight, one which the participants are never likely to forget, with the smoke from bursting bombs and the burning roof billowing about the doomed building, the sudden comparative quite which followed the fierce noise of conflict, and the red, hungry flames shooting skyward. Called upon to capitulate, the garrison replied with a definite 'No Surrender', backed up by a fresh volley of rifle and grenade fire. Instantly 'Seán Forde' signalled the attackers to reopen fire, and the battle was again in full swing. For three further hours a continuous onslaught was maintained against the building, from which the flames increased in intensity every moment. All the while the defenders, who showed remarkable courage and pertinacity, concentrated their main efforts against Clery's Hotel, which they endeavoured to make untenable by continuously directing rifle grenades against it. They were considerably handicapped by the elevated position of the IRA and by the fact that the street between was filled by dense smoke. It was probably largely due to these factors that they failed to place a single grenade through the windows occupied by the attackers whose position was nonetheless difficult, as grenade after grenade struck the front wall of the hotel and burst with terrific force. These repeated concussions occasioned substantial damage to the lower portion of the front of the building.

By six o'clock in the morning the barracks was a roaring furnace, and the position of the defenders had become hopeless, as it was almost impossible to remain in the inferno much longer. Once again the ceasefire signal flashed out, and silence replaced the noise of conflict. Again called upon to surrender, the garrison hurled back defiance, and continued to engage the attackers. Although their barracks was blazing fiercely about them, the RIC continued to maintain a hot barrage of rifle grenades, firing aimlessly through the dense fog of foul-smelling smoke that enveloped the town. Somewhere a cock crew, and a new day clearly revealed an almost gutted building. Higher rose the flames momentarily as the roof collapsed to the accompaniment of frantic cheering by the attackers, and followed by traffic explosions in quick succession, as the valuable stores of grenades and bombs detonated. Flames, sparks and clouds of smoke shot skywards, imparting a weird red background to the scene.

At this stage, instead of the surrender which seemed inevitable, the police withdrew to a small strongly protected building adjoining the barracks at right angles. They were able to effect this change of position without exposing themselves to the fire of the attackers. They left two of their number dead in the flames, as also the bulk of their ammunition and grenades, the bursting of which inside the burning building added to the din and clamour of the fight. Six of the garrison were also wounded. From the small building which was situated at the rear of the barracks, the police continued to put up stubborn resistance, for which they earned the wholehearted admiration of the attackers. They had fought the fight of heroes, and although the IRA were engaged in a life-and-death struggle with them, they readily acknowledged their magnificent stand in face of what was then an utterly hopeless situation. The fact that the police had abandoned most of their reserves of ammunition in the withdrawal from the barracks gave no great advantage to the attackers, who commenced the operation with a pitifully small supply of ammunition and bombs. These supplies were well-nigh exhausted after more than six hours of continuous fighting, and for that reason, and because of the great danger of being trapped by heavy enemy reinforcements, Seán Wall reluctantly ordered his men to retire. It was also found impossible to set fire to the roof of the building in which the Royal Irish Constabulary had taken up their new positions, because of its distance from Carroll's house, from the roof of which incendiaries were hurled to fire the main building. Immediately they were withdrawn from the roof of William Carroll's house, the member of this section who had operated from that position went into the street to have a last look at the burning building. It was then that Captain Liam Scully, the only IRA casualty, received his death wound.

The IRA retired across country in good order, leaving Kilmallock RIC barracks a smouldering ruin. The building was completely reduced, never again to be occupied by British forces. The IRA job was done.

When Liam Scully fell fatally wounded as the IRA were about to withdraw, he lay in the bullet-swept street, but by a single act of bravery Ned Tobin of Ballinalackin, Ballylanders, carried him from the line of fire. Liam was unconscious when taken into the dressing station, which was in the house next to the Munster & Leinster Bank. The station was manned by Mrs Purcell, then Miss Kate M. Sheedy, and by Nurse O'Sullivan. When it was found that Liam, having been shot through the jugular vein, was in a hopeless condition, an Act of Contrition was immediately whispered in his ear, and he was given the last rites of the church by Rev. Fr Wolfe, CC, Kilmallock. The remains were conveyed to West Limerick by his comrades of the western district, who had participated in the fight. A few nights later, when Liam's relatives arrived from Glencar, Country Kerry, he was laid to rest with military honours in a quite little country churchyard which is almost lost in the hills beside Templeglantine. A Celtic cross of Kilkenny marble has since been erected over his grave by his former comrades.

Sergeant O'Sullivan, of the Royal Irish Constabulary, was in charge of Kilmallock garrison, and at one stage after the fight had been maintained fiercely for several hours, it appeared that he was on the point of surrendering. Above the din of battle, he inquired whether the lives of the garrison would be spared if they surrendered, but some one amongst the attackers is alleged to have shouted back words to the effect that the Kilmallock Royal Irish Constabulary would not be afforded an opportunity to repeat the action of the Ballylanders police who identified some of the attackers, subsequent to the fall of their barracks. It transpired that the garrison interpreted that as meaning that their lives would not be spared and, accordingly, instead of surrendering, they continued a most valiant defence. Constables Moreton and King were killed, whilst another constable was seriously wounded through the stomach. Constable Barry was wounded in the head, and the remainder of the garrison had wounds of some sort.

The fighting throughout the entire morning was so terrific that most of the inhabitants of the town were terrorised, and many evacuated it in fear of reprisals before military reinforcements arrived after the IRA withdrawal. Many of the inhabitants became refugees, wandering about in all directions, and the press likened the scenes in the locality to those in Belgium during the war. No immediate reprisals were taken, however, although on the night following the attack, the People's Hall, built in 1916, and outside which the IRA abandoned the oil unit used in the siege of the barracks, was burned down by British soldiers. Sergeant O'Sullivan was immediately promoted to the rank of district inspector of the Royal Irish Constabulary, in recognition of his defence of the barracks. He was subsequently shot dead in Listowel, County Kerry.

BRITISH JUSTICE AS DEMONSTRATED IN KILMALLOCK

by FENIAN

ALTHOUGH THE ATTACK on Kilmallock Royal Irish Constabulary barracks took place on the night of 27 and the morning of 28 May 1920, it was not until 6 August that the customary reprisals took place. During the intervening period the atmosphere in the town remained tense, and rumours filled the air of terrible events to come. When these took material shape the inoffensive townspeople were given a demonstration of British justice and the method of its administration could easily have brought about the total destruction of the town by fire – a catastrophe which, in fact, was prevented only by the bravery of some young men who risked both their lives and liberty to save the homes of the people. On Friday, 6 August 1920, a drunken rabble in police uniforms arrived in Kilmallock, having attended a field general court martial in Victoria barracks, Cork, in connection with the attack on Ballylanders police barracks, which took place in April. Although a warning message had been telephoned to Kilmallock from Charleville that police were on their way in two Crossley tenders, and that they were far from sober, there was not sufficient time available in which to pass on the warning to all who were on the streets of Kilmallock at the time. As the police drove along the road between Charleville and Kilmallock, it was noted that the tri-colour trailed in the dust behind one of the Crossley tenders. The lorries, having entered the town at great speed, were pulled up at the cross and the occupants jumping out, immediately got down to business. Their first victim was the late Bill Hayes, who was standing with his back to the window of the licensed premises of Michael O'Donnell in Sarsfield Street. The police called him, but as he observed their menacing attitude he hesitated and was immediately set upon by eight or ten of the ruffians who knocked him down and beat him savagely on the head and body with their rifle butts. He tried to save himself as best he could by covering his head with his hands, but this was of little avail. His assailants actually impeded each other in their blind fury, and Hayes was almost beaten to pulp when a sergeant intervened and stopped the foul work. Bill Hayes, who had one eye permanently injured never fully recovered from the effects of the beating which ultimately brought about his death. He was a young man of splendid physique, standing six foot three inches, and built in proportion.

The drunken marauders next rushed to the Central Hotel, where they greeted the proprietor, Mr Lyons, with a stroke of a rifle butt that sent him staggering. Recovering quickly, he dashed through the bar and out the hall, closely followed by the yelling constabulary. Fortunately, they were so drunk that even in his semi-dazed state, he easily eluded them and escaped upstairs in the hotel. The police entered the hotel yard, where they beat William Donegan within an inch of his life. He was removed to the Kilmallock Union Hospital and detained there for a long period. In the yard they also beat up Patrick Hennessy.

The next objective of the raiders was the harness-making shop of Con O'Callaghan, a highly-respected citizen and first secretary of the Sinn Féin club in Kilmallock. The raiders entered O'Callaghan's shop and asked his name. When he told them they dragged him into the yard where they beat him mercilessly in the presence of his wife and daughter who, having vainly tried to save him, were hurled aside, knocked down and threatened with similar punishment. Meanwhile inside the shop itself Con O'Callaghan's son had also been receiving attention from the police, but he managed to jump the counter and dash clear to Orr Street. The police pursued him, firing as they went, but he made good his escape. A man named Edwards who entered the line of their fire had a narrow escape as bullets whistled past him. Shortly after the pursuit, the ruffians raided the licensed premises and bakery of Dominick O'Grady, Sarsfield Street; that of Patrick O'Brien, publican, Sarsfield Street, and that of James O'Rourke, publican and victualler, Lord Edward Street. In each case considerable damage was caused to furniture and stock-in-trade, and considerable quantities of drink were looted.

The police next directed their attention to the shops of Con Herlihy and Willie Carroll. Carroll's house and shop stood at the northern end of the Royal Irish Constabulary barracks, and from its roof was directed part of the IRA attack which resulted in the destruction of the building. Mrs Carroll and her young children received no warning as to the intention of the police, but guessing what was afoot, they dashed out the back door and ran down by the river bank to safety in the home of Mrs Carroll's sister, Mrs Agnew. Carroll's house and shop, together with furniture and stock-in-trade, were then completely destroyed by fire. Whilst the blaze raged the drunken rowdies fired volley after volley into the building so that it was neither possible to stay the progress of the flames, nor to rescue any of the Carrolls' belongings. The burning of Con Herlihy's house very nearly produced tragic results, as three girls, who had run upstairs in terror, were trapped in the third storey of the blazing building, and would have certainly been burned to death but for their timely rescue, effected at the back of the house by a number of young men who managed to procure a ladder and place it against the wall. The tallest of the men, standing on the top rung of the ladder, barely reached the girls, who were ultimately brought down in a state of extreme prostration. Shortly afterwards the roof fell in, and the efforts of the brave men, working at the back of the post office, were concentrated in an effort to save the adjoining houses. At that time it looked probable that the entire street would go up in flames, and even before the raiders had withdrawn, many young men were at work, fire-fighting. Ladders were hastily erected and as there was no fire-fighting equipment available, men attacked the flames with buckets of water. Others hacked away portions of the adjoining roofs to prevent the spread of the fire. All through the night and until the early hours of the morning, almost the entire population of Kilmallock was engaged in the great fight to save the town. Those unable to join in the physical effort prayed for the success of their comrades. Eventually the flames were got under control.

Kilmallock had another night of terror on 6 March 1921, when Sergeant Maguire of the Royal Irish Constabulary was shot in Lord Edward Street at nine o'clock, the hour curfew began in the town. As a reprisal the house and business premises of Michael J. Houlihan, creamery manager, were blown up next day. Michael Houlihan was secretary of the Kilmallock Sinn Féin organisation, in succession to Jack Lynch, murdered in a Dublin hotel by British forces a short time after the attack on Kilmallock police barracks. Houlihan's connection with the Sinn Féin movement marked him down for special attention and, as a matter of fact, a sergeant, accompanied by a Black and Tan named Heuton, raided his house on the night before Maguire was killed. Both were in particularly truculent mood, under the influence of drink, and played about with their revolvers whilst they questioned Houlihan and insisted that he had a full and complete knowledge of the whereabouts of a number of prominent Kilmallock IRA men. They threatened to shoot him if he did not disclose the information they required. Ultimately, they tired of the interrogation and departed. On the morning of 7 March a lorry of soldiers from Bruff direction deposited a number of petrol tins outside Houlihan's door, thus indicating that it was their intention to burn the house.

The lorry then proceeded in the direction Kilfinane, and returned some hours later. As the soldiers entered the town secondly they fired several volleys to terrorise the people. Meanwhile, Houlihan, on the advice of his friends, had cleared out of his house and set out towards Bruree. He had only reached Ballygibba Cross when he heard the explosion that blew up his home, furniture and shop, together with his entire stock. That day Kilmallock town swarmed with soldiers from end to end, even the side streets. Officers moved about here and there and conversed in groups. The military were in full war kit and as it was obvious that something big was about to take place, the only question which agitated the minds of the people was where the frightfulness would begin.

It was thought that prominent Sinn Féiners would be shot, and that the biggest of the business houses would be given to the flames. Townspeople remained indoors and business was at a standstill. Towards evening the military entered all houses in the town and ordered the people to assemble at the cross at the intersection to Lord Edward Street and Sarsfield Street. There Colonel Hope addressed the inhabitants whom he had assembled at the point of the bayonet and elaborated on the 'enormity of the many crimes committed by the IRA'. When he had finished, the people were compelled to witness the destruction of Michael Houlihan's home, which was then given to the flames. The military did not withdraw until the roof had fallen in, and all possibility of saving the premises was gone. When the military left the townspeople devoted their efforts to saving the buildings on either side of the burning house. They were successful after a great deal of hard work.

THE FLYING COLUMN ORIGINATED IN EAST LIMERICK

by MAJOR-GENERAL D. O'HANNIGAN

This interesting and historically valuable first-hand account of the East Limerick flying column forms part of a more detailed work which is in course of preparation. The author, now lands officer at the department of defence, was associated with the Volunteers from the inception of the movement and held IRA commands as comdt-general 4th southern division, O/C East Limerick brigade, and O/C East Limerick brigade flying column. He is thus in a position to write authoritatively on a stirring period in the national military effort. In compiling the account he has had the collaboration of Lieut-Col J.M. MacCarthy who, as vice-divisional commander, 4th southern division and adjutant of the East Limerick flying column, was closely associated with him in the events here narrated.

IT IS NOW generally and clearly recognised that the flying column was the spearhead of the Irish Republican Army in its fight for Irish independence, and that the success which attended that fight was in no small measure due to the achievements of these swift-moving and well-disciplined guerrilla units. There is no such clarity of understanding, however, about the place and circumstances of the IRA flying column's origin, for it is not generally known that, for some time previous to the action of GHQ in ordering the formation of flying columns on a country-wide scale, this type of military unit had been operating successfully in the East Limerick area.

East Limerick, therefore, is the place where the first flying column was formed. In this article I shall endeavour to tell how the idea originated; how it was translated into practice, and continued to operate successfully against increasing odds up to the Truce. Incidentally, it is interesting to note that the formation of the flying column in East Limerick was, in effect, the first attempt for several centuries to provide the nucleus of an Irish standing army.

For a clear understanding of the idea which led to the establishment of the column it is necessary to know something of the events which led to the presence of the late Comdt P. Clancy and myself in the West Limerick area in early June 1920. For it was our journey from there to Bruree in East Limerick which gave rise to the idea of an active service unit, as the flying column was first called.

After the attack on Kilmallock Royal Irish Constabulary barracks on the 28 May 1920, the body of Liam Scully, BA, who was killed in that attack was taken to Tournafulla, and was later buried with full military honours at Templeglantine. Comdt Clancy and I were present at the funeral and, after the burial, took part in a discussion concerning an attack on Newcastlewest Royal Irish Constabulary post, which the West Limerick brigade contemplated making at the time. To help in this attack all the available rifles in East Limerick had been sent on loan to the West Limerick unit. It was decided that preparations for the attack were not sufficiently advanced to warrant proceeding with the operation. It was learned, however, that an attack was contemplated on the Royal Irish Constabulary barracks at Sixmilebridge in Country Clare, and at the request of some interested parties, Brigadier Seán Finn (later killed in action), Comdt Clancy and I, together with some of Brigadier Finn's men, went to Pallaskenry and thence across the Shannon to the neighbourhood of Bunratty. The attack on Sixmilebridge was also abandoned owing to the lack of complete plans, and feint attacks on Corofin, Newmarket-on-Fergus and other outlying posts were the only parts of the original scheme which were carried out.

We then recrossed the Shannon into County Limerick, commandeered a Rolls Royce car and travelled over a considerable portion of the brigade area. Comdt Clancy and I were interested in having the rifles returned to East Limerick, but as it was possible they might still be used in West Limerick, we decided to allow them to remain, and to rejoin our own unit pending developments. We set out to march from the neighbourhood of Glin, by Askeaton, Ballingarry and Rockhill to Tankardstown, near Bruree where we were received by Capt. J. Lynch. Our journey was without incident because we took care to avoid the immediate vicinity of towns and were very cautious when seeking food. Next day we proceeded via Kilmallock to Clancy's house at Cush. It was after this march that we realised the full significance of the journey.

Fully armed we had travelled over thirty miles cross-country in daylight without any great difficulty. It occurred to us that since we had successfully done so there was no reason why a larger number, organised and equipped as a unit, could not do likewise. Thus was conceived the idea of the active service unit, which, as already stated, was the original name of the flying column. This idea was revolutionary in its implications in the circumstances then prevailing, for in fact it implied maintaining in the field a standing force for the duration of the struggle. What we had in mind was an efficient, disciplined, compact and swift-moving body of men which would strike at the enemy where and when a suitable opportunity arose. That this intention was subsequently realised is evident from the fact that for the rest of the period until the Truce the major engagements of the column averaged one each month, with many other minor engagements intervening.

As soon as it was decided to put the idea into practice, I visited my home to make preparations for a long absence. While I was away Comdt Clancy, who was assistant creamery manager at Allensbridge,

Newmarket, Country Cork, had got a telegram urgently requesting his return, so that when I arrived back he had left for Country Cork. Comdt Clancy, who was a very dear friend of mine, and a serious loss to our project, had been on hunger strike before the Kilmallock fight and had just been released from Belfast jail. He was afterwards killed in action near Kanturk.

On the day of my return, accompanied by his brother, Volunteer David Clancy and Vice-Comdt P. O'Donnell (these men forming the nucleus of the unit), I set out on another journey to Tankardstown to await further recruitment of men for the column. Comdt Tadhg Crowley of Ballylanders (now Senator T. Crowley) joined us by arrangement and we finally mustered twelve men. These included Volunteers Tom Murphy, David Tobin and Tom Howard, who subsequently saw much severe fighting and were eventually killed in action – three keenly-felt losses and a severe depletion in the ranks of the initial force.

We decided to operate in 5th Galtee battalion area where Comdt J. MacCarthy was in charge. He is now Lieut-Col MacCarthy, GHQ, and I am indebted to him for much assistance in making records of our activities. Comdt MacCarthy set his intelligence system to work and every possible means of harassing the enemy was explored and considered.

There resulted a scheme of action which for the first time committed an IRA unit to keep the field continuously and to engage in a deliberately planned and sustained series of operations. Thus was set a further headline by which the hitherto rather disconnected actions that had been the practice throughout the country were superseded by a definite plan of campaign.

Among the principal engagements which ensued were Ballina-hinch, Emly, Bruree, Kildorrery (County Cork), Cross of the Tree (Knocklong), Grange, Glenacurrane, Dromkeen, Kilfinane, Shraherla, Lackelly, Annacarty (County Tipperary). At Emly, one of our first fights, we were in action against a detachment of the Lincolnshire

Regiment for three and a half hours on 13 July 1920, going into the fight with only five service rifles, one Winchester rifle, seventy rounds of rifle ammunition, three shotguns and three revolvers with a few rounds for each.

Our opponents were extended along the roadway for some hundreds of yards, and, owing to the necessity for conserving our ammunition, the action dragged out for some hours. When finally forced to surrender, one of their number had been wounded and we took eight prisoners with nine rifles and six hundred and fifty rounds of ammunition, a welcome addition to our meagre armament. A Royal Irish Constabulary sergeant and one constable had retreated at the outset and did not come into the area of combat. We could have inflicted heavier casualties, but our object at this stage was to capture arms and ammunition without taking life or inflicting wounds if possible. On this occasion I got a note from the officer in charge of the party as follows: 'On 13 July 1920, we were surrounded by armed men. We fought for a considerable time but were outnumbered and compelled to surrender. We were courteously treated by our captors and we owe them our lives.' At the request of the writer of that note, I gave him a written statement setting out that we had attacked and surrounded his party and that they fought as best they could but were out-manoeuvred and compelled to surrender. These notes were published a few days later in the *Irish Independent*. Similar notes were also exchanged after a number of later actions, but this was the only occasion they were published as the censor intervened.

Our project had not up to this time received the sanction of GHQ. We afterwards got covering sanction, however, for all our activities. I sent regular reports of all operations to GHQ through Brigade Comdt Seán Wall, who was killed while held a prisoner in the course of the fight at Annacarty, County Tipperary.

Towards the end of August 1920, we had an intensive course of training, and general headquarters recommended all brigades to start flying columns similar to ours. In late September the recommendation became an order. We held a brigade council meeting in the neighbourhood of Bruff, Brigadier Wall presiding. An organiser from GHQ attended and delivered the order to us that we were to organise a flying column, and that I, having had experience of this type of fighting, was to be in charge. It seemed rather amusing to all of us to be instructed to bring into being a unit of our organisation which had already existed for three months, but, in the true spirit of military discipline, we wholeheartedly acquiesced.

In February 1921, at Dromkeen our column attacked a convoy of lorries travelling from Caherconlish to Pallasgreen. The convoy personnel had twelve fatal casualties. On this occasion we were assisted by a Mid-Limerick column under Comdt Dick O'Connell. Comdt Liam Hayes (now Major-General Hayes, who was adjutant general of the army up to a few years ago) was wounded and the late David Barry (general manager, ITA), a pioneer of the movement, was also injured in this action. Extracts from my report on this operation were published in *An t-Óglach*.

At Glenacurrane on 17 December 1920, the column attacked and defeated a hostile military detachment. Four of the detachment were killed and the rest were captured, with lorries, rifles, ammunition and grenades. This detachment was conveying military mails from Fermoy to Tipperary. These mails were censored by us and all unofficial documents were re-posted. Among the booty were a number of medals issued to military personnel for 'Gallant Conduct in Ireland'. On the 8 February 1921, part of the column, with Comdt J.M. MacCarthy in charge, captured a British aeroplane and its contents. The aeroplane was destroyed, important documents seized, and the observer taken prisoner and detained notwithstanding – and principally in defiance of – threats of burnings in Kilfinane and Kilmallock. Clancy's house in Cush was destroyed by the enemy immediately after this incident.

Shortly before Easter Week 1921, I received a message from GHQ that it was desirable that we should proceed into West Limerick brigade area. Accordingly we contacted that unit. After a few days there, six of our men, three from East Limerick and three from the west, were attacked by a Black and Tan party in much superior numbers. In this engagement Brigadier Seán Finn was killed and Volunteer Quane of East Limerick very seriously wounded. The engagement lasted for over three hours and although the enemy had the advantage in numbers, transport and terrain facilities which enabled them to envelop us in a pincer movement, we eventually succeeded in out-manoeuvring them and in extricating ourselves from the difficult position. On this occasion Volunteer Seamus Finn distinguished himself for conspicuous bravery in the field and was promoted lieutenant as a result. The hostile casualties on this occasion were one dead and one wounded. In passing, it may be mentioned that a full report as sent by me shortly afterwards to GHQ was published in *An t-Óglach*, also in the *Catholic Bulletin* and *London Daily Herald*.

Early in May 1921, a small number of our men were surprised by a company of the Sherwood Foresters Regiment at Lackelly near Knocklong. We had four fatal casualties. We brought up reinforcements, returned the attack and in a very prolonged fight beat off the attackers, captured all their transport, recovered the bodies of our dead, and could thus fairly claim that the ultimate decision was in our favour despite our grievous losses.

During this particular week we had been in action on five days, and on the Friday of that week Brigadier Seán Wall was killed, as already stated. After his death, I, being in command as vice-brigadier, became commander of the brigade on the order of GHQ. We then began an intensive scheme of reorganisation, and also adopted, as a supplement to our ordinary operation, a method of harassing the hostile forces by forming small parties and sniping on every possible occasion. This proved very effective and was most disconcerting for our opponents. We were making elaborate preparations for a big operation, and I had prepared a report for GHQ in contemplation of a wider scope for our activities by extension of the fight all over County Limerick.

Our brigade organisation had now become as perfect as was feasible in the existing circumstances. We were a small force confronting a powerful foe, with arms mainly captured from him. That opposition had practically unlimited resources in manpower, equipment and arms; we were weak in all these and situated within a hostile ring of strong military posts formed by the large garrisons at Fermoy, Kilworth, Buttevant, Ballyvonaire, Kilmallock, Limerick, Tipperary and Cahir.

I have found it impossible during the time at my disposal and in the space available, to give more than a cursory account of our major military operations. We also engaged in many minor activities throughout the area and there were many incidents of fighting in which the column as such was not actively involved. In addition to military work, assistance had to be given in maintaining law and order. Military courts were also held for punishing criminal offenders. These, however, were few in number. They were minor and major thefts by civilian offenders, all of which tended to detract from the main issue and had to be rigorously suppressed. On one occasion, finding an auctioneer from outside our area holding an auction under permit from the British authorities, I had to declare this an illegal assembly, disperse the crowd and warn the offender not to repeat the performance.

I wish to avail of this opportunity to pay tribute to the parish of Kilbehenny and Anglesboro, on the slopes of whose mountains we occasionally retired for rest and recuperation. That parish had two strong efficient companies of Volunteers and a very good record of nationalism. There were born John O'Mahony, the Fenian leader, and Comdt-General Liam Lynch. I had the honour to be born and nurtured within its bounds, and I should say that the proudest moment of my military career was when the column marched through Anglesboro at night, rested there, and I was hospitably entertained by my old school teacher, Mr P. Kiely.

The flying column worked in unison with the battalions and

companies, and the battalion and company officers were key men in facilitating our movements. The local Volunteers in each area acted as guards and outposts, while the men of the column snatched a few hours of sleep. We had a strenuous time, and it was quite a common occurrence to retire to bed at midnight and be out again under arms at two in the morning. Our men were tough fighters and were adept at outmanoeuvring the opposition, and their enthusiasm to contact him in combat never flagged. The system of reprisals adopted by the enemy added considerably to the anxieties and difficulties of the Volunteers, as not only had they to think of battling their own way, but also the dangers to which their relatives at home were exposed. After the Kildorrery action, a civilian was shot dead as a reprisal; after Bruree, an invalid boy was fatally wounded; shortly afterwards Crowley's house and drapery establishment was burned down, while after Dromkeen, ten homesteads were destroyed by fire.

The people in general loyally supported our forces. Amongst our womenfolk we had many heroines. I can recall one incident of many such; after the fight in Ballyhahill, where one woman, when her house was attacked, coolly handed out rifle and ammunition to a Volunteer who had got out through a back window, while bullets whizzed in through the front windows.

I would like to make personal mention of all my deceased comrades in the fight, and of those who fought and were prominent in co-operating with me in Limerick, and to pay individual tribute as far as I can remember to a people whose patriotism and forbearance under serve hardship, suffering and trial, stood a great test, but I must conserve my efforts for, I hope, a future opportunity.

BALLINAHINCH AND BRUREE AMBUSHES

by VOLUNTEER OFFICER

FOLLOWING THE ATTACK on Kilmallock Royal Irish Constabulary barracks a number of prominent IRA men, particularly from Ballylanders and surrounding districts, went 'on the run' to avoid arrest. They concentrated on the Tankardstown locality between Kilmallock and Bruree, and which is situated about three miles from either town. In July 1920, some of them ambushed and disarmed four members of the Royal Irish Constabulary at Ballinahinch, Kilmallock, and following this latter operation the die was definitely cast for the IRA men concerned, as they could no longer return to their homes. Accordingly, it was natural that they should become the first members of the active service unit, or flying column, then organised by Donnachadh O'Hannigan, Mitchelstown, for the purpose of maintaining in the field a small mobile force to harass and engage the enemy as frequently as possible. To Donnachadh O'Hannigan, therefore, fell the honour of being the commander of an IRA flying column. Within a few months the idea was generally approved by the IRA general headquarters in Dublin, and flying columns were formed soon afterwards in the majority of brigade areas throughout the country. The townland of Tankardstown lies about half-a-mile from the main Kilmallock–Bruree road, and as already stated is situated about halfway between these towns. The pioneers of the flying column were billeted in a number of houses in the locality, and there commenced training in preparation for the task for which their unit had been formed. Their preparation embraced both military and physical training, and part of their work in the latter respect lay in helping the farmers amongst whom they were billeted. Thus, to the casual observe, the men were apparently harmless harvesters.

On 4 August 1920, word reached the active service unit that a British military patrol was proceeding along the main road from Bruree to Kilmallock. A hurried decision having been made to attack the patrol, the men dashed from their harvesting operations, collected their arms and ran the distance between Tankardstown and the main road. There a plan of attack was hastily arranged by Commandant O'Hannigan, and ambush positions were taken up. The country, in no way suited to guerrilla warfare, offered poor cover, but what little was there was availed of by the men of the column before the enemy appeared. The number of the attackers was so small that it was impossible to plan encirclement of the approaching enemy patrol. Immediately the British entered the ambush position they were called upon to surrender, but replied with a volley from their rifles. The IRA immediately engaged them and soon the exchanges were hot and heavy. Fighting continued for a considerable time, and the countryside rang to the reverberation of rifle fire. Things began to get too hot for the British, who began manoeuvres, the object of which the column men were at first unable to discover. It soon became apparent, however, that the enemy's objective was to seek cover in a nearby labourer's cottage belonging to a man named Kennedy. Before the soldiers reached the house Private W. Rogers fell mortally wounded on the road, and his rifle and equipment were seized by Commandant O'Hannigan, who jumped the fence of secure them, in face of British fire.

The rest of the patrol succeeded in gaining the cover of Kennedy's cottage. They refused the occupants the chance of evacuating, knowing that their presence in the building would largely hinder the operations of the attacking forces from which they had retreated. At the same time they broke loopholes in the roof and manned the windows. The IRA maintained the attack, although their efforts were greatly restricted because of their anxiety to avoid injuring members of the Kennedy household. Nevertheless intermittent firing continued for hours during that beautiful summer's evening. In the closing stages of the engagement a member of the patrol, who had exchanged his military uniform for civilian attire, managed to get through the IRA lines, and proceeded immediately to Bruff for reinforcements. Meanwhile, however, the IRA decided that the conflict had proceeded long enough, and that it would be unsafe for them to continue lest the suspicion of the military in Kilmallock should be aroused by the unduly long absence of the patrol, in which event strong reinforcements would be sent in search of it. At that time the IRA were unaware that one of the besieged Britishers had slipped through their lines.

On the same night Bruree had its first experience of the terror when the military reinforcements and the members of the patrol attacked by the IRA shot up the village, killing a young boy named Duggan and an invalid named Harris. Duggan was killed on the street, whilst Harris was bayoneted and shot in his own home. Houses in the vicinity of the ambush were looted and pillaged.

DESTRUCTION OF BRUFF COURTHOUSE

THE FINE TWO-STOREYED structure that was Bruff courthouse stood on the site of the present courthouse, about a hundred yards north of Bruff barracks and with an open space between. In July 1920, the barracks were occupied by Royal Irish Constabulary, Black and Tans and regular military forces. Furthermore, IRA intelligence had ascertained that an additional company of military was about to take up quarters in the courthouse. Its destruction was immediately decided upon, and on the night selected for the job the attackers' rendezvous was at Tompleen, not far from the courthouse. Four IRA men, James O'Connor, W. Moroney, John Moroney and Seamus Maloney, comprising one party of the attackers, arrived about midnight with petrol and other materials. After vainly waiting some time for the second unit, the four decided to go ahead with the job themselves. Having approached the building cross-country, over fences and through gardens, they gained admittance without incurring notice, by forcing the back door. Petrol was immediately spread over floors, windows, benches and stairways. A petrol-saturated sack was laid on the centre of the ground floor, and from it extended a rope similarly treated and which trailed through the back door. The rope was next lighted and shortly afterwards there occurred an explosion which shook the entire town.

At the precise moment of the explosion a British patrol was passing the front of the courthouse building, and its members, thinking that a direct attack was being made on them, fled for their lives, never stopping until almost within reach of their barracks. Then they let loose hell, firing with their rifles and machine-guns. Meanwhile the demolition party, as they made their getaway, could hear leaves and branches being cut from bushes and trees by bullets. Some while previously the second IRA units had arrived at the rendezvous for the attackers and were awaiting their companions to bring the petrol. To their surprise they observed a mighty flash, followed by a tremendous explosion, and heard flying bullets which made them more than a little apprehensive for the safety of their comrades. What they saw next were swift-footed men, flying through the night, their boots hanging across their necks by the laces. So all was well, and another enemy post demolished.

ARMS AND AMMUNITION CAPTURED FROM DEFEATED TANS AT KILDORRERY

by VOLUNTEER

DURING THE SUMMER of 1920 the Black and Tan garrison of the Royal Irish Constabulary barracks in Kildorrery village, County Cork, was most active and its vigilant patrolling of the surrounding countryside constituted a menace to the East Limerick flying column, then operating in the locality. Early in August the Limerick men planned to ambush a patrol of Black and Tans from the barracks, whilst on its way from Kildorrery to Rockmills, a distance of about three miles. The column occupied positions for the attack, but word of the proposed ambush reached the patrol which immediately returned to barracks and telegraphed Fermoy for military assistance. The attacking party, however, having learned of this development in good time, the ambush position was evacuated before the arrival of the military.

On 4 August new positions were occupied by the East Limerick column, as close to Kildorrery barracks as two or three hundred yards. The column was reinforced by local men from the neighbourhood of Ballindangan and Glanworth, and the IRA had with them Miss O'Sullivan, a trained nurse, who had accompanied the column from Country Limerick. She immediately proceeded to fix up an improvised hospital in the cottage of an old couple named Collins, both of whom were eighty-five years of age. When the IRA arrived Mrs Collins was preparing tea for her husband, who was then still in bed, until having learned what was about to take place old Collins jumped out, cheered for joy, and ordered his wife to seek protection in a neighbouring house, as his was then no place for women. He stoutly refused to leave himself, saying he was glad of the opportunity to be present during an attack on the enemy. The IRA knew from previous engagements that the British would not hesitate to seek protection amongst the aged and infirm, so old Mr Collins was compelled to remain behind the barred doors of his own house whilst the fight was on.

During the hours of patient waiting for the enemy a farmer and his workers were engaged hay-making in the field inside which the IRA had taken up their positions. On the request of the column officer they continued about their work as though nothing unusual had taken place. Eventually the Black and Tans appeared in the village street, trailing in the gutter behind them a tri-colour flag. They were in and out of their barracks a good deal before ultimately proceeding in the direction of Rockmills. In a few minutes the column leader's whistle heralded the moment for action, and the British were called upon to surrender. Although surrounded the police took up positions on both sides of the road, and engaged the IRA. A brisk encounter followed but it was of short duration, and when the British surrendered eight Black and Tans had been wounded, two of them fatally. Old Mr Collins, who had cheered in his house whilst the fight was in progress, was then allowed out to view the scene. The IRA nurse attended to the wounded for whose comfort everything possible was done. Two old Royal Irish Constabulary men amongst the police party were held as prisoners and placed temporarily in a labourer's cottage, having been warned not to attempt to leave for a specified time, as their knowledge of the country would be a great asset in the event of possible pursuit of the column by the British. Some months afterwards Black and Tans from Kildorrery murdered an unfortunate man named O'Donnell, in the cottage in which the police had been held prisoners. The ambush at 3 had been carried out within reach of large forces of the British, of whom thousands were stationed in nearby Kilworth camp, Mitchelstown, Buttevant, Fermoy and Ballyvonaire. The column armament having been increased by eight rifles and two hundred and eighty rounds of ammunition, the men moved off in a direction between Shanballymore and Castletownroche. They had a difficult passage as rain fell in torrents and they were wet through when they reached Annesgrove, where they narrowly escaped a British detachment five times their strength. They spent that night in the neighbourhood of Ballyveelick and Shinakilla, and evaded the enemy who scoured the countryside in large numbers on the following day, they marched across the hills, by-passing the British camp at Ballyvonaire, and ultimately arriving in Glenrue, County Limerick, where they were warmly received by Fr Bob Ambrose, PP, of Land League fame.

SHOOTING OF THOMAS MURPHY AND DAN TOBIN

On New Year's Day 1921, Thomas Murphy, Ballylanders, and Dan Tobin, Ballinalackin, two of Ireland's ablest defenders, were shot dead by British forces. Both young men had taken a prominent part in all major operations against the enemy in their locality. They had received Holy Communion at the little wayside church at Glenbrohane that morning, and had returned to Tobin's house for breakfast, where Mrs Tobin, a most hospitable and patriotic woman, looked after their needs. Her other son, Ned, already mentioned in connection with the Ballylanders and Kilmallock barracks attacks, was away with the column.

About twelve noon the purr of a Crossley tender was heard and the boys immediately slipped out the back-way with the intention of heading for the Steav Riog mountains and thus evading the enemy in the road below. This withdrawal might have been successful had not the wily Tans approached Tobin's house ahead of the Crossley tender about an hour previously and sent a section towards the hills to cut off retreat in that direction. The boys were accordingly caught between two fires and tracer bullets did an ugly job. Tobin's body was not discovered until a day later, and by irony of fate he was found within fifty yards of his own house. Murphy made a desperate attempt to break through the enemy lines, but he was killed whilst crossing a road which led towards safety. He fell near the back of Mick Quirke's cottage. The bodies of the IRA men were interred in the republican plot at Ballylanders, where they were later joined by Tom Howard, Glenbrohane, and Willie Rearden of Cullane; the remains of the latter two were transferred from Lough Gur, where they had been temporarily interred. They had fallen in the fight at Lackelly.

MASTERLY OPERATIONS AGAINST VASTLY SUPERIOR FORCES AT GRANGE (BRUFF)

by SEAMUS

THE EAST LIMERICK flying column was resting in the 3rd battalion East Limerick brigade area in the vicinity of historic Lough Gur about two and a half miles from Bruff, in the closing days of October 1920. One day during the column's stay in the locality, a Sinn Féin civil court in session there in an untenanted house was attended by a big number of litigants and members of the legal profession. Three brigade officers constituted the court, and the commonsense justice of the decisions given by these legally untrained men gave entire satisfaction to all concerned. It was some months previously that Ernie O'Malley had presided over the first of such courts, held a few short miles from Lough Gur in the home of David Cremmins, Ballygrennan, Bruff, an officer of the 3rd battalion East Limerick brigade. On the day following the session of the civil court at Lough Gur, the same three brigade officers constituted a military court to try an enemy agent. The trial was adjourned, and a short time afterwards the spy, who was being conveyed further east across country, attempted to escape when the sound of a British Crossley tender was heard in the distance. Refusing to halt when called upon, he was immediately shot dead by the escort.

The IRA of the 3rd battalion were most anxious to engage the enemy, but lack of arms and ammunition prevented their doing so. The advent of the East Limerick flying column to their locality gave them an unexpected opportunity to go into action, and battalion officers approached the column O/C Donnachadh O'Hannigan and 'Seán Forde' (Thomas Malone), about a possible operation. The reliable 3rd battalion intelligence was able to indicate a position where the British might be encountered any day. Martin Conway, vice-officer commanding the 3rd battalion and officer commanding the Grange company, later killed in an encounter with the enemy at Caherguillamore, urged that there was a suitable ambush position in his area, at lower Grange. The position was accordingly visited by the column O/C and his officers, and a meeting was subsequently held in the home of Robert Ryan, captain of the Lough Gur company, to discuss plans for the projected operation. Amongst those present at that meeting were Donnachadh O'Hannigan, column O/C, 'Seán Forde', Martin Conway, Holycross; David Cremmins, Éamonn Treacy, Seamus Maloney, Bruff; Robert Ryan, Lough Gur; Seán Cifford, Fedamore; James 'Benny' Maloney, Kilcullane, and Richard O'Connell, Caherconlish. Donnachadh O'Hannigan, who presided, received reports which detailed the available men and arms. The transport, armaments and routes followed by the British were examined.

On a rough map of the proposed ambush position, the leader inserted a few strokes here and a few dots there and thus were the bombers, rifle and shotgun men and road blocks etched into position. All in attendance contributed something vital to the discussion, and a general plan was soon approved. 'Give attention to every minute detailed', was Donnachadh O'Hannigan's final summing-up to the local commander. 'Have your men get Confession and parade at the gate of Count de Salis at 5 a.m. tomorrow.' At precisely 5 a.m. fifty men of the 3rd battalion paraded and formed up in two ranks. They were addressed by Donnachadh O'Hannigan, who said: 'I have no doubt that we are passing through the most important phase in Irish history for seven hundred years. We are a lucky generation. I am certain that some of you will feel nervous about your first fight; that's only human. We all did, but after the first volley will come the realisation that you are fighting for a glorious ideal, and a feeling of real happiness will be uppermost.'

'Seán Forde' added: 'Remember, men that ammunition is precious, and every bullet must count. I am sure you know what I mean. Right turn! Quick march! In ainm Dé.' Hard man, Seán who came down from Tullamore and liked us so well that he stayed; a man absolutely without fear and idolised by fighting men everywhere. Left, right, left, right, marched the column down the road towards the ambush position where Martin Conway and E. Treacy and their men, having worked throughout the night, had everything ship-shape. It was 8 November, and a cold, bleak morning, when the IRA occupied positions, mostly in the vicinity of John O'Neill's house. Men on both sides of the road were so placed as not to be in danger by their comrades' cross-fire. One mile to the south was outposts to prevent possible surprise from the big British garrison in Bruff, three miles away. A mile to the north was another party to intercept British reinforcements from Limerick, seven miles north, or from Fedamore or Hospital which were only four miles west and east respectively. The IRA then settled down to wait. Every man was on the alert with nerves tensed by nine o'clock, the hour at which two lorries from Limerick usually passed the ambush position on their way to Bruff. By ten o'clock there still was no signal from the outposts, and surely the suspense of the hour spent awaiting action was the worst possible experience.

The men relaxed as the O/C investigated the possibility of attacking enemy forces coming from either direction. Heads popped over the seven-foot high walls, and jokes were exchanged across the road as another hour passed. An aeroplane flew overhead, and nervous tension renewed itself against the men, all of whom were most anxious to get down to the job at hand. At last, at noon, an outpost signalled the approach of British lorries from Bruff and in a short time the sound of lorry engines could be heard by the waiting men. The lorries appeared to stop before they came into view, but before the IRA could contemplate what was happening, engines were re-started and a lorry drove into the ambush position. Five-second bombs were promptly lobbed over the wall by Ned Tobin, Martin Portley, Jim 'Benny' Maloney and Jim O'Sullivan. Volunteers inside a high wooden gate, which gave entry to the road, were thrown several yards by the repercussions of the bombs. Acting under orders, Martin Conway, Seamus Maloney, and Jim Murnane snapped open the gate, first emptied their guns at the enemy, and then pushed onto the road a mobile road block made of two farm carts joined together by a ladder. This was to prevent the lorry getting out of the ambush position. Martin Conway, armed with a revolver, was then in the centre of the road, whilst both rifleman Seamus Maloney and shotgun man Jim Murnane were in the channel. Their minds registered a British lorry capsizing twenty yards away in the Limerick direction, with ten or twelve British soldiers sprawling out of it, some of them apparently dead. The East Limerick column on the west side of the road and the Mid-Limerick men on the eastern side proceeded to pick of the survivors. Suddenly the din of battle increased in tempo, and the IRA men on the road had barely time to size up the situation before an enemy armoured car was upon them.

Quick-thinking Martin Conway saw it first, and managed to get safely to cover with his two comrades, their retreat being covered by David Cremmins and Johnny Moroney. The British armoured car was then only ten yards away, and its machine-guns were blazing at the IRA positions. An officer fired from its running-board, and British soldiers, who had come into the open, fired from behind the cover which it afforded. The officer jumped from the running-board of the armoured car and, with some soldiers, rushed towards the gateway through which the three IRA men had retreated. All were firing rapidly as they advanced, but the officer fell fatally wounded at the entrance, and the soldiers turned and fled, whilst lead was showered into them by the Lough Gur boys under Bob Ryan, Jim Murnane and Ned Daly, and by the Grange contingent under Martin Conway and Éamonn Treacy. The danger that the enemy might encircle the men lining one of the walls was thus averted, but a greater menace arose from the Bruff direction, as eight additional enemy lorries appeared. These, which included two armoured cars, conveyed approximately two hundred well-armed British soldiers, who had a heavy machine-gun mounted on a tripod in one of the lorries. Donnachadh O'Hannigan's whistle immediately sounded the retreat. He had quickly sized up an ugly situation and realised that nothing but the best generalship would extricate his men without serious loss. The east offered the only line of retreat, as an open bog lay to the west. Enemy lorries were to the south, whilst the north was impassable. Furthermore, parallel to the line of retreat ran a river and a road, and were the British armoured cars to reach that road the IRA would be certain to incur heavy casualties.

A small section of the ambushers, four in number, which included Owen O'Keeffe, Billy Burke and Tom Fogarty, engaged the main body of the enemy from positions in Mr Bulfin's house, old home of Seoirse Mac Flanncadha, later murdered when mayor of Limerick. Retreating by the back of the house, that section occupied new positions overlooking the eastern road, and effectively prevented the British forces from concentrating upon it. In a matter of minutes, Donnachadh O'Hannigan, 'Seán Forde' and their men gained the eastern side of the road, and by signals, directed the retreat of the four volunteers. 'You with the rifles, three rounds, rapid,' was signalled. 'You with the shotguns, empty your barrels. What matter if you are out of range; they won't know. Twenty yards to the rear rifles: twenty-five, shotguns'; and so the Volunteers retreated step by step, ever facing the enemy who sent a literal hail of lead in their direction for close on twenty minutes. Billy Burke and Tom Fogarty, two of the little band which operated from Bulfin's, were wounded and conveyed to safety by members of the Grange company. They constituted the sole IRA casualties. The British casualties were unknown, although it was felt that few could have survived the bombing of the first lorry. Furthermore, Lieutenant Watling, who engaged the IRA from the running-board of an armoured car, and who was wounded at O'Neill's gate, died that night in Bruff.

The IRA withdrew to Lough Gur where the men were given a square meal and a rest. The retreat revealed points of great generalship. The British force engaged comprised a convoy of ten vehicles bound from Fermoy to Limerick, a much different proposition to the expected two lorries from Limerick to Bruff. They had observed some of the IRA outposts on the Bruff side, and becoming suspicious, sent ahead as decoy the first lorry which was so expeditiously dealt with by the attackers. The engagement, which had considerable military merit, exercised an uplifting effect on the morale of the IRA who took part in the attack. It was a splendid achievement for a small band of poorly armed men, prepared only to deal with two lorries of the enemy, but instead confronted by over two hundred well-armed men supported by armoured cars and machine-guns in addition to grenades. Moreover the British were travelling in a direction opposite to that for which the ambush had been originally prepared. The IRA armament in the engagement consisted of twenty-one rifles, twenty-one shotguns, and some explosives. Yet, with undaunted courage, they used the arms and ammunition at their disposal with excellent results, and then made a masterly retreat without suffering fatalities, having first inflicted severe casualties on superior enemy forces. On the night of the ambush, the IRA occupied positions around Bruff in case of reprisals but none were attempted.

THE AMBUSH AT GLENACURRANE

by MAJOR-GENERAL D. O'HANNIGAN

GLENACURRANE, IN THE parish of Kilbehenny and Anglesboro, County Limerick, is a picturesque valley about two and a half miles from Mitchelstown, County Cork, and through its runs the main road to Limerick and Tipperary. It became known to the East Limerick flying column that the British military were using that road for the conveyance of mails from Fermoy to Tipperary. Accordingly, on 17 December 1920, the column left Shrove, a slope on the Galtee Mountains above Kilbehenny, and proceeded to Glenacurrane, where they were joined by Commandant Barry of Glanworth, and his men from the Cork area. Positions were taken up on both sides of the glen, and Commandant Barry and Commandant T. Malone ('Seán Forde') arranged the men suitably. A tree almost severed at its base was in readiness for felling across the road, and all other preliminaries having received attention, I personally covered the area and found everything satisfactory.

It so happened that a party was being given by General Franks, a retired British army officer, residing near Knocklong, a factor which increased the number of civilians who passed through our lines during the period of waiting. The guests, who had various modes of conveyance amongst them, motor cars, pony carts and bicycles, were made prisoners temporarily, and were, for their own safety, confined in the house of farmer named Morgan O'Brien, about one hundred and fifty yards from the public road. A Church of Ireland clergyman, his wife, baby and lady friend amongst the number, presented a problem, as I did not like to interfere with movements of a clergyman. I told him that, as we were expecting a fight, it was dangerous for him to be on the road, and that I considered it advisable that he should take shelter and the protection of our troops.

He resented my advice, and was horrified that we should attack British military who would be unaware of our presence, and whom he thought would be shot down without warning. I informed him that he was labouring under a misapprehension of our methods; that the enemy would first be called upon to surrender and given the option of handing over their arms and vehicles without danger to their lives. To his argument that I expected the impossible, as the men were under orders and paid to do their duty, I replied that we were also acting under orders and were bound to carry out our duties, though we were not paid. I proposed to him that he, having a bicycle, could act as intermediary, go into Mitchelstown to inform the enemy of our presence and numbers – sixty men – and offer my challenge to have sixty of their men sent out to fight us. He treated this as a joke and said the British would not consider it. I suggested, however, that they would react by sending out messages to Kilworth camp, Fermoy, Kilmallock, Tipperary and Cahir, where they had thousands of men who would surround the hills as soon as possible, and close in on our position, whilst we would not know of their presence until they had opened fire on us. He then abandoned the idea of dissuading me from attacking the troops, and requested that if any lives were in danger on the enemy's side, he would be allowed to attend to their religious needs, as they would probably be of his religion. I agreed to let him know if his services should be needed, and added that as I thought some of our own personnel were also of his religion, asked whether he would do likewise for them, if they requested his assistance. He consented without demur.

Having left the reverend gentleman with the custodian of the civilian prisoners, we settled down to await the enemy, and in a short time two lorries with twenty men of the Lincolnshire Regiment, stationed in Tipperary, entered the ambush positions. They were called upon to surrender, but refused to do so. A tree felled across the road prevented their advance, and all efforts to reverse out of the danger zone were frustrated by our fire which caught them in the rear. The fight was short, several of the enemy were wounded, four of them fatally. I had the clergyman summoned to the bloody scene where he offered consolation to one man who appeared to be dying.

We took all rifles, some boxes of grenades, and about three hundred rounds of ammunition. A huge consignment of mail for the military in Tipperary was duly censored by us, and the letters and parcels were subsequently posted to their destinations in good time for Christmas.

We rendered what first aid was possible to the wounded, took them about a mile away to Athnaslinga Cross, and put them in a cottage.

RAIDS FOR ARMS AT KILBALLYOWEN HOUSE, BRUFF

by SEAMUS

THE 3RD BATTALION East Limerick brigade had conducted many raids for arms and ammunition, but had little to show for their efforts, except a number of shotguns. In a Bruff public house one night the proprietor was chatting with a young man when a stranger entered whom they knew to be a Kildare man, gamekeeper at Colonel The O'Grady's at Kilballyowen House, Bruff. He was in good form and being most loquacious stated in conversation that there was a large quantity of arms and ammunition stored where he worked. The men in the bar 'stood' him a couple of 'large ones' quickly, following which he became still more informative. He could hardly have known that the proprietor of the bar was most sympathetic towards the IRA, and that the third man at the counter was one of the most able intelligence officers in the 3rd battalion. The intelligence officer immediately prepared a report of the conversation with the gamekeeper which he submitted to Brigade Commandant Seán Wall, at the brigade headquarters in Liam T. Purcell's residence, Uregare.

A raid was immediately planned, and as practically all The O'Grady's staff were in the IRA, further information was readily obtained. On a given night, Bruff company mobilised and proceeded to Kilballyowen House, which they entered through a large window left open for them by one of the female members of the indoor staff. When the IRA had gone indoors the window was then carefully locked and one of the outer doors broken open, in order to divert suspicion from the staff. The O'Grady was ill in bed at the time and madam, his wife, was assured that there were no designs on the colonel's life. Bandolier after bandolier of .303 and revolver ammunition were found and removed, but their lady accomplice informed the IRA that no arms could be secured that night.

Plans were prepared for a second raid, and on the selected night a party assembled north of Bruff and proceeded to Kilballyowen House. They had reached the road at Bruff Hill and were rounding a bend when they marched straight into a patrol of Royal Irish Constabulary and Black and Tans who walked the water tables on either side of the road. Not a word was spoken. No command to halt rang out, and the Volunteer party of approximately eight men marched right through the patrol; ten, twenty, thirty, one hundred yards beyond the patrol, and still no interference by the British. 'Near thing, boys,' commented the leader, as everybody relaxed when the danger zone had been passed. There was only one revolver amongst the IRA, and no one will ever know whether the British or the IRA were the more surprised on the occasion. On arrival at the appointed rendezvous the party reported the incident to Liam Wall who wisely dispersed the men fearing an enemy attack in strength on the house during the arms raid.

A few nights later the Bruff company again raided Kilballyowen House, and this time they bagged the lot, which comprised two machine-guns, one anti-tank gun, two Mauser rifles, and a number of shotguns. The booty was quickly conveyed to a place of safety. On the occasion of the second successful raid the Bruff company was commanded by brigade O/C Seán Wall who directed the operation personally. Amongst other successful raids for arms in the 3rd battalion area were those at Rockbarton Mansion, residence of Nigel

Edward Thomas O'Dwyer, Lord Bishop of Limerick, whose stand against the blood-stained and tyrannical General Maxwell in 1916 gave an invaluable lead to the nation.

Limerick Regiment Irish Volunteers. Photograph: F. Hazelback, Limerick.

Limerick City Regiment Volunteer Officers. Left to right: Captain Robert Monteith, Vice-Commandant George Clancy, Captain Liam Forde, James Leddan, Hon. Colonel and Commandant M.P. Colivet.

Commandant Edward Daly, youngest of the 1916 leaders to face a British firing squad.

General Sir John Maxwell, Commander of the British forces, at a review of loyalist volunteer corps in the grounds of Trinity College, after the suppression of the Rising. It was 'Butcher' Maxwell's secret court martial which ordered the execution of the Irish leaders.

Seán Heuston, one of the founders of Fianna Éireann in Limerick city, died before a British firing squad after Easter Week 1916.

Con Colbert of Athea, rebel of Fenian stock, proudly gave his life for Ireland following the Rising of 1916.

Commandant Seán T. O'Riordan of Kilmallock (left), Battalion Commandant, First Galtee Battalion, who commanded the IRA in the successful attack on Ballylanders Barracks; Lieut-General Donncadh O'Hannigan, O/C East Limerick Brigade flying column.

Patrick Maher and Ned Foley, who were executed in Mountjoy jail in June 1921, in connection with the rescue of Seán Hogan at Knocklong station two years previously. This picture of the executed men was taken in the jail some short time before their execution. With them in the picture is the warder and an Auxiliary guard.

British troops, in full war kit, with armoured and mobile support, stand-to in readiness for emergencies outside Mountjoy jail.

Father Albert, OFM Cap., photographed with Father Dominic, OFM Cap., at the Presbytery door, Church Street, Dublin. It was Father Albert who attended Captain Seán Heuston before his execution.

A group of East Limerick IRA men photographed in 1916.

Dromin Volunteer Corps, 1914.

Volunteers parade at Kilmallock Feis, 1914.

The demolition of bridges, trenching of roads and felling of trees across them were devices adopted by the IRA to hamper the movements of enemy mobile troops. Here some British soldiers are shown repairing a demolished bridge.

Major-General Donncadh O'Hannigan, who commanded the East Limerick Brigade flying column.

An East Limerick flying column.

Mayor Michael O'Callaghan, with members of the Limerick City Corporation, 1920. The story of the last days of his work for Ireland and of his murder by British police, is told in this volume by his wife, Mrs K. O'Callaghan.

Seoirse Clancy, murdered mayor of Limerick, and his wife, Mrs Mary Clancy.

Six Irish mayors bore the coffins of the murdered mayor and ex-mayor of Limerick to the grave. Here is shown the scene at the graveside, with the coffins draped with tri-colours.

Seoirse Clancy photographed in volunteer uniform, with his friends, Commandant M.P. Colivet and Captain Robert Monteith.

Michael O'Callaghan, from a photograph taken a short time before his assassination.

Mrs K. O'Callaghan, widow of Michael O'Callaghan, from a photograph taken in 1921. She tells in these pages the story of her husband's brutal murder by the British.

The home of Michael O'Callaghan, in the hallway of which he was murdered in the presence of his wife, on the morning of 7 March 1921.

Michael O'Callaghan, founder member of the Limerick Industrial Association, speaking to a country audience, 1911.

Seán Hogan.

Mayor Michael O'Callaghan of Limerick, at the funeral of Lord Mayor MacCurtain of Cork, who, in the presence of his wife and five children, was murdered by masked RIC in the early hours of 19 March 1920.

A West Limerick flying column.

Robert Byrne, Adjutant of the Limerick City 2nd Battalion, IRA, who was fatally wounded when rescued from British custody at the Union Hospital, Limerick city, on 6 April 1919.

Funeral of Robert Byrne passing through the streets of Limerick.

Major General Donncadh O'Hannigan photographed in the disguise adopted for the purpose of gaining admittance to interview IRA prisoners in 1920.

Brigadier Seán Finn.

Dan Breen.

Michael Scanlan.

Henry Clancy.

Seán Wall.

Liam Scully.

Patrick Clancy.

Tomás Malone.

Thomas Keane.

Edward Donnelly.

John Moloney.

Éamonn Moloney.

Martin Conway.

Thomas Blake.

Baring, master of the Limerick foxhounds, and at the residence of Count de Salis, Lough Gur, then Britain's envoy to the Vatican.

CROSS OF THE TREE AMBUSH

by VOLUNTEER OFFICER

WHEN KILMALLOCK WAS occupied by British regular troops, following the destruction of the police barracks, Lieutenant Browne, an intelligence officer attached to the machine-gun corps, became notorious in the locality for his activities against the IRA, and against civilians known to be sympathetic towards the movement. A number of unsuccessful attempts were made to shoot him; one at Riverfield, Kilmallock, and another at Ballingaddy, Kilmallock. The spot chosen for the second attempt referred to was in close proximity to Ballingaddy Roman Catholic church, and was abandoned following the intervention by the clergy who feared that the church might suffer as a reprisal.

What is now known as 'Cross of the Tree ambush' was yet another unsuccessful attempt on Lieutenant Browne who appeared to bear a charmed life. As the name suggests, the location of that attempt was a crossroads, in a green space in the centre of which flourished a tree. IRA intelligence learned that Lieutenant Browne with his escort would pass the cross one day in December 1920, and accordingly, preparations were made to ambush the party. The small number of men detailed for the operation fired upon Browne and his escort the moment the lorry in which they were travelling came into view. The British returned the fire and the exchanges became hot and heavy. When the engagement had been about a quarter-of-an-hour in progress the attackers were subjected to an unexpected hail of machine-gun fire, and it was then observed that Lieutenant Browne had managed to get beneath the lorry, from where he was raking the IRA position with a machine-gun.

Plans were hurriedly re-arranged by the attackers, with a view to capturing both Browne and his machine-gun. The necessary fresh dispositions of the attacking party were suggested by Seán Riordan of Ballintubber, Kilfinane, an ex-soldier of the British army in which he held the rank of sergeant-major. Riordan, who had fought through the Great War in France and who had only joined the East Limerick flying column a few days previously, would probably have succeeded in his purpose had not heavy British reinforcements suddenly arrived upon the scene. These include an armoured car and four Crossley tenders loaded with troops.

The position of the little IRA party appeared hopeless, and there seemed no chance of escape for the men of the column, heavily out-numbered and out-gunned as they were. It was then that the value of Seán Riordan's military training became apparent as he ordered the men to fall back and retreat before the superior numbers of the enemy whilst at the same time he issued instructions as to the method which offered the best prospects of escape from the trap. He first saw that each man of the column was in such position as offered favourable chance of a get-away, before he made any move himself, and then with the most conspicuous bravery he personally covered the retreat of the others in the direction of Garryspillane. Fighting every inch of the way, he continued to engage the very large British force until every one of his comrades had got away unscathed. Although he received mortal wounds in the intestines in the course of the action he nevertheless managed to evade the enemy and reached Garryspillane where he immediately collapsed. His comrades placed him in a bed of straw on a horse and cart and conveyed him all the way to Shraharla, where he was sheltered for about five days, until secretly removed to Kilmallock Union Hospital. Despite an immediate operation by Dr Trevor McNamara, who removed the bullets, the valiant soldier died next morning.

THE ENGAGEMENT AT CAHERGUILLAMORE, BRUFF

by SEAMUS

DURING THE LATE fall of 1920 Captain Ernie O'Malley from general headquarters paid a visit to the 3rd battalion, East Limerick brigade IRA. Despite the fact that the presence of Earnán invariable spelt hard work, he had many friends in the area and his advice was eagerly sought. Captain O'Malley, who then possessed a report on the Grange ambush, which had taken place on 8 November, suggested to the battalion staff other points of vantage in the locality from which the British could be successfully ambushed. Following Captain O'Malley's departure a battalion council meeting was held, and amongst those present were Martin Conway, William Leo, and T. Aherne, of Holycross; James (Benny) Moloney, Robert Ryan, John Quinlan, Seán Maloney, Thomas O'Brien, Éamon Maloney and Patrick O'Donoghue. Discussion centred largely on the ways and means of procuring arms and ammunition. Although a good supply of ammunition together with small arms and sporting guns had already been secured in a raid on nearby Rockbarton mansion, service rifles were very badly needed. The battalion vice O/C had been advised by Captain O'Malley as to where rifles could be purchased, though in small quantities. The council accordingly decided to avail of this source of supply in order to equip a battalion column and make life too hot for the British forces in the area. The main problem was to find money to buy the rifles. Somebody jokingly suggested a dance, and other means of securing finances having been found impracticable what was originally a joke was taken seriously, and it was eventually decided to hold a dance. Although the wisdom of this decision was subsequently criticised severely there was not a great deal of opposition to it beforehand.

Ostensibly the place fixed for the dance was Herbertstown Hall; actually, it was decided to hold it in Caherguillamore House, the unoccupied residence of Lord Guillamore, situated three miles west of Herbertstown. Preparations were immediately launched, and the house was inspected by a sub-committee under Paddy O'Donoghue whose father was the caretaker. Every precaution was taken to maintain the secret of the real venue for the dance, and only selected men had the right to issue invitations. Nevertheless, undue activity must have been observed in the vicinity of deserted Caherguillamore. On Saint Stephen's night some hundred ladies and one hundred and forty men arrived at the crossroads at Caherguillamore, where they were met by Volunteers and directed to a point where other Volunteers gave further directions. Eventually having passed through a number of such Volunteer points the party ultimately arrived at Caherguillamore House, outside which picked men from the Grange company mounted sentry. Inside the hall the atmosphere was festive despite the dangerous times, and as friend met friend after a lapse of months in many instances greetings were warm and hand clasps strong. Perhaps for the first time the corridors of Caherguillamore House re-echoed to the strains of traditional Irish dance music played by the brothers Martin of Bruff.

When the fun was at its height, about 1 a.m., scouts glided silently into the house and mingling with the dancers warned those 'on the run' and prominent men, that danger was at hand. A warning shot had been heard; Daniel Sheehan, sentry, true to his trust had challenged and fired, his bullet-ridden body being found later. The house was by that time practically surrounded by a force of seven hundred enemy troops, comprising regular military, Royal Irish Constabulary and Black and Tans, from Limerick, Bruff, Fedamore, Croom and Hospital.

Ascending Verey lights clearly showed Caherguillamore House and lit up the darkened woods and courtyards round about it. Intensive fire was immediately opened by the British who, maddened with blood lust, bombed the buildings and raked them with rifle and machine-gun fire. The trapped IRA men immediately attempted to fight their way through the British lines, and Martin Conway, battalion vice commandant, who had almost passed the enemy cordon when the headlights of a lorry picked him out as he crossed the open road, fell mortally wounded. His revolver was snatched by Éamon Moloney who brought down a Black and Tan named Hogsden before being killed himself. John Quinlan was found outside a wicket gate, rifle clutched tightly in his hands, having died in the cause for which he came from the USA to fight. Henry Wade fell mortally wounded at his post, and Bob Ryan received a rifle bullet through the shoulder from which he subsequently recovered.

Meanwhile, hell broke loose inside Caherguillamore House, and male guests had to run a gauntlet of Black and Tans and Royal Irish Constabulary who used clubbed rifles, table legs and portions of stair banisters to lay upon skulls, smash in teeth and deal savage punishment to all. Men subsequently found by the enemy to be without wounds were quickly put on par with the others. An inquisition took place, too, but despite the beatings no information was given to the British. The terrified girls were held until 8 a.m., when they were released, and at 11 a.m. the men, all of whom were then in a sorry plight indeed, were taken to Limerick together with their dead. They were subsequently tried by court martial, under Major-General Eastwood, and given terms of imprisonment which varied from three months to ten years. Those given the longer sentences were still in Dartmoor when the Treaty was ratified. During the break through the British cordon Major J.F. O'Dwyer received a bullet wound in the hand, and a bullet passed through the hat of his brother, Nicholas O'Dwyer. The IRA swore vengeance, and in a short time a three-to-one toll of the Tans was exacted at Dromkeen.

AEROPLANE BROUGHT DOWN NEAR KILFINANE

by VOLUNTEER OFFICER

EARLY IN 1921 when the nation's struggle for freedom against the might of the British Empire was at its height, there took place in the Kilfinane district, then a veritable hive of British military activity, an operation without parallel in the history of the War of Independence. It was carried out by a section of the flying column numbering about half-a-dozen men, under the command of Seán McCarthy, adjutant of both the East Limerick flying column and the East Limerick brigade, and now lieut-colonel attached to the army general staff. McCarthy and his men were billeted in a district which lay between Kilfinane, Martinstown and Cush, when they observed flying low, an aeroplane which, it transpired later, was flying from Oranmore in Galway to Fermoy, County Cork. As it was apparent that the pilot was in difficulty the column commander decided that they should make an attempt to bring the aeroplane down. Accordingly, as it flew low over the position which they occupied they opened rapid fire upon it, and in a few moments were thrilled to see it land about half a mile from the spot from which the attack was made. It was never learned whether the plane came down directly as a result of the IRA fire. The attackers immediately rushed towards the spot where the plane, a British military type, had landed, and around which a number of local people had already congregated. Shots fired into the air by the approaching IRA men prompted the pilot to comment, 'these are our men'; but the people answered back, 'no, they are ours'. The assembled civilians immediately dispersed and the IRA called upon the pilot to surrender, but he refused to do so. He took up a position in a hollow in the field, but as he appeared to be unarmed the IRA did not wish to injure him. However, they immediately proceeded to set the plane on fire, having first removed the pilot's equipment and a number of military documents. Having achieved their objective by the destruction of the plane the IRA withdrew without delay, taking the pilot with them. His observer had got away before they reached the scene of the crash, and as British reinforcements were expected at any moment, there was no point in the members of the column unnecessarily delaying their departure. It was not intended to hold prisoner for an indefinite period the pilot whose name was Flight Lieutenant Mackey; rather it was intended to keep him merely for as long a period as the safety of the column dictated.

Following the destruction of the aeroplane and the capture of the pilot, an ultimatum from the British military forces to the people of the town of Kilfinane was conveyed by the Black and Tans stationed there. The ultimatum threatened that the town would be bombed from the air unless the pilot was released within a specified time. Upon receipt of the ultimatum the IRA decided that they would not release the pilot until such time as it pleased themselves to do so and, consequently, he was brought about with them from billet to billet, for a number of days. Flight Lieutenant Mackey turned out to be a decent fellow, and many humorous stories recall the period during which he was a prisoner of the IRA. He was treated with every consideration during captivity, and could not understand why the IRA should be operating in flat country, as it had been his belief that all 'Shinners' confined themselves to the mountains. He was amazed, too, to find a number of ex-British soldiers in the flying column, and considered their's the 'grossest disloyalty'. Ultimately when told of his release, he asked Seán McCarthy for a letter to his commanding officer in Fermoy, indicating that he had been held against his will. That was given to him and, in turn, he gave Seán McCarthy, as officer in charge of the column, a letter thanking him for the favourable treatment he had been given by his captors, and because of which he promised to do them no harm when he re-joined his unit. In that respect he kept his word because, subsequently the Fermoy Black and Tans brought him on tour of the area to discover the location of his captivity and, if possible, to identify his captors. Brought to a stud farm where he had been held a prisoner, he saw in the dining-room racing trophies which he had admired a short time previously. When asked by the Black and Tans if he had been previously in that house, he answered 'no'.

Prior to the release of the pilot the Black and Tans did everything possible to terrify the people of Kilfinane by every means at their disposal. Their efforts were augmented by a squadron of aeroplanes which appeared over the town and dropped what appeared to be bombs. Loud explosions followed, but no material damage was done as apparently only smoke bombs had been used. All the while the local IRA company in Kilfinane was mobilised and in readiness to protect the town from further hooliganism by British forces.

BLACK AND TANS ANNIHILATED AT DROMKEEN

by LIEUT-COLONEL J.M. MacCARTHY

FLAUNTING DEFIANCE FROM the highest point of a large, detached building in the village of Pallas, County Limerick, a conspicuous flag in the sombre colours of black and tan strikingly, if unconventionally, identified the local police barracks throughout the winter of 1920–1921.¶ Here, also, was the headquarters of a police district in charge of an officer ranking as a district inspector, RIC, but whose special category, and that of the greater part of the large garrison, was plainly indicated by the unofficial emblem so prominently displayed. The hoisting of this banner reflected fairly well the tension prevailing in the area at that period, and was expressive of the challenging sentiments of the garrison towards the countryside at large, but particularly towards the East and Mid-Limerick brigades, IRA. These two units were equally involved through the fact that, though Pallas itself was in the East Limerick domain, the inter-brigade

---

¶ *Author's Note:* This is the form of the name by which the village is normally known except when necessary to distinguish it from Old Pallas, 1½ miles to the south-west. According to local usage, it then becomes New Pallas. The ordnance survey map versions are respectively Pallas Green (New) and Pallas Green, but in some map editions Old Pallas is given as alternative to the latter name. This is a fair example of the confusion that can sometimes arise in relating map reference to local usage, and of the pitfalls to be watched for in that connection.

boundary ran close by, while the police district – and, needless to say, the police activities – extended into both areas.

For long the operations, and more especially the methods, of this garrison, besides making its personnel exceptionally feared by the general public, had proved a very sharp thorn for the two brigades and faced them with a challenge that had to be met. The police were definitely in the ascendant when, early in 1921, they scored what, in the circumstances of the time, was a big success, and for the local IRA a correspondingly serious reverse, by locating and capturing the arms dump of the Mid-Limerick brigade. Incidentally, the police raiding party took good care to celebrate their feat by visiting the house of the 'on-the-run' O/C, of the brigade's active service column, and staging a *feu-de-joie* with the captured weapons in the presence of the occupants paraded to witness, so they were assured, this proof of defeat and final end of the column's activities.

These events brought matters to a head. Consultations, already in progress, between the two brigade staff with a view to common action, were hastened to a conclusion. Plans were considered for an attack on the barracks, but in view of the pitiably poor armament of the IRA, disclosed serious difficulties to be surmounted. The nature of the building, its position and defences made for difficulty of approach and ensured a protracted fight if the defenders were to be overcome. Despite the fairly extensive experience of the East Limerick column in conducting prolonged and successful barrack attacks, such as that Kilmallock in the previous May, when the attack was sustained for over six hours, the time factor in this case was a definite obstacle to success. The proximity of Pallas to large military and police centres (Limerick city, ten miles; Tipperary, twelve miles) made it probable that the garrison would be relieved long before the barracks could be destroyed or captured, notwithstanding all that might be done to impede the arrival of reinforcements. With a mere sniping, or demonstration, attack being of no value since the situation required that the IRA should register a clear-cut success, an awkward problem seemed to defy solution when the I/O, of the Mid-Limerick column came to the rescue. He was able to report that a considerable portion of the Pallas police garrison regularly travelled with a lorry convoy to Fedamore, eleven miles distant, making the return journey on the same day. Further, he was able to indicate the route normally followed, and even to the usual date of the movement as the first Thursday of each month.

With this information the decision to attack and destroy this convoy was taken, the first Thursday of February being fixed for the effort as a joint operation by the East and Mid-Limerick columns. An examination of the route led to the further conclusion that a carefully laid ambush along a particular stretch of road at Dromkeen, some three miles from Pallas, offered the best method of attack. Here a straight section of the route extended for three hundred yards, slightly downhill, from a bend at its western (Fedamore) end to a road junction at its eastern (Pallas) limit. Dromkeen House at the bend afforded observation both over the whole ambush position, and westward for a considerable distance towards Fedamore. The road junction presented almost full right-angled turns to vehicles travelling in any direction, and was an obvious site for barricades which would be out of sight until the turn was about to be taken. From this point, too, observation over the entire position, and extending as far as the western bend and Dromkeen House, was feasible from a ruined house at the road fork.

These facilities, and the lay-out of the road section, were definite advantages in the light of a number of factors. The basic decision being to effect complete destruction of the convoy, a fairly lengthy stretch of the route had to be held in order to ensure that all the vehicles were within the position before the action opened. The position had also to be capable of being sealed off at both ends once the convoy had entered it. The length, at first sight over-long, was therefore not excessive in the circumstances, especially when there was no certainty as to the number of lorries likely to be encountered, nor as to the distance between the lorries.

To reduce this uncertain element to the minimum, and for other reasons, it was decided to intercept the convoy on its return, rather than on its outward journey. In this way its strength would be known on its departure from Pallas and, though it had varied somewhat on occasions, might be counted on to be approximately the same when it set out on its return trip from Fedamore. With this knowledge any necessary last-minute adjustment in dispositions could be made. Further, the later in the day the action opened the better from the standpoint of the column's withdrawal, which it was desired to effect under cover of darkness as far as possible in view of the elaborate military and police reactions anticipated. The other grounds for interception on the return journey were that it made actual occupation of the position unnecessary until confirmation of the movement of the convoy was received, and, by that very fact, lessened the possibility of a long and perhaps fruitless wait in the position itself. Also, by ensuring that occupation would not be effected at all if the convoy did not move out, possible disclosure of intentions was avoided, and the same site could be used another day. This alternative was important in view of the suitability of the location, and the distinct chance that the intelligence officer's estimate as to the date of the movement might not be borne out by events.

Keeping this valuable alternative in mind, as well as the special caution needed in this particular area, the arrival of the two columns, and their junction with one another, was so timed that neither would be in the immediate vicinity of Pallas longer than was absolutely necessary. The more distant of the two, the East Limerick unit, was mainly concerned in this 'approach march'. By the day preceding that fixed for the attack it had reached a billeting area, nine miles away, near Emly, on the Limerick-Tipperary border. At nightfall it moved forward some four miles to the neighbourhood of Kilteely. Here it remained for a few hours before continuing, while still dark, to a previously agreed on 'assembly area' and rendezvous with the Mid-Limerick column.

THE COLUMNS MAKE CONTACT

AT THIS POINT, situated in a secluded locality away from dwellings, and a little over a mile short of the selected Dromkeen position, contact was made between the two columns just before dawn. The combined force, some forty riflemen strong, then lay up to await developments, a dilapidated shed affording the shelter needed both because of secrecy and because of the fact that the weather during the moves on the preceding nights had been very bad and had so continued. Communication was soon established with the local scouts who, from early morning, were keeping movements in Pallas, and on the adjoining roads, under observation. It was not, however, until close to noon that calculations were in great part fulfilled by the news that two lorries, carrying about twenty policemen, with the district inspector in charge, had started out along the road towards Fedamore.

DISPOSITIONS

A MOVE WAS at once made to the site for the intended interception through which, as further information soon indicated, the lorries had passed, travelling fast and close together. The weather had now cleared, and luckily as matters developed, little time was required for taking up positions, these having been assigned beforehand. Excepting the farmhouse at the turn of the road to Old Pallas, all the houses and the barn provided fire positions, and were occupied in varying strength accordingly to accommodation and field of fire available. The farmhouse, left unoccupied, was used to detain passers-by, some half-dozen being thus 'interned'. Dromkeen House, on road bend at the western end, held a party detailed to observe the route towards Fedamore, signal movements from that direction, and prevent a withdrawal by the lorries or their occupants by that route.

What amounted to the CP was set up in the ruined house facing the road junction. Small detachments also took positions at intervals on both sides of the straight stretch of road along its low boundary walls, in the yard of the farmhouse used as 'a place of detention', and at the fences covering both the road-fork and two barricades erected there. These barricades were made with farm carts in preference to other forms of obstruction so that no outward signs need have remained should there have been postponement. For the same reason no artificial fire positions were constructed except at the northern boundary wall of the road where loose stones, readily replaceable, permitted a limited number of loop-holes. Elsewhere fire was to be brought to bear from the top of the walls and the fences, the hay in the barn, and the windows of the houses.

These steps completed the dispositions except for two other measures intended to secure the authors of the projected surprise against being themselves surprised. One was the occupation by a party of armed local Volunteers of a position near Dromkeen across the intended line of retreat to keep open that route and cover the withdrawal of the column. This step was considered essential in view of the heavy military traffic in the vicinity. The other security measure was the use of a screen of scouts provided over a wide area by the local Volunteer companies to warm of hostile approach from an unexpected direction. The frequency of enemy patrols in the locality generally, and on the main Limerick-Tipperary road, only three-quarters-of-a-mile distant, made such an outcome not improbable. Whether or not it was appreciated at the time, the fact is, however, that these scouts had no effective means of delaying, or rapidly communicating, the progress of any hostile formation should the latter, as was likely, have been motorised. Consequently, had an occasion for action by the scouts arisen, this protective measure would in all probability have broken down badly.

It was now a little after 12.30 p.m., with all in readiness. After an uncomfortable night and morning, and a seventeen-mile cross-country march to their next billeting area in prospect, the Volunteers hoped for an early end to their vigil. In this they were not disappointed, for nearing one o'clock the approach of lorries was signalled from Dromkeen House. Hardly had the signal been amplified to indicate the number of vehicles as two, when the first lorry appeared around the road bend, quickly followed by the second at about fifty yard's distance. Orders had provided for the opening of fire when the first of whatever number of lorries might compose the convoy took the turn at the road-junction. In the event, fire was opened a few seconds before this occurred, due probably to the riflemen in the western half of the position having difficulty in judging the exact moment of the leading lorry's arrival at the road fork. As matters were, this was of no consequence, though it might have been otherwise had there been a larger convoy, or a wider interval between the lorries. This point, however, serves to emphasise the necessity of a checking up on details lest the larger plan be wrecked through a small oversight.

THE CONVOY ENGAGED

AFTER THE OPENING volley, the first lorry continued along the short distance separating it from the road-junction. Confronted with the barricade as he was taking the left-hand turn on the usual route – that leading to Dromkeen station – the driver swerved violently to the right in an effort to take the other turn. Faced here with the second barricade the lorry struck both it and the fence adjoining the ruined house. Thrown or jumping clear, the driver, who happened to be the district inspector, and another policeman, both unwounded, reached the adjoining field. Aided by the fact that they alone among the police party were wearing civilian clothes, they succeeded in making good their escape, and eventually proved to be the sole survivors of a total police party of thirteen. A stronger police escort had been expected but a reduction in the original number had probably been made at

Fedamore. Of the five occupants of the first lorry three remained, one of whom was mortally, and two slightly, wounded at the outset. The latter two took cover at the roadside, but shortly after were again hit, this time fatally.

The second lorry contained eight policemen. It had arrived a little beyond mid-way in the ambush position when the first shots were fired. Halting at once, its occupants began to dismount. Some were hit while doing so, others as they took up positions at the roadside. Five were killed outright, and one sustained severe wounds that proved fatal some days later. Two managed to get into positions beneath the lorry. From here, firing from behind the wheels, and refusing to surrender, they maintained a steady exchange of shots. Difficult to hit in this situation, they were eventually struck and killed by fire brought to bear from new positions on the road level taken up by a few of the attackers. In passing, it is both of interest, and but fitting to record here that the two policemen responsible for this determined fight against hopeless odds were two of the only three members of the 'regular' RIC in the police party. It was in the course of the attack on this second lorry that the Volunteers sustained their single casualty, a Volunteer officer on the wall near the church having his hand shattered by a bullet.

This casualty somewhat complicated the pre-arranged cross-country withdrawal and the 'evasive action' to counter the widespread military and police 'round-up' that now ensued. For a great part of the march various forms of transport had to be called on to permit the wounded officer keeping up with the column. By using field-paths and avenues, however, the move was effected mainly across country as planned, with the result that nightfall saw the Volunteers safely through the cordons and installed in billets some seventeen miles from Dromkeen.

IRA SURPRISED AT SHRAHARLA AND LACKELLY

by VOLUNTEER

FOLLOWING THE ARRIVAL in East Limerick of the combined East, Mid and West Limerick brigade columns, arrangements were made to ambush a cycling column of the enemy which usually consisted of from fifteen to twenty men and which had for many weeks previously terrorised the people of the countryside by murders, raids and robberies. The enemy detachment was known as the 'Green Howards', and the East Limerick column had waited vainly in ambush for it on many occasions. On Saturday night, 30 April 1921, the combined columns were divided and sent to various billeting areas while further efforts were made to contact this enemy column.

On 1 May 1921, Seán Carroll and some of the Mid-Limerick flying column were on the march to take up ambush positions not far from the old churchyard at Shraharla, situated on a steep hill, one side of which overlooked the road along which the enemy cyclists were expected. As it approached a main road whilst crossing fields on its way towards the site selected for the ambush, the little IRA party was suddenly surprised by four lorries of enemy troops accompanied by an armoured car. The enemy force, which appeared around a bend in the road at great speed, had been investigating an incident which took place in the Kildorrery (County Cork) district on the night before. Having unexpectedly interrupted the ambush preparations they immediately opened fire on Carroll's men who were taken completely off guard and entirely exposed to the enemy fire. Some of the British cars advanced along the main road, and their occupants jumping out, engaged the Mid-Limerick men front and flank. They killed three of them, Captains Paddy Starr, James Horan and Tim Hennessy. Volunteer Casey, whose ammunition had become exhausted, was captured, taken immediately to Cork; tried by drumhead court martial, and executed next morning.

Carroll and his Mid-Limerick men maintained the unequal fight for hours until ultimately the enemy boarded their vehicles and withdrew. They feared the arrival of reinforcements of IRA from the East and West Limerick column whom they knew to be somewhere near the locality. The night the members of the Mid-Limerick column who participated in the engagement, together with the East and West Limerick columns who later came up, withdrew towards Knockaney and were billeted in houses in the Kilteely, Mitchelstown and Lackelly districts.

IRA SURPRISED AT LACKELLY

ON THE FOLLOWING morning a scout brought word to the IRA section billeted at Lackelly, under Vice O/C Dan Allis, that a strong patrol of Black and Tans was on the Emly road. The scout departed and later returned to state that the enemy had gone towards Emly. The IRA abandoned the defensive position which they had taken up and were speaking to the scout when Miss Mai Moloney arrived with further news of the patrol. She volunteered to go for the O/C Donnachadh O'Hannigan and other IRA, with a view to attacking the enemy patrol on its return journey. She mounted her bicycle and had only barely rounded the bend of the boreen when she dashed back and shouted: 'They are on top of ye!' The IRA party, twelve in number, got over the fence into a haggard and emerged at the far end, where they were immediately observed by the enemy, who opened fire at about fifteen yards range. Four of the IRA were killed immediately, whilst others who included Dan Murphy of Abbeyfeale, had amazing escapes, their clothes having been cut in many places. Those killed were Lieutenant Jim Frahill, Pat Ryan and Riordan of Mid-Limerick; and Tom Howard of East Limerick. The IRA survivors fought their way to a sunken drain which afforded some cover and whilst they occupied that position, the enemy endeavoured to surround them.

Seán Carroll, who had figured so prominently in the fighting the previous day, arrived on the scene with two or three companions and engaged the enemy on his right flank and thus gave the IRA party a better chance to reach the cover of a low bank. These men were then on a slightly wider front but their position was still desperate. They exchanged round after round with the Black and Tans at practically point-black range, and that rapid fire gave Seán Carroll and his men the opportunity to link up with the others. Whilst fighting their way through the enemy lines the IRA waded through mire up to their waists along a sunken drain which provided their only cover. The firing attracted further contingents of the enemy, but by that time Miss Moloney had succeeded in getting word to the O/C Donnachadh O'Hannigan, who arrived with IRA reinforcements, and a heavy engagement which then took place over an extended area lasted from noon until about six o'clock in the evening.

The Black and Tans fired explosive bullets. During the engagement some of them took cover in a farmhouse, and when observed approaching that house they appeared to have prisoners. It later transpired that the 'prisoners' were a couple of Tans who had removed their tunics to give the impression that they were prisoners, and so escape the IRA fire. That party of the enemy was later dislodged from the farmhouse. Some of the original ambushed part of the IRA were allotted the task of covering off the railway line as it was feared that enemy reinforcements might be rushed to the scene by train. When the fighting ceased, the IRA, attracted by signals from three ladies, Miss Mai Moloney and the Misses McGrath, returned to the scene of the ambush, where they were assisted by the ladies to remove the bodies of the four fallen IRA men and also sixteen bicycles abandoned by the enemy, to a farmyard about a mile away. The removal of the bodies was a grim task even for men, as the heads were practically blown off by the explosive bullets of the enemy, and one body was mutilated after death. That night the remains were removed in two traps, and members of the column, who rode the captured bicycles, acted as escort. They were buried next evening in a temporary grave in a field many miles from where they had met their deaths. May they and all who died for Ireland rest in peace. A number of the enemies were wounded in the Lackelly fight.

On 3 May 1921, a column section under Jim Colbert surrounded near Emly managed to force its way through the enemy lines. Next morning movements of an enemy patrol were again reported to the IRA. The patrol consisted of eleven men with a machine-gun. It was decided to attack them and one section of the IRA was moving to take up positions for that purpose when they met an IRA officer who was recuperating from a wound received some time previously. He informed the IRA that it was only a decoy section of the enemy, of whom there were about forty lorries in the vicinity. The section returned to the main body of the IRA and all moved across country to the cover of double banks or fox covers. Some of the captured bicycles were dumped in a hollow in a corner of the first field entered. A party of the enemy actually entered the field later but did not see the bicycles.

THE LIMERICK CITY CURFEW MURDERS OF 7 MARCH 1921

ASSASSINATION OF MAYOR CLANCY, EX-MAYOR O'CALLAGHAN AND VOLUNTEER O'DONOGHUE

Contributed by Mrs O'Callaghan, Mrs Clancy, and comrades of the murdered patriots

On the morning of 7 March 1921, Seoirse Clancy, mayor of Limerick, and Michael O'Callaghan, his predecessor in office, were foully murdered by British police in their homes, and in the presence of their wives. The mayoress, Mrs Clancy, was wounded during the assassination of her husband. The murder of Michael O'Callaghan took place about 1.10 a.m. and that of Seoirse Clancy about 2.30 a.m. Some hours previously Joseph O'Donoghue of the IRA was murdered and his bullet-ridden body was found in the street in morning.

THE QUESTIONS WHICH this article is written to answer are: (1) Who was George Clancy? (2) What were the circumstances of his death? (3) What manner of man was he?

His relatives, the companions of his early manhood, and his friends and fellow-workers of later years, have contributed towards the answers given here to the first question and to the third. His wife sets out in detail the answer to the second question.

WHO WAS GEORGE CLANCY?

IN BOYHOOD: Born in the village of Grange, County Limerick, Seoirse drank in the tenets of militant Irish nationality with his mother's milk. She was the daughter of a Fenian, his father was scout and recruiter for Stephens, Luby and O'Leary in the early 1860s, his uncle was captain of six hundred men at Grange on the fateful night of 6 March 1867. While yet a child he learned many things from his grandfather – also George Clancy – whose mind was stored with the history and legends of his native place, with the tales of Ireland's heroic age, and with the facts of Irish history at home and abroad. Seoirse received his early education at Grange national school and St Patrick's seminary, Bruff, where he proved himself an apt pupil, studious, bright and intelligent. To the knowledge acquired in the schools, he added knowledge of the Irish language, laboriously learned from the old people in the neighbourhood, and an intimate acquaintance with the history, traditions and legends of Ireland, more particularly of his native place.

IN EARLY MANHOOD: In 1899 he went to Dublin, entered the Royal University, graduating in 1904. With most of those whose names loom large in modern Irish history, he was associated while in the capital. He met two obscure young men named William Rooney and Arthur Griffith in the Celtic Literary Society, where they were sowing the seed that has since received such a marvellous fructification. He joined the Gaelic League; and his first Irish teacher was a shy, studious-looking, very earnest young man named Patrick H. Pearse. He knew and loved old Michael Cusack, founder of the Gaelic Athletic Association, whom he often met in An Stad, an Irish tobacco shop kept by the famous Irish humorist, Cathal MacGarvey, in North Frederick Street, Dublin. Seoirse took a large part in founding Cumann na bPáirtidhthe (The Confederates' Club), which on the social side held weekly debates on national subjects and organised *ceilidhthe* and excursions in the various seasons. On the athletic side it had a hurling club, of which Seoirse was captain, and Na Suibhlóirí ('Tramps') who walked along distances during the weekends among the Wicklow hills and to whom Seoirse was guide, philosopher and friend.

THE YOUNG MAN AT HOME: After Dublin, Seoirse went to Clongowes college as language teacher, but he fell ill and had to return to Grange. There he taught Irish classes and organised indoor and outdoor entertainments that were thoroughly Irish in character. In 1906 he was the person mainly responsible for the agitation to divide up untenanted land on the de Salle estate near his own home, among the small farmers and the landless, which ended successfully with a monster meeting at Grange in September 1906. John Redmond, struck by the outstanding capacity of the young organiser, offered him the secretaryship of his Party, which Seoirse refused, as he had no faith in parliamentary action. Three years later he was offered the representation of East Limerick, which he also declined.

THE TEACHER: In October, 1908, Seoirse came to Limerick as teacher of Irish in the schools and Gaelic League. For more than ten years he taught the Irish language and Irish nationality to the children of Limerick. The sweetness of his personality and the strength of his character, with earnestness and patience and careful method, bore fruit in time.

Every school-going child in the city knew him and loved him. An old Christian Brother prophesied of him in those days that the boys whose teacher he was would eventually make him mayor of Limerick and so it proved. One of his last his acts was to make arrangements to inaugurate a special class for Irish teachers in the Gaelic League, but when the appointed day came, Seoirse had fallen a victim to the assassin's bullet.

THE IRISH VOLUNTEERS: Before the formation of the Irish Volunteers, Seoirse was connected with the different national societies of the time. He had a share in establishing the Fianna Éireann (Irish Boy Scouts) with Seán Heuston (executed in Dublin after Easter 1916), and others. From 13 December 1913, when the Volunteer movement was started in Limerick, he was a member of the committee, and as such, he welcomed Patrick Pearse and Roger Casement in February 1914, when the Volunteers were formally and publicly established. The first need was a supply of arms, and it was arranged that a cargo would be landed in the Shannon. Seoirse went to Glin, County Limerick, to watch for their coming, but circumstances diverted the ship's course, and the arms were landed in Howth. During the summer holidays he organised a Volunteer company in his native place, and later acted as commandant in a Volunteer camp at Kilkee, County Clare. Returning to Limerick, flushed with hope and of good spirits after his camp experience, he was faced with a new situation. The war had broken out, Redmond and his followers had declared for unqualified co-operation with England and, obviously, the Volunteers were about to be split into two antagonistic bodies. Seoirse's spirited answer to the pessimists put new heart into them: 'Even if we can muster only fifty men, we must stand our ground.' When the split came and those in Limerick who chose to stand by Ireland went on parade, two hundred and eight were present.

MARRIAGE: In the July of 1915 he was married to Máire Ní Chillín, whom he had met at Coláiste na Mumhan, in Ballingeary, and later in the Limerick Gaelic League.

AFTER 1916: The Rising of Easter 1916, was followed by anxious days and nights for a handful of men waiting orders, and for their leaders, heavily burdened with responsibility, in a city full of troops and in the midst of a population openly hostile. No one felt the situation more keenly than Seoirse. His arrest followed in May, but he and the others taken with him were released after a few days. At the historic election of de Valera for East Clare in 1917, Seoirse did effective work as a speaker at the meetings and as personation agent on the day of the poll. Prominent among the speakers during the campaign was Thomas Ashe, who received the answer to his prayer: 'Let me Carry your Cross for Ireland, Lord!' when he died in the September of that year during the first hunger strike at Mountjoy jail. The immediate result of the Mountjoy tragedy was the revival of public parades of Volunteers, met by the government by arresting the officer in turn. First, Commandant Colivet was taken, then Seoirse, who stepped into his place, and so on with others.

IN JAIL: The prisoners were taken to Cork jail and there Seoirse met Thomas MacCurtain, murdered in 1920 when lord mayor of Cork, and his successor, Terence MacSwiney, the martyr of Brixton whom Seoirse had already known at Ballingeary. The numerous Cork prisoners were being tried by court martial in turn, and it was agreed that the courts should not be recognised. Seoirse contended that in no case should an address be made to the court and that non-recognition would be best shown by a short replay when the prisoners were asked to plead. He suggested the Irish phrase: *Níl meas madra agam ar an gCúirt seo,* and after some discussion, his proposal was agreed to.** However before the time for their trial came, the prisoners went on hunger strike, were released, and the Limerick men received a popular ovation on their arrival in the city.

CONSCRIPTION YEAR: The year 1918 was occupied with the estab-lishment of Sinn Féin club and the various other activities for the strengthening of the movement. As the year advanced the need for intensive organisation became more apparent. Ireland was threatened with conscription and the country resolved to resist. To prepare military resistance in the Limerick district was Seoirse's task, as his senior officers were in jail or 'on the run'. He had also to continue his work in the schools, to do the routine work of his battalion, and to attend meetings of all kinds. The strain of those strenuous months from May until October, when finally England abandoned Irish conscription, told on Seoirse's constitution and highly strung temperament. He fell a victim to the severe influenza epidemic which came that winter, and was seriously ill for some weeks. When

---

** An expression of utter contempt, literally, 'I haven't a dog's respect for this court'.

he regained his strength he had give up teaching work, and, instead, became local superintendent of the Irish National Assurance Co. Within a year he had established a fairly remunerative business.

IN MUNICIPAL LIFE: At a municipal election of 1920 Seoirse was elected senior alderman of the city. His poll was more than double that of any other candidate. He had the votes of his former pupils, who had grown to be men and women, and of the parents of his later pupils. Said one poor women: 'I'll vote Clancy who never closed his eyes on my child.' Seoirse was offered the mayoralty but he declined it, as he had yet no experience of municipal life. Michael O'Callaghan was elected mayor for 1920.

I.R. LOAN: Seoirse was appointed organiser in the city and liberties of Limerick for the Dáil Éireann Loan of 1919. He visited the country districts to help the collection, took charge of all monies received and kept the accounts – a matter of unexampled difficulty, as house searches were frequent and personal searches in the streets of common occurrence. In June 1920 Seoirse was in a position to go to Dublin and hand the money intact to the finance minister, Michael Collins.

In January 1921 George Clancy was appointed mayor of Limerick. In his address to the corporation after his election he said he was 100 per cent Sinn Féin, and when the time would come, he would be found pure wool and unshrinkable. Those words recalled themselves to his wife while he stood without a tremor before his murderers, and she realised in a flash that he was about to die.

HOW GEORGE CLANCY DIED

WHAT A 'RAID' WAS: Raids and searches were an outstanding feature of the English campaign against Irish nationality in the years 1916 to 1921. They usually took place late at night when the people had retired, or in the early hours of the morning, and the searchers were not provided with anything in the nature of a search warrant. At first the armed force were usually accompanied by a responsible police or military officer, and were duly authorised by the military governor of the district, but as time went on unauthorised raids freely took place, and the forces employed, whether sent officially or otherwise, conducted themselves without any regard for the persons or property of the occupants of any house they chose to enter. In the final stages of the terror armed forces of the crown raided private houses with the set purpose of murdering prominent republicans.

In Limerick the raids began in May 1916 after the military had taken possession of a number of rifles, the property of the Irish Volunteers. In various part of the city during the night, parties of soldiers and police searched houses and arrested men – a score of citizens, including Seoirse Mac Flanncadha. So frequent were the searches in that and the following two years at the Clancy home that no record has been kept of them.

MRS CLANCY'S NARRATIVE: Towards the end of 1919 Seoirse made it a point not to sleep at home so that his activities might not be interrupted by another term of imprisonment. One November morning at 3 a.m. there came loud knocking, awakening the household. I got up, called the maid, and together we went to the door. I asked who was there and got the answer 'military' followed by 'if the door is not opened in thirty seconds it will be broken in'. I opened the door and in rushed a military officer, a number of soldiers and one member of the RIC. The officer asked for my husband, and I answered that he was not at home. He then placed his men all over the house, in the garden and back yard. He searched the house himself minutely, examining every place, even the hen run. This search lasted about two hours, and as the night was extremely cold I was feeling pretty bad when it was over. When going, the officer informed me they would come again. Nightly expecting another raid my husband and myself had not very much rest for the next few months, but strange to say, were not again visited for a considerable time.

How women suffered: My only sister died in September 1920, and then my parents came to reside with us. On the night of 7 December 1920, at 10.30 p.m. the long expected summons came. I went to the door and I asked who was there. In reply to my question they said they were police, so I opened the door. The hall was quickly filled with RIC, Black and Tans and cadets in uniform and mufti, all carrying rifles and revolvers, a number of them being under the influence of drink. They were led by a man in civilian clothes, brandishing a revolver in one hand and having a flash-lamp in the other. They spread through the house, even invading the privacy of the room in which my mother and father were in bed. My poor mother got up and dressed, but my father, being an invalid, could not do so.

The raiders asked for my husband and when I said he was away from home on business, they replied I should tell them where he was. I repeated I did not know, and they then said if I did not tell them they would burn me out. I was detained in the dining-room for over an hour surrounded by ten policemen and a cadet in uniform, who sat on the table dangling his legs and enjoying the insults and abuse poured on me. They told me we were murderers, that we knew all about certain ambushes, and that we brought my parents to live with us so as to cloak our misdeeds, and so on. One of their number, an RIC sergeant, ordered two men to go upstairs and carry my father out of the house to the avenue, so that they could, as he said, 'blow the place to pieces'. At the same time he ordered others down to the lorry for petrol. Another sergeant went into the sitting-room and took a picture from the wall – a camp group of Volunteers, with my husband and myself in it – and called me to walk on it. I refused, he then asked the maid to do so, but she taking her cue from me, also refused. He walked on it himself, and tearing the picture out, burned it. This same man put the maid, a young girl of about eighteen, with her back to the wall of the sitting-room and questioned her about her home and people. Then in a threatening manner he told her to clear out of my house before six the next evening and tell her father to get her 'decent' employment. Some of the raiders then left the house and returned in a short time with two women searchers. My old mother of seventy, the young girl and myself were then sent into the sitting-room to suffer the humiliation of being searched while the men went through the house and ransacked every corner of it. Before leaving, the RIC sergeant, who had trampled on the photograph and who seemed to be in command of the raiders, officers and cadets included, told me to the evident amusement of the cadet before mentioned that if my husband did not report at William Street barracks before seven o'clock the next evening, they would come again the next night and actually burn us out.

THE AUXILIARY OFFICER'S RAID: On 27 February 1921 at 10.30 a.m. we were saying the family Rosary before retiring when we were startled by a frantic knocking at the front door. My husband jumped up and told us not to be frightened as it was probably a raid, for Michael O'Callaghan had told him that on the previous Tuesday night raiders at his home said that they intended giving his successor a lord mayor's show. My husband went to the door, asked who was there, and received the reply 'military'. I followed him to the door and when he opened it I saw a number of soldiers in charge of an officer in mufti, the same who had been in charge of the raiders at Michael O'Callaghan's home on Tuesday 22 February. The avenue outside was lighted up by the searchlight from the car on the road. The officer asked my husband was he Mr Clancy, and being answered in the affirmative, expressed surprise at finding him at home. My husband said there was no reason why he should not be in his own house, adding that he had no choice but to be indoors after curfew. The officer said he had come to search the house and stationed some soldiers in the hall. He first visited the sitting-room, which he searched minutely, then asked my husband to accompany him to the dining-room. Here he again expressed surprise that my husband was at home and received the same reply. My husband afterwards told me that he learned from this man that he was in the Auxiliary division, and remarked to me what a charming cultivated voice he had. Before this officer completed his search of the dining-room he went out to the hall door and called in Cadet ——, whom he sent upstairs with me to search the bedrooms. A soldier with a rifle accompanied us. My husband explained that my father was an invalid confined to bed and the officer said he would not be disturbed, but that he wanted to see our room. This cadet was the same that had come with the police on the terrifying raid of 7 December 1920. When we got upstairs the cadet said to me that he was surprised to find my husband at home. On my replying there was no reason why he should not be in his own home, he said, 'but he was not at home on previous occasions'. I then said my husband's business took him frequently from home. His next remark was that they, the government forces, intended giving us a lord mayor's show. I then said was not this visit a lord mayor's show, to which he replied 'Not at all – a lord mayor's show, when we all come dressed in our best as we do in London', adding that he would bring his most powerful searchlight. After a short time the Auxiliary officer came up, looked around the room, and then they both went to my father's room where they remained only a few minutes. In the hall as they were leaving, my husband referred to the bad raid we had when there were only women in the house. The officer expressed sympathy, adding that this was an official military raid.

THE MURDER RAID: My father died on the 4 March 1921 and was buried on Sunday 6 March. That night friends remained with us up to curfew hour, 10 p.m. Then we had the family prayers and we chatted for a little while before going upstairs. Seoirse insisted that I should sleep in my mother's room that night so that she might not be lonely. He came in with us and remained some time consoling her and trying to lighten her sorrow. Before getting to bed I discovered that the candle in his room was still alight and I went in as I was anxious about him – he had a slight cold for some days. I found him awake reading Keating's *Defence of the Mass* in Irish. He promised me that he would get to sleep quickly, so I wished him 'goodnight' and left him. It was then midnight, and, though we didn't know it, Joseph O'Donoghue was at that time dead and his murderers were making their way to Michael O'Callaghan's house. When I got to bed I fell almost immediately into a deep sleep, for I was very tired and lacked sleep for over a week owing to my father's illness and death. About 1.30 a loud noise awakened me. I jumped up startled and asked what the matter was. My mother said, 'Oh God! It is a raid, they are hammering at the door.' I got on my dressing-gown and slippers, calling out to my husband as I did so, 'Seoirse, I will open the door.' He answered 'No, Moll, I will,' and went down the stairs ahead of me. He held a candlestick in his hand and said back to me, 'It's all right, Moll, only a raid.' Before opening the hall door he asked who was there, and got the answer 'military'. I was just behind him at the foot of the stairs, and when he opened the door I saw three tall men wearing goggles with caps drawn well down over their faces and the collars of their coats turned up. Two stood at one side of the door and one at the other; one of the two held a flashlight. Even then I did not realise the murderous work they had come to do. The man at the right asked 'Are you Clancy?' pointing a revolver at Seoirse. My husband answered 'Yes, I am,' and stood straight in front of him. Then this man said, 'Come out here, we want you.'

Seoirse asked, 'What for?' and the man said more loudly, 'Come outside.'

'No I won't,' Seoirse answered, and stepped back a pace or two, opening the door still wider as he held the knob in his hand.

The spokesman then stepped into the hall and shouted, 'Then, take this,' and before I could move fired three shots at him. I then dashed between them screaming and trying to move Seoirse back and push the man away, but even as I did so, he emptied his revolver. I heard in all seven shots. The men then rushed off and banged the hall door, leaving me in the dark, as the candle Seoirse held had fallen and the gas was not lighted. I did not know then that I was wounded. I thought the sting I felt in my wrist was a blow I got in the struggle. I groped about with my hands to find my husband, but could not. Then I saw the door at the end of the hall and also a door beyond it leading to the yard were open. I called Seoirse by name and getting no answer I rushed round the yard still calling him but could not find him. I opened the gate leading into the garden and ran across to a friend's house, falling many times on the way. I knocked at Mr Barry's bedroom window and asked him to come and help me as my husband was shot and I could not find him. I went back immediately and passing in through the gate I stumbled over my husband's feet. He had fallen in the yard and I had passed without seeing him. The maid, who was now up and dressed, came into the yard when she heard my cry on discovering him. Between us we tried to lift Seoirse up but failed, as my hand was useless. I then discovered I was wounded and the blood was streaming from my wrist. I ran back again to Mr Barry and told him I could not lift Seoirse as I was wounded in the wrist. He was dressed by this time and came to me immediately, and with the help of the maid we lifted Seoirse into the kitchen. My aged mother had come down stairs in her night attire and had been wandering about the yard in her bare feet looking for Seoirse and myself. She was a pitiable sight, with her poor feet covered with his blood and mine.

My only thought now was to get the priest to my poor Seoirse while he was still alive. I then asked Ned – Mr Barry – to go for the priest, and he went off not knowing but that he himself might be shot on the way. I knelt beside Seoirse and tried to say the Act of Contrition in his ear – he was breathing very heavily but seemed unable to speak. In a few minutes Canon O'Driscoll, who had prepared Seoirse's mother for death, arrived and administered the last sacraments to the pupil he had encouraged and taught at Bruff seminary twenty-five years before. After this Seoirse opened his eyes and looked at me, then he looked at the canon and back again at me. I was now faint from loss of blood so the canon led me away just as Seoirse expired. During this time another friend, Miss Renehan, had come in and had gone upstairs with my nearly demented mother, washed her feet and dressed her. At about half-past two Canon O'Driscoll decided to go to the Strand barracks and ask the military to phone for a doctor as my arm was still bleeding, and I was getting weaker. After a short time he came back accompanied by three military officers, from them he learned that Michael O'Callaghan had also been murdered. They said it was a dreadful occurrence and that they had phoned for Dr Dundon at Barrington's who would be with me immediately. The military had scarcely left when some police arrived including a district inspector and sergeant, the men who had already conveyed Rev. Fr Philip, OFM, to Mrs O'Callaghan's.

THE DEAD MAYOR: As the morning advanced friends hurried to me, and, as the news spread to the city, hundreds poured from every side to weep and give me sympathy. Early Fr Philip, OFM, arrived and, then and afterwards, he was a source of help and consolation to me during all that terrible time. The nuns of St John's hospital came to do the needful offices of the dead. Seoirse's friends and comrades – Gaelic Leaguers and Volunteers – gathered to take charge of all arrangements, to keep guard in and about the house, and so save me from as much inconvenience and worry as possible. For two days there was a constant stream of people who came to see their dead mayor and to say a prayer for his soul. The lord bishop said the Rosary in Irish by his side, and hundreds of the little children who loved him so paid a last tribute to their master. During the two nights – Monday and Tuesday – his comrades stood guard in the room where he lay, and the Rosary was recited almost without intermission. On Wednesday he lay in state at St John's cathedral with his murdered comrades and next day six Irish mayors bore his body to the grave.

THE MURDER OF MICHAEL O'CALLAGHAN

MICHAEL O'CALLAGHAN LOVED Ireland, worked for Ireland, and died for Ireland. Knowing well the danger, he chose the hard road of service to his motherland, and his logical end was murder by the hand of a hired English assassin. His passionate interest in Irish affairs was not the growth of these last few tortured years. As a boy, he was proud of the fact that it was his grandfather, Eugene O'Callaghan, who in 1843 proposed the repeal of the Union in Limerick corporation. His collection of books shows how deeply he read and thought on Irish history and economics. In politics, he was a member of the first Sinn Féin club in Limerick in 1905, and died a member of The O'Rahilly club of the same city. He was a member of the Irish Industrial Development Association and was one of a gifted group of Limerick men, who, Sunday after Sunday, for some years, addressed meetings in Limerick and the neighbouring counties, impressing on the people the importance of supporting native goods. He was a member of the Gaelic League, and during his mayoralty presented the local branch with a scholarship for its students. He believed that the Gaelic League was the training ground for the men who were to save Ireland and in the midst of his business cares he made time to take lessons in the Irish language from the man who met his death on the same tragic night – George Clancy.

In January 1914, he was present at the meeting in the Athenaeum to establish the Irish Volunteers in Limerick, and spoke on the platform with Patrick Pearse and Roger Casement. He was on the executive committee of the Irish Volunteers from 1914 to 1916, and spoke at Pearse's last lecture in Limerick in February 1916.

After the 1916 Rising, he was one of the small band that kept the heart of the country alive. He was treasurer of the local branch of the National Aid Association. He threw himself into propaganda work for which he was so fitted and helped to circulate throughout the country thousands of copies of Bishop O'Dwyer's letters, and other seditious pamphlets. He was one of the founders of the National League, and was instrumental in getting the abstention policy carried by that league and accepted by the country. He fought for the release of the 1916 prisoners interned and jailed in England, and used his wonderful gift of eloquence in the East Clare election in 1917.

He was the friend of the extremists, and well realised the need for a military as well as a legislative and constructive side to the national movement. He helped in the general election in 1919, and, aided by George Clancy, wrote the election address for M. Colivet, who was in jail at the time.

He entered Limerick corporation in 1911 as a councillor for the Irishtown Ward, and took a keen interest in municipal matters. This training was of value to him when, in 1920, he was elected mayor of the city of Limerick by the newly elected corporation. He and the corporation at once pledged allegiance to Dáil Éireann and the Irish Republic, and he was proud of the fact that he was the first republican mayor of Limerick.

MAYORALTY, 1920

WE ARE INDEBTED to Mrs K. O'Callaghan, widow of the murdered ex-mayor, for the following story of the last days of his life.

My husband, Michael O'Callaghan, was elected Mayor of Limerick on Friday, 30 January 1920, and his first official act was the pledging of his allegiance and the allegiance of the Limerick corporation to Dáil Éireann. Owing to the critical and difficult time, and for the credit of the Republic, he devoted himself entirely to the work of the corporation, and it is admitted that no mayor of Limerick was ever so successful in managing the city affairs. He had a sympathetic understanding, and appreciated the point of view of the different groups of citizens. A member of the manufacturing class and an employer, he was yet, as a working man said to me on one of the first sad days, a labour leader; a Sinn Féiner and a Republican, he tolerated the Unionists of the Chamber of Commerce and hoped to win their service for Ireland.

From the very first day of his mayoralty, he was noted for his uncompromising national stand, and it led to his murder. In the first week of his mayoralty, two citizens – Miss Johnson and Mr O'Dwyer – were shot by the crown troops. My husband, at a meeting of the corporation on Thursday 5 February, said that under the present regime, men's homes were no longer sacred nor their lives safe. He would say to the British government: 'Clear your soldiers out of the country and we will see to it that every citizen is safeguarded. Withdraw the soldiers, place the police under municipal control, and we will look after our own city.'

At the inquest on these two victims, he stated that he had not been consulted in an advisory or in any other capacity about the preservation of the peace of the city. 'The elected representatives of the people,' he said, 'have only one connection with these armed patrols that parade our streets; as taxpayers, they have to foot the bill.'

FIRST DEATH NOTICE

On Friday, 18 March, he attended a meeting of the governing body of University College, Cork and lunched with the mayor of Waterford and Lord Mayor MacCurtain. He returned to Limerick that night and heard next day with horror of the murder of his friend, following the receipt of a threatening letter. He went to Cork on Monday 21 March, to attend the funeral ceremonies, and on his return received a similar threatening letter on the morning of Tuesday 22 March. This letter he published in the local press. It bore the Clonmel postmark, was in typescript, and read as follows:

Prepare for death. You are a doomed man. Rory of the Hills.

On advice from the Volunteers, he left his house and went to stay in the George Hotel, and a guard of Irish Volunteers watched at night across the street in the Sinn Féin club rooms over Herbert's boot shop. The mayor occupied the end front bedroom in the first floor corridor. One night he was given another bedroom. That night, a motor car stopped at the hotel, a tall woman got out, interviewed the night porter, and said she was looking for an eloping couple who were sleeping in Room X

– the room in which my husband had been sleeping. The night porter protested, the lady pushed past him, and entered the bedroom to find – as she told the porter – that the people there were not her friends. By this time others were roused, and the motor drove away. My husband laughed at the incident, but the Volunteers thought that he would be safer in our own house, so he moved back to St Margaret's Villa, and slept at ease while the Volunteers changed guard outside.

This arrangement lasted for some months. Much has been said by General Cameron and others of the British government regarding the way in which my husband kept the peace of the city. I would like to put on record that General Cameron's armed forces baptised my husband's year of office in the first week with the murder of Miss Johnson and Mr O'Dwyer, and marked his last week with the blood of Tom Blake, IRA. How far the year 1920 was a peaceful one in Limerick is known through the press to the public. During the first six months of the year, there were more 'shootings-up' and more crown outrages in Limerick than elsewhere in Ireland. It was reported in the issue of the *Limerick Leader* for 30 June, that owing to the tension due to outrages there was an abnormal number of patients suffering from nervous complaints and diseases. During this time of 'peace', Michael O'Callaghan was the people's champion against crown aggressors and law-breakers. It was to him citizens went when their homes were robbed, wrecked or burned by the crown forces; it was to him they turned when they themselves were brutally beaten by members of the English garrison; it was he who enlightened foreign newspaper correspondents as to the truth of happenings in Limerick and district; it was he who forced the truth on the notice of General Sir Neville Macready in an open letter on 21 August 1920. A sentence from that letter gives his attitude:

> I know you have no real right to exercise any authority in this country, and I address you simply to insure that your professed ignorance of outrage and atrocity shall be culpable, and that you shall not be able to assume ignorance of what has occurred in my city.

General Cameron spoke so strongly at the military inquiry about the help my husband gave him in keeping the peace of the city that it was thought that they had many meetings and discussions. The only meeting between Michael O'Callaghan and General Cameron was of General Cameron's seeking. The English garrison broke barracks on Monday 26 April, a riot followed in which a soldier of the Welsh Fusiliers was killed; the troops did a certain amount of damage to property, and the general called on the mayor at the Town Hall to discuss plans for keeping order in the streets. The mayor said that he could keep the peace of the city with Volunteer peace patrols, if the English soldiers and police were confined to barracks. General Cameron put that suggestion aside as impossible, but suggested instead that both bodies could work together, the Volunteers to wear a distinguishing badge. Michael O'Callaghan knew only too well what treatment awaited Volunteers so badged, and the discussion ended there.

FIRST RAID

IN JULY AND August 1920, raids on private houses in Limerick became more frequent. My husband, knowing that it would be a serious matter if his armed guard fired on the crown forces coming on a 'legal' raid, decided to do without them, and relied for safety on the presence of the ordinary guests, Americans and others, who came and went during the summer months. We had decided to take a three weeks' holiday in London from 1 September, and on the night of Monday 30 August, when there was neither guard nor guest in the house, we had our first search. On that night, at 11.45, a mixed party of soldiers, police and Black and Tans, accompanied by some military officers in uniform and in civilian clothes, in charge of Mr E——, the local district inspector of police, also in civilian clothes, having fired off volleys of shots at the Sarsfield Bridge, climbed over the front wall of our garden and knocked at the door. Hearing the shots, I got out of bed and, watching from my bedroom window, saw the dark figures coming over the wall and rushing up the grass in the moonlight. Long before that night, we had decided that Michael should never go down to open the door at night, so it was I who went accompanied by the maid. I asked who was there, and the answer was 'police'. When we opened the door and saw the crowd in mixed uniform and civilian clothes, armed with revolvers and rifles, the maid, Brigid, said to the man who was in front: 'Oh, sir, you are not going to murder the master.' When I was convinced it was a 'legal' search, not a murder raid, I called my husband, and the search began, but not before I had handed to them the key of the garden gate which was kept locked at night. The district inspector said that he was most anxious that there should be no looting, and asked Michael and me to accompany the men into the different rooms, but as they poured into all the rooms in the ground floor, the drawing-room floor, and the bedroom floor, that was impossibility.

A few days after, I wrote the district inspector the following letter, which he acknowledged :

St Margaret's,
i/ix/1920.

Sir,

After your search of my house on the night of Monday, August 30th, the following articles were missing: Silver Drawing-room Clock, Silver Pepper Castor, Silver Cigarette Case and Match-box, Silver Butter Fork, two Tea Spoons, Cards, Toilet Soap, Cork screw. All the articles, with the exception of the clock, were taken from the downstairs portion of the house, where your men also helped themselves to claret and stout. I am telling you this, not that I want restitution, but merely as a matter of information for you, because you personally seemed anxious that nothing like this should occur.

'ON THE RUN'

WE LEFT FOR London on 1 September 1920, and while there received letters pressing us to stay away as long as possible. My husband wrote to say that he intended returning to Limerick after three weeks. Again we were urged to take at least six weeks, if not the three months' rest we needed. My husband agreed with me that there must be something behind all this, but he said that his post awaited him, so back we came to Limerick on Saturday 25 September, to learn that secret information had been got from Colonel —— that my husband's life was in great danger, and that it would be folly for him to sleep at home. From Saturday, 25 September, until Christmas Eve, my husband never slept a night at home. That is to say, he attended during the day to his mayoral duties at the Town Hall, walked home to meals unattended through the public streets, but at night, owing to the information we had received, he dared not sleep in his own house. It meant that, if there was a corporation meeting at 6.30 p.m., he left his home about that time and did not return. If there was no meeting of the corporation, he left his home about nine o'clock – curfew being at ten o'clock – and walked to the house he had selected for that night. On such nights, I stood in the hall with my sister and waited for ten minutes or a quarter of an hour. If there were shots – and very often there were – my sister ran out holding an electric torch and searched the roadway as far as Sarsfield Bridge. Coming back she used say to me: 'Well, he's not there tonight.' It was a trying time, but for my husband's sake, I pretended not to mind.

FINAL DEATH NOTICE

HE RECEIVED HIS final death notice on 15 October 1920. It read as follows:

Final Warning. Whereas, it has come to our knowledge that the Sinn Féin organisation of which you are a prominent official through the so-called IRA, or murder gang, has been committing outrages in this hitherto God-fearing and law-abiding country.

This reign of terror must be stopped. You are, therefore, most earnestly warned that in the event of the continuance of these heartless and cowardly crimes you will be personally held responsible and punished in such a manner that others will be deterred from criminal courses. – By order.

We examined it very carefully and noted the typing and postmark. I put it aside for future reference. Some weeks afterwards, about 10.30 one night, there was a telephone call to say that my husband could have the trunk call that he was asking for during the day. I knew nothing about this, but I said that my husband was not at home. Next day, Michael, on being told of the matter, said that he had not asked for a trunk call. I wondered if the authors of the final warning wanted to find him at home that night. Here, to show my husband's close connection with the IRA in these autumn and winter months, I wish to state that he was one of the three persons who supported financially ——, the local commandant of the IRA. When —— was arrested, the newly-appointed officer called at once on the mayor to tell of his appointment, and to keep up the necessary relations between the military and civil sides of the republican government. My husband, was, too, in constant communication with all the departments of An Dáil, and carried out their orders. When in Dublin, he got into personal touch with the cabinet ministers, and their relations were most cordial.

On Christmas Eve, we decided that even the British government kept some rules and that assassins would stay their hands for the time commemorating the birth of the Prince of Peace. So my husband slept at home that night. On Christmas Day, however, he decided that, no matter what the risk was, he was not going to leave home again. It worried him that I had stayed by myself all the winter, though I pointed out that there were three of us women in the house.

On 19 January 1921, my husband got a copy of *The Weekly Summary* through the post. We were interested in the wrapper, and getting out the envelope that brought the final warning on 15 October 1920, we could see that the postmarks were the same, and that there were the same peculiarities in the typing and punctuation of the addresses. They had been typed by the same machine. The final warning and the anonymous copy of the police gazette, *The Weekly Summary*, published in the Castle, came from the same source; I have these two, the wrapper and the envelope.

ELECTION OF GEORGE CLANCY
TO MAYORALTY

As THE END of the mayoralty year drew nigh, pressure was brought to bear on my husband to continue in office a second year. He pleaded that he was not a strong man that he had put his own business aside for 1920, and that one year of the mayoralty under difficult circumstances was the most that could be expected from even the best citizen of the Republic. George Clancy was elected mayor on Monday, 31 January 1921.

After the mayoral election, my husband at once plunged into the affairs of his firm, the city tannery. We had been promising ourselves a holiday in the south of France after the worry and strain of the year, but pressure of business decided him to postpone such a holiday. He was, besides, full of the propaganda work he was now free to do for the cause, and he insisted that the time was ripe for a genuine boom in home manufactured goods. He felt that this was just as much a means of attack as military operations, and that it had the advantage of putting, as it were, every Irishman and every Irish woman on active service.

SECOND RAID

ON SHROVE TUESDAY night, 8 February, my husband and I were having supper in the dining-room at a few minutes after ten o'clock. There was a frantic knocking at the hall door and at the service door. The maid and I went to the hall door, and I asked who was there getting the answer: 'police!' I opened the door, and in rushed a body of policemen, armed with rifles and revolvers. They shouted as they rushed past me in the hall, and up and down the stairs: 'Who lives here?' 'Hold the doors.' I noticed that they were very red in the face and excited, their clothes were dusty and untidy, and some of the men were drunk. I ran into the dining-room, and said to my husband, who was standing with his back to the fire: 'Have you that relic in your pocket? Oh, I'm afraid. They have come to do something dreadful. They are very drunk.'

'Come over here,' he said, 'and stand near me. Whatever it is, it will be all over in a minute.' After a little time, the police came down the stairs from the bedrooms and up from the kitchen floor and my husband asked the meaning of their visit. I cannot describe this raid, for it was like a nightmare. There were both English and Irish police, and we owed our lives to two members of the old RIC, who seemed to have a slight restraining influence. All the others rushed about, shouting and pulling things out, overturning vases, jeering at the long agony of Terence MacSwiney, threatening to put a speedy end to my husband's propaganda, yelling that there was no God, God was dead, asking me how I would like my house to 'go up', saying that I would soon know more about murder. I had to accompany one man who went off on his own initiative to search the bedrooms, though all the time I was afraid for my husband's safety downstairs. This constable found a military whistle and the mourning armlet which my husband had worn at the funerals of Lord Mayor MacCurtain and Lord Mayor MacSwiney, so I had to go downstairs with a rifle to my back. They all agreed that I was treasuring the whistle because it had been robbed from a policeman killed in an ambush. When they had been an hour and a half with us, they asked for the key of the gate as they did not want the trouble of climbing out over the gate and wall. My husband asked them why they came at night like this, frightening his wife and pulling the house about; adding, however, that he was glad they came so early. 'We'll come later the next time,' they replied in a threatening manner.

After this raid I was frightened for the first time, for again and again during it, when my husband was quietly and courteously answering the questions shouted at him, I saw hate and murder in the faces of a few of these men. It appalled me that anyone should feel so towards my husband, and next day, when I met one of my sisters, we walked along the quayside, while I told her of the raid. 'Our bad time is in front of us,' I said, and, overwhelmed by some vague terror, I broke down and cried. Women do not cry much in Ireland during this war: the trouble goes too deep. My husband said during the following day, as he had said so often since the trouble started, whenever he heard of the brutal treatment of prisoners at the barracks, or of brutal murders: 'I hope they will neither beat nor torture me. I am not afraid of death, but I must confess that I should like a quick one.'

THIRD RAID

On Tuesday 22 February, just a fortnight after the last raid, we were visited again. There was the usual knocking at the door about 10.30 p.m.; the maid and I having asked who was there and getting the usual answer, 'police', opened it. On the steps were a crowd of police and soldiers, and shining over the wall at the end of the garden, I could see the searchlight. The man in front, in mufti, armed with a revolver, was the Auxiliary cadet whom I had seen at the dance, whose name had been given to me and about whose conduct at Tom Blake's house I had heard. Tom Blake had been murdered since then, so I looked at the man with interest and apprehension. He was obviously in charge of the raid as he was in front of the others, and asked 'Who lives here?' On being told, he said that he had come to make a search. Then he said, 'I want the key of the gate.' My husband, having heard that it was merely a search, came out of the dining-room. I walked back to the hall table in view of all who were standing at the door, and, taking the key from the little tray, handed it to him.

In a few moments I saw the need for opening the gate, because three women searchers came hurrying in; also the searchlight, shining now through the open gateway, lit up the whole house, and gave ample light for the search of the front rooms. I could see that the garden was full of soldiers in war outfit. They stayed outside, and the search was carried out by about twenty English police, in the charge of the cadet I mentioned, and another young officer. At once, the women hurried the maid and me upstairs, while my husband was led into the dining-room. The women searched the wardrobes, linen press, cupboards, drawers, beds, etc., etc., very carefully; even the heels of my boots and the shoes and the hems of my gowns were examined. The manner of the senior woman searcher was insolent in the extreme. At last she searched me personally. This seems a small matter, but the circumstances – the time, eleven o'clock, the place, my own house, the insolent manner – were such as to cause me great humiliation. This woman, I could see, had learned her methods and her manners in London dealing with a class of English crime very different from my offences under the Restoration of Order Act in Ireland.

All this time I was anxious about my husband downstairs. Afterwards he told me that the second officer said to him: 'We were thinking of giving the new mayor a lord mayor's show.' Michael, scenting a jeering note, flung back: 'Well, you could have done so. You have the power, the guns, the armoured cars, the tanks.' Even then, my husband's 'peaceful' character was being built up, for the officer replied: 'I hope he'll keep the city as quiet as you kept it.'

The cadet in charge and the second-in-command then came upstairs, and the cadet asked me particularly which was my room. I pointed it out, overlooking the front garden. Then they noticed the disposition of all the rooms, and meantime, the soldiers were examining all the windows opening onto the next garden and the back of the house. In the hall, when the Auxiliary cadet, intelligence officer, or whatever he really was, was leaving, I said: 'Are you aware that we were raided just a fortnight ago?' He hesitated a little, but replied at length, 'Yes.'

Then I complained that it was a drunken raid, and that the attitude of some of the men taking part in it was most hostile and threatening. I pointed out that it was not really a search, for some of the rooms were not entered, so that I could only conclude that it was an 'irregular' raid, merely to worry and frighten us. He was sympathetic about this, and very polite, and left saying 'good night', having made arrangements to have the gate locked by one of the Black and Tans, who would bring us back the key and get out over the wall. After they had gone, my husband and I had a chat about the raid. We discussed the cadet in charge, and my husband remarked that he had a charming cultivated voice, and wondered if he were English. We could come to no conclusion about his nationality as his name suggested that he might be of Jewish extraction. 'Anyhow,' said Michael, 'the rascal has a nice voice, but a very dirty job.'

MURDER RAID

ON THE NIGHT of Sunday 6 March, Michael and I went to bed about eleven o'clock, having spent a very happy day together. After a morning visit to his mother, I wrote letters while he attended the funeral of George Clancy's father-in-law. In the afternoon, Mr William Hard of America called, and my husband never was in a happier humour nor in a better vein for brilliant talk. Later, my two sisters and my brother-in-law came, and when they left before curfew, we sat, and read, and chatted at the drawing-room fire. As we were going to sleep, I said: 'This has been a happy day.'

'Very happy, thank God,' he replied.

I fell asleep, and was wakened by a loud knocking at the hall door. I got up and, throwing up the bedroom window, said: 'Who's there?' It was a darkish night, and I could see nothing, but a voice from the steps, a voice I recognised, replied: 'Who lives here?' I said, 'Michael O'Callaghan.'

'We want him,' came immediately, two voices this time. My mind stabbed me with the thought that this formula preceded murder in Ireland, and I felt faint with horror, but I said calmly enough: 'Well, you can't see him at this hour of the night.'

The voice I knew said again: 'We want him, and we're coming in anyhow.' I grew fainter at this, but when the voice said in the tone of words I had heard on the previous raid, 'and we want the key of the gate', I felt reassured, thinking at once of the women searchers. Turning to my husband who was getting out of bed I said: 'It's the usual thing. What shall I do?'

He said, 'Oh, I wish they would not worry us like this, but ask them is there an officer in charge.'

I bent out again, heartened by his calmness, and asked: 'Is there an officer in charge?'

'Oh, yes,' came the answer, 'one officer.'

'Two officers,' said the other voice.

In spite of myself, while I put on my dressing-gown and shoes, I cried a little, and my husband said: 'Don't bother about Brigid tonight. You're nervous, and I'll come down with you this time. 'Tis the usual thing, don't be afraid, dear.'

'I'll bring my Rosary beads,' I said. He had lit the candle, and put on his gown and shoes, and we went downstairs together. I heard Brigid's door opening, and she told me afterwards that she wondered to see the master going down with me in spite of all our arrangements. She heard him say to me on the stairs: 'Don't worry, dear. It will be all right.'

He lit the hall gas, and put the candlestick on the hall table, and, as I went towards the door, I said: 'Don't stand there in the middle of the hall. You never know what is going to happen.'

He said, 'It's all right,' and stood just behind me while I unlocked and unchained the door. I opened the door wide and when I saw the two men with goggles, and hats pulled down, and coat collars up about their ears, my heart leaped in my breast. I knew it was murder. Both men said together, waving their revolvers at Michael: 'You come out here. Come out.' My mind worked like madness. I thought of the dark garden, of the river, of all the horrors, and stretching out both my arms to cover Michael and pushing him back behind me, I shouted: 'No. No My God! Not that.'

I heard Michael say, 'No, no' just twice, as the men advanced after us in the hall. I caught at their hands as they tried to get me out of the way; there was a struggle for a second, and the man on my right hand, the man with the clear glasses and the blue eyes, freed his right arm and fired over my shoulder. I turned to see Michael stagger from the hall table, against which I had pushed him, and fall onto the mat at the foot of the stairs. In my agony, I relaxed my hold of the man, and that same devil slipped past me and emptied his revolver into my dear husband's body as he lay on the ground. I was struggling with the other man – the man whose voice brought me downstairs – but as the man who had shot Michael was passing us to go out, I flew at him. I had the strength of a maniac. We three fought together in the hall, while I screamed all the time. I knocked them twice as our feet slipped on the polished floor; my shoes fell off; I tore at their faces and heads instinctively; they never said a word, but beat me with their hands on the head, shoulders and arms. We fell against the umbrella stand, and at last with an effort, they threw me off, and I fell heavily on my hip on the floor.

I shall never forget the agony I suffered as I lay there screaming and helpless while I watched them running down the grass in the shaft of light from the hall door.

I crawled back to my husband and fell across his body, all my being crying out to God to spare him to me. I had never seen any body die, so I hoped, where from the first shot there was no hope. His eyes were closed, and he gave just a little sigh. Brigid had flung on a coat, and was on the landing when she heard the first shot. Others followed, and she knew what it meant. At once, she got her Rosary beads with the cross blessed for the hour of death, my crucifix and holy water, and ran down to find us both lying at the foot of the stairs. At first she thought us both dead. She roused me, and I asked her: 'Is this a bad dream?' She held the crucifix to my husband's lips, and said the Act of Contrition before I could think.

I went mad at times during this night, but I can remember some things only too well. After that one little sigh, my husband did not even moan, thank God. I refused to let Brigid move him, lest we should hurt him, and knowing that I would lose my reason if I saw his wounds or his blood. We got pillows, put rugs over him, and placed a hot water bottle to his feet. The brandy bottle we neither of us could open, so we broke the neck off, and I bathed his poor forehead. In a distracted state, Brigid ran down the garden to go for help, but hearing talking outside the garden wall, on the road, she did not like to leave me. When we had done all we could, it was she also thought of the telephone. While she was looking up the numbers, I saw on the table the glasses I had pulled off the murderer in the struggle. I did not know I had done so, yet here they were lying folded on the table.

I got the exchange at once, and, telling the operator what was the matter, tried to get onto the Jesuit Fathers, for I knew Fr Hackett would come to Michael. I failed to get an answer from them, or from my husband's doctor, whom I tried next. Then the operator suggested Dr Roberts, whom I did get. He seemed to think from what I said about the number of shots that there was no hope, but I asked him to come for God's sake, and he said he would chance it. Then I thought of Fr Philip, of the Franciscans, who had been my husband's chaplain and friend when he was mayor. He would come to Michael if I could only get word to him, so I asked the operator at the exchange to walk down to the Franciscan Friary and call up Fr Philip. It is but a few minutes' walk from the Telephone Exchange to the friary, but, though he was kind and wanted to help, he could not leave his post; besides he could not risk the curfew streets. He suggested ringing up the lying-in hospital in Bedford Row, which is just across the street from the friary; the night nurse there could call Fr Philip. There was no answer from the lying-in hospital.

Then I thought of the fire station: I rang them up and the man on duty answered. I told him that my husband had been shot and that I wanted Fr Philip, and I asked him to walk down from the fire station and call up Fr Philip. He said: 'I would do anything on God's earth for Mr O'Callaghan, but I dare not go out into the streets during curfew.' Next the operator suggested asking Dr Roberts to call up Fr Philip on his way to my house. I rang up the doctor, and his wife answered that he had just left the house. Then my husband's words flashed back to me: 'If anything ever happens, throw the matter over on to them at once. Remember their number 184.' I rang up 184, William Street police barracks, and when I got on, I said: 'This is Mrs Michael O'Callaghan, of St Margaret's, North Strand, speaking. My husband has been shot and I want the priest and a doctor.'

The voice asked: 'What name?' I repeated what I had said before. 'What name? What name?' came the voice again. I repeated in desperation: 'Mrs O'Callaghan, wife of Michael O'Callaghan, who was mayor of the city, of St Margaret's, North Strand. I want a priest. My husband has been murdered.' Again came the question: 'What name?' I threw down the receiver and cried to Brigid: 'O, they are mocking me. They will not understand what I am saying.'

I went to kneel down beside my husband, when the telephone bell rang. I took the receiver and repeated that my husband had been shot, and that I wanted a priest. A decisive voice replied this time, and I explained where Fr Philip lived on the way from the barracks to my house. Then I rang off. Brigid went down to the gate again and again to find if the doctor was coming. At last she heard footsteps. She called out: 'Is that the doctor?' He answered, so she unlocked the gate and they came in together. I was crouching near my husband's body, so the doctor took me up and led me into the drawing-room. Then he went back to the hall to examine Michael, closing the door behind him, while I knelt in the dark praying and in agony. I knew, and yet I hoped. In a moment he was back in the room, telling me that there was no hope. I cried out, and would not could not believe him. He lifted me from the floor, and he and Brigid did what they could for me. At last he said: 'I can't do anything for him, but I can get Fr Philip.' When he was gone, Brigid and I knelt and prayed that my husband would live until Fr Philip came. The time passed, and Brigid, watching, cried out: 'Here's Fr Philip.'

He knelt at once to anoint Michael, while I went to the hall door holding the glasses in my hands. Knowing who the murderers of my husband were, I wanted to keep the police out until all was over. There were four men on the steps – a district inspector, a sergeant, and two constables – all looking coldly and curiously over my shoulders into the hall, where at the foot of the stairs my husband was receiving the last rites of the church. They saw what was happening, that a man, whom they afterwards described as a man of peace, was dying, murdered, and they did not remove their caps; nor was there a single word of sympathy for a woman in sorrow. Pictures of soldiers saluting the dead bodies of their opponents flashed through my mind, pictures of men saluting the dead all the world over. No salute here, only cold curiosity.

'Have you any idea who has done this?' asked the district inspector.

I replied: 'I will not say, but I have these glasses belonging to the murderer.'

He seemed interested in them, and put out his hand, but I drew back, saying I would keep them.

'When did it happen?' he continued.

'I don't know,' I replied.

'Ten minutes past one,' said the sergeant. 'We heard the shots at the barracks, turned out, but could not locate them.'

Fr Philip finished his work, and then made me go into the drawing-room where he lit the gas. I could hear the police moving round the hall and the kitchen stairs, looking for bullets. 'Find the puzzle,' said one to the other. After a little time, the sergeant came into us with a note-book, and asked me to tell him what happened. 'The district inspector is a new man,' he said, 'he does not know what to do, so I am forced into the work.' I told him simply what had happened, for I was exhausted. He said he would come back the following day for more information, to which I made no reply. He also questioned Brigid, but she had seen nothing till she came down to find us lying together at the foot of the stairs.

Suddenly a thought seemed to strike Fr Philip; he walked with me to the drawing-room door, and called out: 'You can't help Mrs O'Callaghan. Why not go and see if the mayor, George Clancy, is safe.' The police left at once. I dressed, we made up the fire, and I tried to face the overwhelming tragedy that had come on me. Time seemed to stand still. At last, Fr Philip telephoned to the William Street police barracks for a motor and escort to take him to Eden Terrace to break the news to my sister, and to my husband's brother. In a very short time, the car came, and he went to Eden Terrace.

In the car, as part of the escort, was the sergeant who had been with us some hours before, and he chatted with Fr Philip on the way out and back. My sister and her husband, my brother-in-law and his wife all walked over together, and their coming was a help to me. Fr Philip left to say Mass at six o'clock, and at the same time my sister's husband went to tell the mayor, George Clancy, that Michael had been murdered and to make arrangements. At the six o'clock

Mass, Fr Philip prayed for Michael's soul. After the Mass, a woman rushed to him. 'You have made a mistake,' she said, 'it is not Michael O'Callaghan who has been murdered; it is the mayor, George Clancy.' My sister's husband learned the same news at the mayor's house.

As the morning grew, other friends flocked to my aid, and at last, about 9.30 a.m., I was put to bed exhausted, and in need of the doctor's care, for I was bruised all over and my hip hurt me.

All Monday and Tuesday, the people of Limerick streamed into the house to look at my dear husband's face and to kiss his dead hand. All Monday night and all Tuesday night, members of the IRA, 'wanted' men from the flying column, stood guard in his room. All night long. I could hear them saying the Rosary. On Wednesday the bodies were placed before the high altar in St John's cathedral, and on Thursday 10 March, they were laid to rest in the republican plot in the city cemetery. I am proud to think that my husband lies beside the Gaelic Leaguer and the Irish Volunteer, the two types he loved most in the Ireland of today, the types who were making the dream of his life come through. God speed the day.

MURDER OF VOLUNTEER JOSEPH O'DONOGHUE

DURING THE NIGHT that Mayor Clancy and ex-Mayor Michael O'Callaghan were assassinated, another brutal murder was perpetrated by the Royal Irish Constabulary, on the person of Volunteer O'Donoghue. Joseph O'Donoghue, a native of Ballinacarrigy, Westmeath, had been in Limerick about two years. At the time of his death he was twenty-six years of age, and was employed as manager of the River Plate Meat company, William Street. An ardent worker in the Gaelic League and the GAA, he was but a brief time in Limerick when he became attached to 'E' company 2nd battalion IRA, of which he was to prove himself a loyal and active member.

About eighteen months previously, Joe O'Donoghue had gone as paying guest to 'Tigh na Fáinne', the residence of Mrs B. Lyddy, situated in the then sparsely populated district of Janesboro, in the southern suburbs. It should be noted that both Mayor Clancy and Michael O'Callaghan resided on the north side of the city, approximately at a distance of one and a half miles from Janesboro.

On the night of the murders, the Rosary had just been finished at 11.40, and the household was preparing to retire for the night, when there came a loud knocking at the door. It was opened to some twelve members of the RIC led by the infamous Detective Leech, and accompanied by bloodhounds. All poured into the living-room, and one of them demanded in a loud voice: 'Are there any rebels here?' Another of the party approached Joe O'Donoghue and asked him his name. When he gave it, his interrogator cried: 'You are the man we want.' Thereupon violent hands were laid on him, and he was hurried from the house.

What happened subsequently is known only to God and the murderers. Early next morning, the body of Volunteer Joseph O'Donoghue was found lying some distance away on Janesboro Avenue. He had eighteen bullet wounds in his body.

THE IRA CAMPAIGN IN WEST LIMERICK

by VOLUNTEER

WEST LIMERICK WAS not found wanting when Ireland sounded the nationwide clarion call that was to prelude the Rising of Easter 1916. For more than a year before that epoch-making event, young men and old, from the towns and villages, hills and valleys of the West Country had been rallying in ever-increasing numbers to the ranks of the Irish Volunteers. Despite the confusion which preceded the great climax on that fateful Easter Sunday morning, approximately three hundred men assembled ready for such action as they might be called upon to take, with the background of storeyed Glenquin Castle as the focal point of their mobilisation. It was a proud day for the Volunteers of West Limerick, the final promise of fulfilment of many months of hard training and unceasing endeavour. None of the rank and file was officially aware of the real purpose of the mobilisation; but all sensed that something big was in the offing. Every man and boy was ready to do his part, however humble or unpretentious it might prove to be. Such was the proud spirit which animated the men as they assembled in Glenquin on Easter Sunday morning, in response to the summons sent forth by dispatch riders to the remotest corners of the area on the previous day.

The men were under the command of Brigadier Charles Wall, now a well-known and esteemed merchant in Dromcollogher. His second-in-command was Captain McEnery, of Limerick, who, because of previous military training, was appointed director of operations. Two chaplains were in attendance, Rev. Michael Hayes (RIP) then CC at Newcastlewest, afterwards parish priest of Ardagh; and Rev. Tomás Wall, now parish priest of Ballingarry and a canon of the Limerick cathedral chapter. Some of the leaders had been more favourably disposed towards the selection of Barnagh as the assembly point, on the grounds that from there the Volunteers could control the railway line from Limerick to Tralee. Glenquin, however, was decided on; and so, on Easter Sunday morning the men rallied to a total strength of approximately three hundred. All were not armed. Only a small number were equipped with shotguns and buckshot. Supplies of arms were expected from the ill-fated *Aud*; and in any case, the men, armed or otherwise, were anxious and ready to play whatever role they might be called on to fill.

The main purpose of the mobilisation at this juncture, it would seem, was to ensure a clear line of communications through West Limerick for the arms that were expected to pass that way from Kerry. All day long, ever on the alert for the warning that never came, the Volunteers maintained unceasing vigil by the walls of the old western stronghold of the De Laceys. Hour after hour passed, and still no news, came from 'The Kingdom'. By nightfall it had become painfully evident to the leaders that something had gone seriously wrong with the original plan of campaign. Having received the blessing of their chaplains, the men were reluctantly disbanded though not without hope that the morrow might bring better and brighter news from the western skyline that shielded Kerry from view.

The West Limerick Volunteer companies which assembled at Glenquin included: Monegea company (under the command of Dan Conway and Dan Collins); Templeglantine company (Mossie Leahy); Killoughteen company (Jim Sommers and Dan McCarthy); Newcastlewest company (B. Moone and M.J. O'Gorman); Tournafulla company (M. Hartnett and T. Leahy); Ashford company (Mick Begley and Jackie Noonan); Raheenagh company (Dick Anglim); Broadford company (—— Brennan); Ardagh company (Paddy Drinane and P. Ambrose). Athea company was also ready for the march to Glenquin, but did not arrive there in time for the mobilisation due to delay in the arrival in Athea of the summons.

CON COLLINS OF MONEGEA

ONE OF THE most gallant, sincere and, at the same time, least spectacular of the men who paved the way for the freedom of Ireland was Con Collins, who came of a West Limerick family which contributed much to the movement that led to the establishment of the present state. Like the great Mick Collins, Con was a member of the staff of the post office when Ireland was deciding its new and great destiny. Born at Arranagh, Monegea, Newcastlewest, he was one of six sons, nearly all of whom played a big part in the fight for Irish freedom. His mother was one of the Mulcahys of Meelin, a family which was steeped in the traditions of nationalism. When following the tragic triumph of 1916, she was informed by neighbour Dan Conway that her son Dan had followed her elder boy, Con, on the road to prison, she merely commented: 'I would not begrudge it if my six sons were taken out and shot against the wall in the fight for Irish freedom.' Little wonder, then, that her son Con was a willing student in the academy which produced so many patriots in the period that preceded 1916. Receiving his early education at Monegea national school, he passed on later to Newcastlewest Courtenay school where he received the full benefit of the teaching of that intellectual genius, the late James D. Musgrave.

In due course, Con entered the post office service in Dublin where he became acquainted, probably through the Gaelic League, with the illustrious Seán MacDermott, with whom he shared lodgings, and with whom he was associated in the production of *Irish Freedom*, one of the advanced journals of the time. It was inevitable, perhaps, that Con Collins should become a member of the Irish Republican Brotherhood and that he should later have been a 1916 leader. Indeed, the extent to which he was trusted by the men of Easter Week is amply shown by the fact that, on the fateful days before the Rising, he was entrusted with the all-important and difficult task of travelling to Kerry to meet Roger Casement and Austin Stack, with a view to contacting the *Aud*. The circumstances associated with that tragic chapter of our history are now too well known to bear repetition. At all events, for his part in the Rising, Con Collins was subsequently tried by British court martial and sentenced to life imprisonment. On his release, following the general amnesty of 1916 prisoners, he continued to take an active part in the national struggle.

He was elected Sinn Féin TD for West Limerick in the historic election of 1919, and was again much to the fore in the fight against the Black and Tans. He was still a member of the Dáil when the Truce came, and in the fateful decision he voted against the Treaty. Although he continued to serve the republican cause during the Civil War he took no further active part in politics and later resumed his connection with the civil service, as a member of the Limerick post office staff. He was still working in that capacity until his death.

No record of West Limerick's contribution to the 1916 effort is complete without reference to Dónal Sheehan, a native of Rollision's Bridge, Templeglantine, Newcastlewest. Dónal, who was working in the post office in Dublin, was one of the three men chosen to travel by car from Dublin to Kerry with the object of making wireless contact with the *Aud*. The sequence of events which caused the driver of the car in which they were travelling, to take a wrong turn and plunge into the River Laune with the loss of Donal Sheehan and his two companions, is dealt with by a contributor to *Kerry's Fighting Story*. West Limerick men, who took part in the fighting in Dublin in 1916, included Con Colbert, Athea, one of the executed leaders;

Éamonn Dore of Glin; Garrett McAuliffe, Newcastlewest; Matty Flanagan and James Flanagan of Killoughteen.

YEARS OF RE-ORGANISATION

THE RE-ORGANISATION YEARS 1917 to 1919 were continuously active ones for the Limerick Volunteers who, in addition to their intensive training, assumed responsibility for guarding Sinn Féin courts, and collected arms. They drilled and manoeuvred openly under the ever-watchful, hostile eyes of the Royal Irish Constabulary. Even the smallest movement of the Volunteers was reported to Dublin Castle by the police, and, during these years, many Volunteer officers and men were arrested. It was obvious that the nation had taken on a new outlook, and a new spirit animated by the sacrifice of the 1916 men.

The Volunteer movement had the enthusiastic support of the vast majority of the people who put their best efforts behind a Dáil and the Volunteer Force, to rid the nation, once and for all, of the British invaders. In the summer of 1920 Brigade Commander Seán Finn, Garrett McAuliffe, 'Slope' Reidy, Pat O'Shaughnessy, T. Madigan, and Con Cregan, crossed the Shannon to Clare, to participate in an attack on Sixmilebridge Royal Irish Constabulary barrack. Later, Jim Doody, Owen Sullivan, Mick Sheehy, Ben Sullivan and Con Foley, made the long march into Cork for the Clonbanin ambush, which had just ended when they arrived. The late Captain Jack Brosnan of the Ballygrane company, co-operated with both the North Cork and West Limerick flying columns, in their operations against the enemy.

By 1920 the Irish Republican Army had made great progress in West Limerick, its five battalions in that area having formed one brigade known as the West Limerick brigade, Irish Republican Army. The late Seán Finn was O/C, with Garrett McAuliffe of Newcastlewest as vice-brigadier. James Colbert of Athea, brother of Con Colbert, who was executed for his part in the Rising, was quartermaster, and Paddy Roche of Rathkeale was adjutant. Jim Liston, Castlemahon, commanded the 1st battalion; Mossie Harnett of Tournafulla, the 2nd battalion; Con Foley of Broadford, the 3rd battalion; Jimmy Halpin of Pallaskenry, the 4th battalion, and J.T. O'Connor of Ballyhahill, the 5th battalion. Amongst brigade officers and men who were on active service with the flying column were: Jimmy Collins, Abbeyfeale, afterwards brigade adjutant; Con and Edward Cregan of Monegea; Ben Sullivan of Dromcollogher; Thomas Leahy and Jack Aherne of Tournafulla; Michael Colbert of Athea, company captain; T. Wallace of Pallaskenry; S. Brouder, L. MacNamee, J.J. Leahy, 'Slope' Reidy, P.J. O'Neill, D. Murphy, L. Harnett and J. Moloney of Abbeyfeale; Con Boyle, Johnny Glenny, Jimmy and Paddy Roche of Rathkeale; Denny Lane of Mountcollins; James Roche and Paddy Aherne of Templeglantine; Paddy Naughton, Denis Collins, Johnny Harnett, Jim Guiney, Owen McAuliffe, A. Reidy, Tadhg Collins, John R. Leahy, T. Regan, O'Mahonys, Quins, Denis Harnett, T. Liston, 'Sonny' Quaid, J. McAuliffe, D. Curtin, D. Lenihan, D. O'Donnell, Tom Bouchier, J. Wrenn, J. Sullivan, Richard B. Woulfe and J. Shine, who was sentenced to death when captured by the British, but whose life was saved by the Truce.

SOLOHEADBEG MEN IN LIMERICK

ON 13 MAY 1919, a young Tipperary boy named Seán Hogan, who was captured by the British following an ambush in which he had taken part, at Soloheadbeg in County Tipperary, was being conveyed by train to Cork jail, a prisoner under escort of Royal Irish Constabulary. The train was attacked at Knocklong railway station, by young Hogan's comrades, amongst them Seán Treacy, Dan Breen, Seamus Robinson, Edward O'Brien of Galbally, and others from the borders of Tipperary and Limerick – many of them men who subsequently played prominent parts in the campaign against the Black and Tans in East Limerick. Hogan was rescued and a couple of the Royal Irish Constabulary were killed, including Sergeant Wallace who had charge of the escort. News of this successful rescue electrified the country and stimulated the zeal and daring of the Volunteers. Following the rescue at Knocklong young Hogan with Treacy, Breen and Robinson, were conveyed to safety, first in County Limerick and subsequently in Kerry.

The hue and cry rang through the country, and the entire County Limerick was intensively combed for the wanted men by military and police. The arrival in West Limerick of such fearless exemplars of the new revolutionary movement thrust grave responsibility upon the local IRA. The victors of Knocklong were first moved to Danganbeg, where Breen and Treacy, who had been dangerously wounded, received shelter and protection in the home of the Kennedy family, subsequently proprietors of the Eden Vale Hotel, Harcourt Street, Dublin. Some days later the wanted men were removed to the house of Mossie Harnett of Tournafulla, where they remained for nearly a fortnight whilst recuperating from their wounds. They were then conveyed to Knocknagoshel, County Kerry, to convalesce amongst the O'Connors and the Hickeys and, having regained some of their old form in the hills of 'The Kingdom', they moved to Gale View, Athea, where they stayed at the home of Jim Colbert, ex-TD. That, also, had been the home of Con Colbert, one of the youngest of the 1916 men who paid the extreme penalty following the suppression of the Rising.

Whilst the wounded men were at Danganbeg they were attended by Dr Edward Harnett of Abbeyfeale, and by R.B. Woulfe, MPSI, both of whom subsequently followed their movements to the other places mentioned, in order to continue daily medical attention. The three removals were not without incident. The retreat into Kerry became an urgent necessity when Mossie Harnett was given information by an old Royal Irish Constabulary friend of the

Volunteers that it was the intention of the British to employ a large force of police and military to search Tournafulla. In the dead of an intensely dark summer's night the Tournafulla IRA requisitioned half-a-dozen horse-traps, and armed with shotguns and revolvers set out to convey the 'wanted' men to Kerry, The exceptional darkness of the night, and the rough road, added to the hazard of the undertaking, caused renewed suffering to Dan Breen who had been very severely wounded. It was known that a large force of the enemy was stationed in Abbeyfeale, and it was accordingly decided to by-pass that town on the way to 'The Kingdom'. The alternative route lay along the 'Hill-Road' overlooking the town on the south, but because of the intense darkness and the fact that the escort was not familiar with the locality, the party went astray. Instead of continuing directly towards Feale bridge, leading into Kerry, they descended the high road known as 'Betty's Road', into Abbeyfeale.

Daybreak found the company only a few hundred yards from the town – the very last place they would have wished to find themselves in if they were not in search of trouble. It was a serious predicament, made more complicated by the fact that one of the horses fell, throwing Danny Curtin of Tournafulla, head foremost, onto the road and rendering him unconscious. Mossie Harnett, who was in charge, consulted with the others, and it was decided to push on straight ahead through Abbeyfeale. Accordingly, the hair-pin bend just ahead led not alone into the town, but also past the back and front gates of the Royal Irish Constabulary barracks. It was about 4 a.m. when the order was given to advance. Each man looked to his gun, muttered a prayer, and hoped for the best. The drive past Abbeyfeale barracks on the dawn of that glorious summer morning was something not readily forgotten. No challenge from the police broke the tension, and the open country having soon been gained, the wounded men and their convoy breathed freely. In a short time all were ready to enjoy the cheerful welcome that awaited them on the Kerry side of Feale bridge.

POLICE AGGRESSION

EARLY IN THE year 1919 the Royal Irish Constabulary in Tournafulla adopted a determinedly aggressive attitude towards the district IRA. One dark night Constables Lyons and Hearst, armed with revolvers, lay in wait outside the village for the purpose of capturing Tommy Leahy, captain of the local Irish Republican Army company. As he walked past them along the road, both policemen jumped at him, but Leahy managed to evade them, and ran speedily for some yards with the policemen at his heels. Suddenly he wheeled about and fired at Constable Lyons with his revolver. In doing so, he slipped and fell on the road with Lyons on top of him. Leahy managed to get on his feet again, and engaged both Hearst and Lyons, wounding the latter, before making a safe get-away. Accordingly, he became one of the first men on the run in West Limerick, and was one of the firm friends whom Seán Hogan made during his time in the West. Tommy fought right through the campaign, but was ultimately surprised and captured by the Black and Tans at Mountcollins creamery in the summer of 1921. Found in possession of arms, he was sentenced to death, but his life was saved by the advent of the Truce.

SHOOTING OF RIC IN
RATHKEALE HOTEL

SOME TIME BEFORE the formation of the first flying column, small groups of IRA, driven from their homes, began to take offensive and defensive action against the enemy. One such action took place at the March fair of Rathkeale in 1920. Early in the day, Liam Scully, who was in Rathkeale doing Gaelic League work, informed Commandant Seán Finn that there were two Royal Irish Constabulary men from Tralee in Ward's Hotel in the town. These were Sergeant George Neazor and a constable named Doyle, who were escorting an enemy civilian. Commandant Finn assembled a small group of Rathkeale IRA men who were then 'on the run' with a view to holding up and disarming the police. These men included Jimmy Roche, 'Patro' Shaughnessy, J. Reidy, T. O'Regan, P. Roche, Johnny Glenny, Larry McNamee, D. Guiney, with Garrett McAuliffe, of Newcastlewest, who was also 'on the run', and Seán Hogan of Knocklong fame. Commandant Finn told his men that he had reason to believe that Sergeant Neazor had taken part in the arrest of Austin Stack and Con Collins in Tralee during Holy Week, 1916, and that it was his intention to take their weapons. There was to be no shooting, except in self-defence. Scouts were posted in the streets to prevent surprise from the military encampments at Mountbrown, or from the local Royal Irish Constabulary barracks. The group of IRA entered the hotel and, having boldly walked into the dining-room, where the police were sitting, gave the order 'hands up'. To the surprise of the IRA, the sergeant drew his gun and aimed at one of them near him. The other IRA men fired simultaneously, killing Neazor and wounding the constable. The arms of both men were then collected, and the attackers withdrew. Great military and police activity followed, but the IRA units got safely outside the British ring.

ARMS FOR THE COLUMN

DURING THE EARLY summer of 1920, Commandant Finn and the West Limerick brigade staff were busily engaged in an effort to secure rifles to arm and equip a flying column. A deputation led by the commandant himself, at great personal risk, travelled to headquarters in Dublin for this purpose. Eventually, after some delay, caused no doubt by the great difficulty of procuring arms, a consignment of seven rifles arrived at the Devon Road railway station, consigned as creamery merchandise. The late Fr Dan O'Sullivan, CSSP, then a young student and member of a patriotic Springmount family, collected the rifles at the railway and brought them in a pony trap from Devon Road to Richard O'Sullivan's house at Cooleygoman Cross. Larry McNamee, on a bicycle ahead of the pony, acted as scout, as the road travelled was frequently patrolled by enemy forces.

Whilst the rifles were being conveyed to O'Sullivan's, there were dramatic happenings a few miles away in the parish of Clouncagh, where Jim Noonan of Newcastlewest IRA and Paddy Naughton, of Limerick city IRA ran unexpectedly into a large Royal Irish Constabulary patrol. The IRA men had been approaching the main Clouncagh road from the by-way leading to Mrs Airey's house at Teernahilla, where the boys 'on the run' were always welcome. The police patrol comprised between twenty and thirty men, who immediately dismounted and fired upon the two IRA men. Although hopelessly outnumbered, Noonan and Naughton sought cover and, with the small arms they carried, replied to the policemen's fire. In an effort to confuse the enemy, they retreated in different directions.

Ultimately, Jim Noonan was seriously wounded and captured, but Paddy Naughton succeeded in getting clear away. Whilst the skirmish was in progress, Commandant Finn, who had been to Rathkeale on brigade business, had one of his frequent providential escapes from capture as he returned via Clouncagh to his temporary headquarters at Raheenagh. He was taken into a pony trap driven by David O'Brien, creamery manager, Clouncagh, who was returning from a funeral. They had not driven far when they were informed of the engagement at Clouncagh, and warned that there was a big enemy concentration in the locality. Seán Finn thereupon altered his route, and avoiding the roads as much as possible, travelled cross-country in the direction of Cooleygoman. Meanwhile, big British military forces from Newcastlewest had penetrated as far as Bunoke bridge, when the late T. Sullivan of Cooleygoman, went to Raheenagh to warn the IRA of the Clouncagh happenings, and of military raids on houses near Bunoke, not very far from Cooleygoman Cross. Knowing that the rifles were at the Cross, the IRA men procured bicycles and, having cycled there as fast as they could, found the weapons safe in O'Sullivan's. L. McNamee and S. Brouder then took them (the ammunition had not yet arrived) cross-country to O'Keeffe's, and were joined there at midnight by Seán Finn, who told of the happenings at Clouncagh, and how he had eluded the military and police by wading the broad and deep Deel River near Feohenagh, after nightfall. Next morning the IRA moved to Templeglantine, and that night, in an unoccupied farmhouse overlooking Abbeyfeale, the West Limerick flying column was formed.

THE ATTACK ON KILMALLOCK BARRACKS

EARLY IN MAY 1920, the possibilities of attacking police barracks and capturing arms and ammunition were examined, and it was finally decided to make an attempt on Kilmallock Royal Irish Constabulary barracks. This attack was arranged by the East Limerick IRA who invited the co-operation of the West Limerick men. The last attempt of this kind had been made in 1867 when the unknown Fenian fell. The proposed attack on Kilmallock barracks was discussed at a brigade council, held in the farmhouse of Mrs McEnery, Camas, Monegea. Amongst those who attended were Seán Finn, Michael Brennan, Clare; 'Seán Forde', East Limerick; Mossie Harnett, Tournafulla; Jimmy Roche, Rathkeale; Garrett McAuliffe, Newcastlewest; Tom Wallace and several others. The plan of campaign was decided upon, and the men appointed to take part were selected. About a dozen West Limerick men were chosen to participate in that famous attack, and during the engagement they occupied the houses opposite the barracks. All during the night of the attack heavy fire was concentrated on the front of the barracks, which fell as a smouldering ruin on the following morning.

It was there that Liam Scully, the Irish teacher from Kerry, fell a few minutes before the engagement was broken off. He was attended in his last moments by the late Rev. Fr P. Woulfe, PP, Cappa, then curate of Kilmallock. Motor cars had been provided to convey the attacking party from West Limerick to Kilmallock, and one of the cars belonged to Michael O'Mahony, creamery manager, of Devon Road. Two cars returned to Tournafulla with the remains of Liam Scully, and with 'Seán Forde', Michael Brennan, Seán Finn and others, weary from the fight, but exultant because of the destruction of such a strong enemy post. Guards were posted by Mossie Harnett that night, and a large number of IRA from West Limerick occupied positions along the road, to engage any military or police who might venture to raid the district.

When O'Mahony's car was being returned next day, Larry McNamee, the driver, nearly ran into a police patrol of ten men at Devon Road. He observed the patrol just in time, and quickly turned the car up a narrow road to avoid capture. The police seemed more alarmed than Larry and, fearing that something was wrong, they mounted their bicycles quickly and returned with all speed to Abbeyfeale. Liam Scully's remains were interred with full military honours by the shade of the ivied ruins of the Old Temple in Glantane churchyard. Fr McCarthy, CC, of Loughill, performed the last rites of the church, and once again the soil of Ireland was sanctified by the blood of a heroic son. Liam Scully was sadly missed by all, having endeared himself to everybody by his gentle and unassuming nature. He loved his native land intensely, and cherished and fostered her language by his teaching.

WEST LIMERICK MEN IN BROSNA BARRACKS ATTACK

IN JUNE 1920, anxious to emulate the successful attack on Kilmallock police barracks by the combined East and West Limerick columns, the East Kerry IRA, under Dan O'Mahony, enlisted the aid of the men of West Limerick. Owing to its remoteness, and being in the midst of bogs and hills which offered favourable possibilities for its capture, Brosna barracks was selected for the attack. Once previously arrangements had been made to take this barracks, but the police were informed of the intended attack, and, under cover of night, a surprise party of military from Castleisland captured a large body of the IRA on their way to Brosna village.

The second attempt took place on 5 June 1920, and on this occasion the attacking party met in a large field across the river from Brosna. T.M. O'Connor and Dan McCarthy were in charge of the Kerry column, and Mossie Harnett of Tournafulla had under his command sixteen West Limerick men armed with police carbines and rifles. These men included Paddy Buckley, who subsequently lost his life at Ballyseedy; James Roche, Tommy Leahy, Con and Ned Cregan, Paddy Mulcahy, Jack Aherne, Paddy Aherne, J. Kiely and T. Bouchier. The men were divided into sections and marched to various positions round the barracks.

Fire was opened from the barracks before all the men were in position, as the police were warned of things to come by the noise caused as some of the IRA got into vantage points prematurely. Soon the village resounded to the continuous discharge of rifle fire from and against the barracks, which occupied an isolated position at the south-eastern corner of the square beside the local cemetery. Some of the West Limerick men were placed in front of the barracks near the church, and the remainder in an old house at the back. Humphrey Murphy of East Kerry directed the attack on the barracks himself in person, and made every effort to break in the roof and gable with grenades and bombs. The attack lasted all night and continued into early morning. The sound of shouting and firing re-echoing back from the hills and valleys around was deafening. Verey lights were sent up by the police at intervals, rendering the scene more weird and terrifying. Inside the barracks the police and Tans could be heard distinctly playing a melodeon and shouting 'Come on the Rainbow

Chasers'. Counter slogans were lustily slung back by the besiegers. The morning was advancing and considerations of inadequate equipment dictated the advisability of raising the siege. Necessity demanded this step as an engagement with the superior numbers of the reinforcing military, surely on their way to the relief of the beleaguered garrison, was to be avoided. It was decided to withdraw and as a preliminary the attack was intensified while the different sections were withdrawing. There were many hair-breadth escapes at this stage. Later, over a soldier's breakfast of bread and cheese, incidents of the night were jokingly interchanged.

That morning the West Limerick column narrowly escaped being wiped out. They were saved by the courage of some IRA members of the Abbeyfeale company under James Collins. On the night of the Brosna attack some seven or eight of these men were assigned positions at Glenesrone Wood to keep an eye on any supporting movement of the Abbeyfeale Royal Irish Constabulary, and if possible to frustrate it. In the early morning the 'look-out' at the Abbeyfeale barracks reported to his sergeant the appearance of Verey Lights over Brosna. As a result nine of the Royal Irish Constabulary were dispatched by the nearest route for Brosna. This happened to be by the old road at the rear of the barracks, known as Betty's Road. This cut across the line of retreat from Brosna of the West Limerick section engaged there. It was vital to intercept the police and prevent them cutting off the retreat of those returning from Brosna, and the men entrusted with the responsibility succeeded in accomplishing this at Glenesrone Wood. The brunt of this fight was borne by Jerry O'Sullivan of Springmount, William O'Connor of Mountmahon, and the late Jim Leahy of Ballaugh. They were armed only with double-barrelled shotguns. At close range, they opened fire on the advancing police, seriously wounding Constable Martin, and slightly injuring some others. The police halted when challenged and returning rapid rifle fire, they retreated to their barracks, firing as they went. Reaching the barracks they maintained an intense fire in the direction of the hill. None of the IRA suffered casualties either at Abbeyfeale or Brosna.

ENEMY PATROLS ATTACKED

ONE EVENING IN the early summer of 1920, the presence of an enemy patrol was reported in Tournafulla. Word was sent to the local IRA that a sergeant and five constables, armed with carbines and revolvers, had cycled from Abbeyfeale, and it was decided to ambush them as they left Tournafulla to return home. The police left earlier than was expected, however, and when they reached the point for which the ambush had been planned, only two of the attacking party had arrived in position. The two IRA men on the spot, armed with a service rifle and shotgun, engaged the enemy, but failed to inflict casualties. The Royal Irish Constabulary dismounted and returned the fire for some minutes. Luckily for themselves, they broke off the engagement before the main body of IRA arrived on the scene. From that time onwards, the police realised that it was no longer safe to travel the country except in large, heavily armed groups.

In the summer of 1920 a detachment of police was in the habit of patrolling the roads from Foynes to Glin. A party of IRA under Seán Finn, and which included 'Slope' Reidy, Larry McNamee, J. Regan and J.T. O'Connor, lay in ambush for them. The police patrol consisted of eight well-armed men, and they rode into the ambush unsuspectingly. Fire was immediately opened upon them, and Constable Fahy fell mortally wounded. The other Royal Irish Constabulary men immediately returned the fire and, having worked themselves into positions overlooking the attackers, they enfiladed the IRA positions. Continuous fire was maintained for some time, and eventually it was with extreme difficulty that the IRA extricated themselves from their precarious situation. They retreated in good order.

Early in the autumn of 1920, a number of daring raids were made by a small group of IRA officers attached to the 1st battalion. The group of officers included Jim Liston, O/C, Tadhg Collins, Owen McAuliffe and Con Cregan. Although 'on the run', they entered the town of Newcastlewest, despite the fact that details of military, Black and Tans and Auxiliaries regularly patrolled the streets. Collins and McAuliffe fired on and wounded a daring British ex-serviceman who had publicly associated himself with the enemy. After this and other IRA activities in the area, the Auxiliaries and Black and Tans ran amuck and set fire to the creamery, the Carnegie Library, O'Mahony's and Reidy's houses in St Ita's Road. Jim Kelly of South Quay, an active member of the IRA, had a narrow escape when an enemy patrol broke into his home and smashed it up.

It was about this time that the Black and Tans were making their appearance amongst the old Royal Irish Constabulary, and already they were playing a leading part in the general campaign of terror. In Abbeyfeale, a fiend in human shape, named Huckerbery, led in this lawless campaign. Before coming to Abbeyfeale he had been stationed in Shanagolden where he had murdered an old man, named Reidy, in cold blood. It was decided to attack the police in Abbeyfeale and, if possible, to eliminate this ruthless Black and Tan. Spearhead of the attacking force was the West Limerick active service unit, or flying column, and which, formed in Athea in September 1920, comprised approximately thirty men, all of them 'on the run'. This column, with a section from each company of the 2nd battalion, moved into positions on the outskirts of Abbeyfeale, on a dark night in September. Nine had rifles and revolvers, and the others were armed with shotguns. There were ten or twelve Black and Tans in Abbeyfeale town at the time, and they usually turned out in full force to patrol the outskirts. On the night in question, the IRA lay in ambush in positions covering the road leading to Mountmahon.

They were barely in position and were without orders, when the police patrol came along in loose formation. Moving in the darkness, the police must have heard noise emanating from inside the fence, because they stopped and looked into the fields. A revolver shot was immediately fired, and Constable Mahony fell mortally wounded. The fight was on and continued fiercely for some time before the enemy retired, leaving one Black and Tan dead and five wounded. That night the IRA column retreated safely to Athea, six miles away. The coolness and daring of Captain P.J. O'Neill, under difficult circumstances, was mainly responsible for the IRA victory. The much sought for Black and Tan Huckerbery, never came into the line of fire, but escaped to spread terror in Abbeyfeale next day. Inside a week he had shot dead two young men named Harnett and Healy, as reprisals for the ambush. Mick Collins, brother of James and Denis Collins of the flying column, was arrested and chained to a tree in Bourne's field, where machine-gun fire was played about him. He was badly beaten up, and later thrown from a fast-moving lorry onto the main Limerick road.

On 27 May 1920, the mail train was held up in broad daylight at Barnagh railway station. Amongst those who participated in the raid were Paddy Aherne, Jim Roche and Tom Bouchier of the Templeglantine company; James Collins, P.J. O'Neill and 'Bird' Collins of the Abbeyfeale company. 'The Bird' hopped onto the engine and held up the fireman and driver. The raid on the mail train gave the Royal Irish Constabulary the long-sought excuse to raid the premises of the late Seán Quirke, at Templeglantine.

About a fortnight after the Abbeyfeale ambush, a postman was held near Tournafulla creamery, a mile from the post office, and the mail taken from him. The raid was carried out by the battalion adjutant, Jack Aherne, together with Tommy Leahy and Bartholomew Wrenne, all of whom were armed with revolvers. They took the mails behind a fence nearby and began to sort them out at their leisure, Meanwhile, the postman, who had been permitted to return to the post office, reported the seizure of the mails, and an urgent message was telephoned to the British authorities in Newcastlewest. Inside half-an-hour two lorry loads of police and military, together with the postman, pulled up on the exact spot where the seizure of the mails had taken place. All unconscious of any approaching danger, the IRA letter sorters were still at work inside the fence, and their first intimation of anything being amiss, was the approach of the enemy lorries which halted beside them. The IRA men started to run across country, but were sighted by the British, who opened fire on them. Jack Aherne, who was shot through the neck, and Bartholomew Wrenne were captured. Tommy Leahy dodged inside the fence, and although pursued for about a mile, made good his escape under heavy fire. The other two were sentenced to long terms of imprisonment which they served in Ipswich prison, England.

CAPTIVITY OF GENERAL LUCAS
IN WEST LIMERICK

Shortly after his capture by the IRA in North Cork, in June 1920, General Lucas was transferred to the custody of the West Limerick brigade. Brigade Commander Seán Finn, 'Seán Forde', 'Patro' Shaughnessy, S. Reidy, J. Crowley and Larry MacNamee went up to North Cork and took him into custody from the North Cork men. Seán Moylan and Daniel Clancy accompanied the West Limerick men and their prisoner as far as Templeglantine. Travelling in two motor cars the party boldly drove past Abbeyfeale RIC barracks in broad daylight. During a stoppage on the Limerick side of Abbeyfeale Seán Finn enquired of the general whether he would be surprised to learn that the car in which he was travelling had been captured from a district inspector of the RIC. Lucas replied: 'I would be surprised at nothing now.' Having been detained for some short time in the hillside home of the Sheehan family, near Templeglantine, Lucas was later moved to the farmhouse of Michael Dore, Balliston, Shanagolden. About six o'clock one summer morning, the general and his escort arrived at the Dore home, then one of the principal headquarters of the IRA. He was conveyed in a car driven by Larry McNamee, now an ambulance driver at the County Hospital, Croom. Fatigued by their long vigil over the distinguished captive, the general's escort retired early to bed, leaving James E. Dore, now a well-known draper in Glin, to watch over the prisoner. Some hours later Dore was relieved by Captain T. Madigan of the Shanagolden company, who was afterwards killed in action; and by Volunteers O'Brien and O'Shaughnessy, also of the Shanagolden company. Michael Dore then set out for Newcastlewest, to report the general's arrival at his home, and also to procure for him night attire and other personal equipment.

The disappearance of the general had created great excitement, and there was intensive activity by the enemy who carried out exhaustive searches, in the counties of Limerick and Cork, during their endeavours to locate them. Actually, he had been transferred from Cork to West Limerick quite openly and, so to speak, under the very nose of the British. Whilst on his way to Templeglantine, the car in which he was travelling pulled up opposite the premises of R.B. Woulfe, MPSI, in New Street, Abbeyfeale. While parked there patrols of Royal Irish Constabulary passed by the car, never suspecting that it held the distinguished captive for which the British were combing the country. It was a source of great wonder to the general that the men 'on the run' could move about so freely, and could joke, sing, laugh and dance, as though the waging of war against the mighty British Empire was an off-hand matter of every-day occurrence. Blissfully unaware of anything unusual about Balliston House, a servant-boy employed there began one morning's work with the chorus from the popular parody of the day, 'Can anybody tell me where General Lucas went', sung to the well-known air of 'The Blarney Roses'. The singer would certainly have been astonished to know that, listening to him, inside a window overlooking the yard in which he was singing, was General Lucas himself. Amongst the

IRA men then at Balliston House were: Seán Finn, Tom Malone ('Seán Forde'), Clancy, McSheehy, Jim Liston of Knockaderry; Tim Madigan, David O'Brien of Shanagolden; Jimmy Roche, Paddy Roche, Johnny Glenny, 'Slope' Reidy, 'Patro' O'Shaughnessy, Con Boyle and the Quinn brothers of Rathkeale; James E. Dore, Glin; J. Goode, a Londoner; D. Clancy of Kilfinane; and Jim Listen of Athea.

During his captivity in West Limerick General Lucas was accorded the respect and privilege due an officer of his rank and standing. According to one of the men who had charge of him, he endeared himself to his captors by his gentlemanly demeanour and attitude of friendliness and respect. Whilst in the Dore home he played cards a good deal and talked freely about the military situation in Ireland. 'I think you are going the right way about it this time', was his comment on the policy of ambushes and attacks on barracks. Having been held for some considerable time in West Limerick General Lucas was transferred to East Clare on instructions received from headquarters. Despite very considerable military and police activity the general was first brought to Melon, a point adjacent to Limerick's big foreign garrison, and later taken by boat across the Shannon to Hogan's of Cratloe, then headquarters of the East Clare brigade.

His sensational capture having served its original purpose, the general, who was frequently moved from place to place to avoid his friends, became a burden on the active units of the IRA, and his continued detention was not considered a matter of importance. Whilst still a captive he seldom missed an opportunity to enquire about his former captors in West Limerick. During his detention in East Limerick the newspapers carried an announcement that his wife had given birth to a baby son at her home in England. His captors felt that the occasion should not be permitted to pass without affording him an opportunity to celebrate the event. Appropriate liquid refreshments and a box of cigars were produced, and General Lucas and the Volunteers sat round in happy mood.

THE GENERAL'S ESCAPE

FOLLOWING HIS ESCAPE General Lucas was besieged by English newspaper-men, no doubt in anticipation of a sensational story of brutal ill-treatment at the hands of the IRA. They were rudely disappointed as the general's brief comment on his captivity was much to the point: 'I was treated as a gentleman by gentlemen,' was all he said. His successful break for freedom took place on the night of 29 July, and he wandered about the countryside until morning, when he reached the police barracks at Pallas. There he was taken aboard a military lorry by which the mails of the British garrison were carried to and from Limerick Junction in County Tipperary. As it happened, Seán Treacy and the 3rd Tipperary brigade had arranged to ambush this lorry and its special military escort, that very morning, near the village of Oola, six miles from Tipperary town. It was arranged that the ambush would fall into two parts. First, a military cyclist, who generally came in advance of the lorry, should be held up by a minor obstruction as he came round a bend of the road; and second, that the lorry should then be attacked by another party of men stationed behind a ditch. Several mishaps, however, nearly turned the ambush into a trap for the ambushers. General Lucas was in the first lorry which was closely followed by a second. The motor-cyclist's machine had been punctured and he and it were aboard the first lorry. Moreover, the main attacking parties were armed mostly with Martini-Henry rifles, and by an oversight had been supplied with the wrong ammunition; at a critical moment this ammunition was to stick in the breach and fail to be ejected. The first lorry came round the bend and surprised the men lying in wait for the motor-cyclist scout. Some distance ahead, the main barricade had been placed in position. The main party opened fire on the first lorry and shot two soldiers dead, and then their guns jammed. The remaining soldiers jumped from the lorry and took cover. The second lorry came quickly on the scene. The alarm had already reached the

Royal Irish Constabulary barracks from which an armed body of constabulary could be seen hastening. The fire opened by the military was concentrated on the main body who could not, for the most part, reply. They broke from their positions and ran from cover over the open fields. They were exposed to the fire of the military, and their position would have been critical because they were easy targets in their flight across this open space. The coolness of Treacy saved them by a daring diversion. He saw the danger and advanced to within sixty yards of the nearest lorry, stationed himself on a ditch on the right-hand side of the road, and opened a rapid fire on the military with his parabellum. Firing coolly and deliberately, Treacy retreated slowly as soon as the rest of the party had found cover. His attack distracted the military and prevented them from picking off at their ease the retreating ambushers. Three of the soldiers were wounded by Treacy's shots, and General Lucas was shot in the nose. The presence of General Lucas, or indeed his escape, was at that time, of course, unknown to Treacy.

Shortly after the capture of General Lucas, there was a fierce outbreak by the military in Newcastlewest town. About an hour before dawn one morning, a party of armed military with officers and accompanied by some members of the Royal Irish Constabulary approached the residence of Seán Brouder, in Upper Maiden Street. They immediately proceeded to smash in the door and windows of the house. A district inspector of the Royal Irish Constabulary, who lived in a hotel across the street, and who had just been transferred from Newcastlewest, approached the British forces and appealed to them to desist. As they responded by threatening to shoot him, he had to make a hasty retreat. Having smashed in the front door, the attackers rushed through the house, shooting wildly as they went. They obviously sought the editor of *The Observer* newspaper, and were much chagrined to find that he had escaped them. Having scattered petrol throughout the rooms, they set fire to the house, after which they proceeded to *The Observer* office where they smashed machinery and type. As this attack had many new features, the propaganda department of the First Dáil made full use of it, and the press of America and other countries featured the story. An apparently well-informed writer in the *Bulletin* of the First Dáil attributed the attack to the fact that a section of General Lucas' personal regiment was stationed in Newcastlewest at the time.

IRA LOSSES IN BURNING OF CROOM COURTHOUSE

THE COURTHOUSE, CROOM, stood as a monument to British mis-rule until June 1920, when it was burned by local IRA under the command of Captain W. Burke, a well-known hurler. When that operation took place there were in Croom a large detail of regular British soldiers, Black and Tans and RIC, who occupied the police barracks and adjoining houses. Unfortunately, the burning of the courthouse ended in tragedy. Everything worked smoothly until a false alarm was raised and the men engaged in sprinkling the build-ing with petrol were withdrawn. The plan having been thus upset at the outset, the men, over-eager to complete their task when they returned to the building, started the fire before making good their arrangements to retreat. When the petrol was ignited, the vacuum formed caused the only door to shut tightly and become locked. In an instant the courthouse was a raging inferno. Two badly burned Volunteers managed to escape, but three others were trapped and burned to death. They were Edward Donnelly, Honeypound Road, Croom; John Moloney, Honeypound Road, Croom, and James Hogan, Fanningstown, Croom. Timothy Quirke and Simon Howard were those who received serious, burns. The latter, a well-known hurler, and brother of Garrett Howard, of All-Ireland fame, never fully recovered his former health, and died a few years later – the fourth victim of the tragedy.

At the commencement of 1921, several attacks were made on small patrols of police and Black and Tans. The West Limerick column was poorly armed and equipped, and was not in a position to engage large enemy forces. The number of small patrols of police or military which ventured outside the garrisoned towns was very few.

AMBUSH AT BARRYGONE

INFORMATION WAS RECEIVED by Brigadier Seán Finn that it was the intention of a detail of Black and Tans to travel by the morning train from Foynes to Limerick. A council of officers was immediately called and plans were made to attack the train. It was arranged that a young man named Liston, would travel from Foynes on the same train in order to ascertain the strength of the enemy, and signal this information from his carriage window as the carriage approached the ambush position. If the enemy was definitely travelling, it was planned that Con Boyle of Rathkeale would walk along the railway tracks towards the train, and attempt to halt it with a red flag. The signal pre-arranged with Liston was one wave of his cap through the open window to indicate each Black and Tan abroad. The column was immediately mobilised near Ballyhahill, and the men marched through the night to occupy advantageous positions on high rocky ground overlooking the railway track at a place called Barrygone. The column numbered eighteen, and included amongst others, Jimmy Collins, Johnny Collins, Jerry Moloney, Michael Colbert, Danny Murphy, Owen McAuliffe and Larry Harnett, John T. O'Connor, C. Cregan, D. Collins, Johnny Harnett, Garrett McAuliffe, Dan and Maurice Quinn, J. Liston and David O'Brien.

The column having waited anxiously some hours for the approach of the enemy, tension was eventually broken when the train came into view. From the window a hand was seen frantically waving a cap. Con Boyle commenced his delicate task, and carried it out successfully, stopping the train exactly at the ambush position. Heads thrust through carriage windows to ascertain the cause of the stoppage were quickly withdrawn when it was seen that the rocky embankment was lined with rifles and shotguns. The cutting was a deep one, and as Con Boyle mounted the embankment, fire was opened on the train from both sides. The rifles of the Black and Tans barked quickly in reply, and chips of rocks were seen flying in all directions. Passengers had a terrifying experience as they lay on the floors of compartments to escape the hail of bullets. Ultimately, a daring Black and Tan jumped down from a carriage, and although under heavy fire, managed to reach the engine which he compelled the driver and fireman to re-start. The Black and Tans were lucky to escape with a number of wounded.

EAST LIMERICK COLUMN IN ATHEA

IN FEBRUARY 1921, it was decided by the West Limerick brigade IRA officers, that a smashing blow could be dealt the military and Black and Tans, amongst the hills of West Limerick. At that time, when the British forces in the area moved out of the garrison towns such as Newcastlewest and Rathkeale, they invariably travelled in strong force in Crossley tenders and were usually accompanied by armoured cars. They were guilty of innumerable outrages, such as the murder and beating of civilians and the burning of private houses and public buildings. A conference of the officers of the West Limerick brigade took place in February, at which decision was taken to tackle the mobile enemy forces somewhere on the road between Newcastlewest and Foynes, near Shanagolden area, or on the Abbeyfeale–Newcastlewest road, as opportunity offered. Headquarters offered the assistance of the North Cork or East Limerick flying columns for the engagement, and Brigade O/C Finn decided to enlist the assistance of the East Limerick men. Accordingly, towards mid-March, 1921 the East Limerick flying column, under its commanding officer, Donnachadh

O'Hannigan, began the march, still remembered in rural homes, across the wide plains of Limerick from the Tipperary border to that of Kerry. The column comprised some fifty well-armed men, and at its rear a horse-drawn vehicle carried mines and other explosives. The march was boldly carried out, along the main roads leading to the west of the county, and the column actually passed quite close to two big enemy military encampments at Mountbrown and Smithfield. On arrival in Athea, the men were billeted in farm houses round the district, whilst a favourable opportunity was awaited to carry out the planned attack upon the enemy.

Amongst the members of the West Limerick flying column then in Athea were the following: Brigade Commandant Seán Finn; Vice-Commandant G. McAuliffe; Jim Colbert, Michael Colbert, Jimmy Collins, Con Cregan, Ned Cregan, Tom Wallace, Richard Woulfe, MPSI; P.J. O'Neill, Larry Harnett, John E. Harnett, Dan Murphy, John J. Leahy, Jim Liston, Amos Reidy, Paddy Roche, Seán Brouder, Joe Mahony, William Mahony, Owen McAuliffe, Paddy Naughton, Denis Collins, Tom Markham, Jim Guiney and Michael Murphy. Some members of the West Limerick column had been captured during a night raid a little while previously, and were at that time being carried about as hostages. A number of others were ill.

On Easter Saturday all the men of the combined columns went to confession in Athea parish church, in preparation to receive Holy Communion on the following morning. About midnight a dispatch came from the late Tommy McDonagh, then acting captain, Newcastlewest, stating that there was extraordinary military activity in Newcastlewest, and that it looked as though there was about to be a big military movement against the combined IRA columns in the Athea district. Commandant Finn immediately sent out two IRA men who had been on guard duty in order to call all the members of the columns who were billeted over a wide area in the hospitable homes of Athea. In less than twenty minutes all members of the two columns had mobilised at Direen Cross.

Scouts had been posted earlier at the cross to prevent a possible surprise, and each group of IRA men was challenged as it approached in the darkness. The columns had barely got into formation when the distant rumble of enemy lorries and armoured cars could be heard along all roads which led from Newcastlewest, Rathkeale, Limerick and Listowel, and converging on the Athea area. It appeared that an all-out effort had been launched to capture or wipe out the columns. It was decided by the IRA officers that the men should occupy the high ground above Knocknagonna school and, if necessary, to fight it out with the enemy even though there were the great advantages of numbers and armament on his side. It was a bitterly cold night, with driving sleet beating against the heather, as the men stood to arms and awaited the arrival of the British. Vivid flashes of lightning repeatedly lit up the dark hills around, and now and again enemy searchlights played upon the valleys between.

Apparently the British failed to locate the positions of the IRA, and towards dawn a report reached the column headquarters that the enemy had withdrawn his forces. There remained but one armoured car which appeared to be in trouble, on the bog road near the Black Heights. A small number of soldiers remained to guard it. It was immediately decided to attack the armoured car and capture it if possible. Both columns mobilised for the attack on the road near Knocknagonna schoolhouse. I retain a vivid recollection of Seán Finn's handsome face and soldierly bearing, as he stood at the head of his men and hummed Michael Scanlon's 'The Bold Fenian Men'. In open formation, the columns advanced cross-country, directly towards the enemy position. The terrain afforded them little cover, and the advance was made cautiously. Suddenly the scouts ahead signalled the return of big British forces in lorries and armoured cars. The columns were then in an extremely difficult position, in very open country almost devoid of cover, and which could easily be swept by the quick-firing guns of the enemy's armoured cars. By successful manoeuvring, the IRA forces were withdrawn to their original positions without being observed by the enemy.

Later in the night, the IRA marched to Ballyhahill where they obtained badly-needed rest. It was a difficult task to find billets for such a large number of men in the sparsely populated rural area and, consequently, groups of two or three, or more, were accommodated in different houses by the patriotic people of the district. These billets extended over a very wide area, stretching more or less in a circle which extended five miles from Whiskey Hall to Teenakilla Cross in Glin parish.

THE FIGHT AT BALLYHAHILL

DURING THE FOLLOWING day the men rested from their hardshipping operations of the previous night. About four o'clock that afternoon some of the East Limerick men, who were billeted on the south-east of Ballyhahill went to a crossroads house nearby in order to have their shoes repaired. They had not been long there when scouts reported the rapid approach of enemy forces in Crossley tenders, and in a matter of seconds the roar of the lorries could be heard.

Having left their rifles at their billet, the men rushed out of the shoemaker's house, and were immediately fired upon from the British lorries, as they ran to get their arms. Back in their billet, the three IRA men were immediately engaged by over forty of the enemy who besieged them. At that stage, Brigade Commandant Seán Finn, of West Limerick, and East Limerick column leader Donnachadh O'Hannigan, together with Volunteers Seamus Finn of the East Limerick brigade and Jim Colbert of West Limerick brigade, heard the shots and rushed to engage the enemy forces. It was an unequal battle from the outset, with the small group of IRA men entirely isolated from their comrades. The main body of the East Limerick flying column was billeted at the far side of the White River in

Ballyhahill village and above it; whilst the West Limerick column, which knew every inch of the ground, was still further away, in townlands near Glin district.

The first intimation that anything was wrong reached Vice-Commandant G. McAuliffe, in a casual manner. He was billeted in the same house as Michael Colbert, Paddy Roche, Richard Woulfe and S. Brouder, and in the evening the *bean-a-tighe* told them that she had just heard shots in the direction of Ballyhahill. The vice-commandant and his comrades collected their arms and set out immediately; listening intently, but no sound of firing reached them from any direction. It was decided, however, to call out the entire West Limerick column immediately. Two IRA men who knew the country well were dispatched post-haste to the scattered country houses of the district, to mobilise the West Limerick forces. Swiftly, the column assembled, and the position was explained briefly to the men.

Having spread out in open formation, they advanced at the double cross-country towards Ballyhahill village, the direction from which the firing had been reported. As they approached the village, they came upon the main body of the East Limerick column, standing to attention in close formation in a field near the village. An officer was giving the men the password for the night in case night fighting should develop. Commandant Hannigan was not there, nor was Commandant Finn, and inquiries were immediately made as to their whereabouts. Somebody said that they had gone to Danaher's the night before, and this was taken to mean Dan Danaher's, Monomohill, who had very frequently sheltered Seán Finn; whereas it was to Mr Danaher's, Woodlawn, the men had gone. Nobody in the East Limerick column knew the reason for the shooting which had been heard. Scouts had been sent out to ascertain what had happened – if there had been fighting and, if so, where. Suddenly, the tragic news came through. The local battalion commandant, John T. O'Connor, who knew the country well and who had gone out to reconnoitre when the first alarm reached Ballyhahill, returned to report to his comrades the heartrending news that their gallant and chivalrous young commandant had been killed in action, and that Volunteer Quane of East Limerick was dangerously wounded. I have never seen strong men so deeply moved as were these men of the two IRA flying columns, as dusk fell over the countryside on that March night of 1921. In a few minutes the wounded man was brought in, almost bleeding to death. Swiftly and gently he was moved to a place of safety near Glin. He was ultimately nursed back to health under the care of the late Dick Woulfe, MPSI, and James Dore, Glin, both IRA men with medical knowledge. Dr Phil McGrath of Athea, and Dr Enright of Listowel, also attended him, despite great British military activity which continued in the district for many weeks after the shooting.

When survivors of the engagement came in, the men of the columns learned how the fight had developed. The shooting commenced originally when the party of Volunteers dashed from the shoemaker's house to their billet, in order to recover their arms. These men, all of whom belonged to the East Limerick column, were Volunteers Quane, Walsh and Howard. Having reached their billet, they were attacked on three sides by over forty of the enemy forces. The sound of firing reached the four men billeted in Danaher's house, and they immediately dashed out and took up positions on the fourth side of the besieged house.

It so happened that Donnachadh O'Hannigan carried two whistles which gave different sounds well-known to his men. When these whistles were blown, the three besieged East Limerick men evacuated the house and fought their way in the direction of their four comrades. The two little forces linked up, and a running fight with the enemy developed. The superior British force pressed hard, and in a short while moved very close to the IRA. The fight took place between two public roads, and the British were thus able to utilise their transport to send forward sections to cut off the retreat of the IRA men The battle had raged for about half-an-hour, when Volunteer Quane of Redchair, Ballyorgan, East Limerick, was shot through the neck, the bullet making its exit through his teeth and cheek. The wounded Quane urged his comrades to continue the fight and permit him to fall into the hands of the enemy, as he could fight no further and would thus be an impediment. His comrades vehemently refused to do. They brought him along with them, and thus the fight continued, 'One for all and all for one'. The English repeatedly demanded surrender, but there could be no yielding, especially to the merciless Black and Tans.

THE DEATH OF SEÁN FINN

ALTHOUGH THE TERRAIN favoured the British, the IRA fought on against powerful odds, in the vain hope that the flying columns in the neighbourhood of Ballyhahill would hear the firing and come to their relief. The battle had proceeded for over two hours when Brigadier Seán Finn fell mortally wounded. His hands went up, his rifle whirled in the air, and his last words are as clear today as the moment in which they were uttered: 'Goodbye, lads; carry on; I am done.' He fell on the field of battle, his rifle beside him, his young life given in the cause he loved. When the brigadier fell, a Black and Tan who crossed a fence with the obvious intention of approaching the body, was calmly shot down by Volunteer Tom Howard, who remarked to O'Hannigan: 'I have shot him, boss.'

In every battle there comes a crucial moment which calls for brave deeds and quick action. That moment had come for the small IRA party when eighteen-year-old Volunteer Seamus Finn, of the East Limerick column, informed his O/C that all his ammunition was spent. The situation was then desperate. Of the original seven, one was dead, one was wounded, and now a third was unarmed. And so young Finn was given the desperate order to recover the rifle and ammunition of his dead comrade. The opposing forces were then about forty yards apart, and the dead IRA man was about midway between them. The four IRA effectives maintained a heavy fusillade of fire against the English whilst young Finn dashed out and, to the amazement of all, recovered the rifle and ammunition of the dead brigadier. It was an extraordinary achievement, and the hail of bullets which ploughed ridges in the bare pasture land remained for weeks as evidence of Finn's remarkable escape.

Following that incident, there was a definite easing off by the English, but the fight still continued, and a strong party of Black and Tans was observed approaching from fresh positions, crouching for a new attack. But the gallant little band was still full of fight, and, with rifles at the ready, they doubled towards the enemy on this new front. Reaching the centre of a fairly high fence which momentarily screened them from view, they suddenly changed direction and took cover behind a rath on another side of the field. They were not long in this precarious position when a welcome fog crept from the shores of the lordly Shannon and completely screened the attackers and the attacked. The Black and Tans were too nervous to move about the unfamiliar locality in the fog, and made no further attempt to locate the IRA men.

Eventually, Jim Colbert observed a local farmer surveying the scene of the battle, and it was decided to chance an interview with him. It was learned that the enemy had withdrawn from the locality, and the little worn out force was thus enabled to leave the field of battle and proceed to the house of a hospitable farmer who provided welcome refreshments. Later in the day enemy whistles were again heard, and the IRA moved on a further distance to another farmhouse where they were served with hot tea, 'oneway' bread, and fresh eggs. Volunteer Quane, who all the while had borne his sufferings bravely, lost an enormous quantity of blood, and under the circumstances it was impossible to administer anything beyond elementary first aid. Volunteer Finn was promoted to the rank of first lieutenant for conspicuous bravery in the field of battle, promotion which was afterwards confirmed by order of general headquarters. The chief breadwinner of a widowed mother and young family at that time, Lieutenant Finn has since been called to his eternal reward. Volunteer Tom Howard was subsequently killed in action at Lackelly, on 2 May 1921. Howard, who was noted for his wonderful store of Irish wit and humour, became a member of the East Limerick flying column when it was formed in June 1920, following the attack on Kilmallock police barracks.

THE MARCH TO EAST LIMERICK

WHEN THE MAIN body of the flying columns was notified of the gallant fight at Ballyhahill, new positions were occupied about the village which were held until 3 a.m. on the following morning, in anticipation of the return of the British. Early next morning definite information was received from a friendly source in the enemy camp that the British authorities had ordered a mass concentration of troops from Limerick and Tralee in the Athea–Ballyhahill area, for the object of capturing or eliminating the combined columns. With the enemy about the district in such overwhelming numbers, the IRA were fortunate to retreat safely to Kilbaha, in County Kerry. On the morning of the successful retreat, the British wrecked many houses in the Athea district, and in the mortuary chapel attached to the Athea church they opened the coffin of a person awaiting burial.

The death of the gallant young Brigadier Finn cast a gloom over the IRA in the west, and checked their military activities temporarily. Ultimately, a council was convened, and it was decided that as the surprise element would be absent and consequently an attack on the big British force out of the question, the combined columns should march to East Limerick, where the terrain was more favourable to guerrilla warfare. The march east was planned and carried through successfully in March 1921, and amongst the West Limerick men who participated, under the command of Michael Colbert, column O/C, were Jim Colbert, Jim Liston, Jim Guiney, Danny Murphy. Jimmy Collins, Denis Collins, Larry Harnett, John J. Leahy, Paddy Naughton, Michael Murphy, Owen McAuliffe, Amos Reidy, James Sullivan and the Fitzgeralds of Askeaton; Con Cregan, Johnny Harnett, M. Neville.

The West Limerick men engaged in close on six weeks strenuous campaigning whilst in the east, in the course of which they participated in the fights at Lackelly and Emly, which are described in the section of this volume devoted to the struggle in East Limerick. At the end of that period, they were recalled home as developments in the west demanded their presence in their own district. They reached Athea by two night marches from the Galtee Mountains. When resting in the vicinity of Ballinaleena during the march west a brigade council meeting took place in a house at Woodcock Hill where a British ex-soldier suspected of being a spy was under arrest. The prisoner, who was guarded by members of 'H' company (Granagh), 4th battalion, West Limerick brigade, was found guilty and sentenced to face the firing squad. At that time the area was under curfew, and enemy patrols were frequent. Whilst on the way to the place of execution the prisoner and escort came upon a patrol of British soldiers from Ballyvonaire camp patrolling the Ballinaleena–Bruree road. The British challenged the IRA party to halt but the latter, thinking that the challenge had emanated from other members of the column, continued to approach until stopped by a fusillade of lead. Second Lieutenant Michael O'Shea, who had charge of the escort, fell dangerously wounded, as did also one of his men, Volunteer Patrick Benson. Seizing his opportunity in the confusion that followed their prisoner crawled to cover and succeeded in making good his escape to join the British patrol. Both wounded IRA men were captured and conveyed by lorry to Charleville, where Lieutenant O'Shea died shortly afterwards. Volunteer Benson, who was wounded in the neck and left shoulder, hovered for a long time between life and death. He ultimately recovered and was released in a weak state of health after the Truce. The remains of Lieutenant O'Shea were handed over to his relatives and were conveyed to Granagh church where a guard of honour of his comrades watched by the catafalque. Impressive scenes were witnessed at the funeral in Shanavogha next day, as the coffin, wrapped in the tri-colour, was borne on the shoulders of his fellow soldiers and a huge funeral procession of relatives, sympathisers and Volunteers followed. At the graveside an oration was given by company officer Captain Michael Madden, All the while the British military, posted on a hill overlooking the churchyard, prepared to swoop in case a volley was fired over the grave. The Rosary was recited and all that was mortal of a fearless comrade was laid to rest. In the words of Terence MacSwiney:

> Let us be free and proud
> Or roll me in my shroud.

BLACK AND TANS SUCCESSFULLY ATTACKED IN ABBEYFEALE

IN MARCH 1921, a West Limerick flying column arrived at Meenahela, Abbeyfeale, to ambush a police patrol in the town. Almost at the same time an enemy mobile force comprising over one hundred military swooped upon the locality and as the IRA were greatly outnumbered the move against the police had to be abandoned. It was then decided to enlist the assistance of the North Cork IRA flying column to help attack the police in Abbeyfeale town. A meeting was arranged near Meelin, Newmarket, between Mossie Harnett, battalion O/C, and Michael Sullivan, a prominent North Cork IRA officer. As a result of the meeting a big contingent of men from North Cork were brought to Meenahela one night towards the end of May. They were in the charge of Paddy O'Brien, Liscarroll, then battalion commandant, and included amongst them were Michael Sullivan, Meelin, the late Bill Moylan, Con Moylan, Newmarket; Connie D. Curtin, Rockchapel, and about sixteen others. They were met at Barrett's house at Meenahela by officers attached to a West Limerick service unit and men of the 2nd battalion. Arrangements were made for the combined columns to occupy positions about half-a-mile from the town on a steep road frequently patrolled by Black and Tans. For several days prior to the arrival of the Corkmen, notices were posted on gateways and other places in the vicinity of the town ordering the Black and Tans to leave the country immediately. Some of the notices were posted very close to the police barrack itself.

The columns moved to Abbeyfeale Hill, where they were billeted in three or four farmhouses nearby. Previously prepared positions were taken up at dawn and at about ten o'clock in the morning the Black and Tans were observed to leave their barracks and proceed through the town along the Newcastlewest road. Wherever they came across the IRA notices they stopped and tore them down.

Returning along the Newcastlewest road they walked directly towards the ambush position but surprisingly turned back for no apparent reason before they reached it. They did not move out of their barracks again that day. The IRA remained in position until nightfall and then the West Limerick men withdrew to Mountcollins and the North Corkmen to Rockchapel. Although the IRA were on the alert during the days that followed the Black and Tans were loath to leave their fortress, and ultimately the North Corkmen returned home.

A meeting of the local IRA officers then took place and amongst those who attended were Jimmy Collins, Mossie Harnett, Johnny Harnett, P.J. O'Neill and Jeremiah Moloney. It was decided that the only way to get to grips with the Black and Tans in Abbeyfeale was to enter the town in the early hours of the morning and to occupy houses converging on the square. On the morning of 5 June 1921, about twenty of the West Limerick column marched into Abbeyfeale from the Newcastlewest side. They halted at the Protestant church, where they were met by John O'Connor, Pete Collins, T.J. O'Connell, Edward Sheehy, Michael Shannon, D. Cullinane and Michael Collins. Eight selected men of the column removed their shoes, crept into the town on their stockinged feet and occupied positions allotted them in certain houses. The remainder of the column entered the town noiselessly shortly afterwards. One of the notices ordering the Black and Tans to quit the country was posted on the very door of the barrack by Thomas O'Connell and P. Collins.

The Tans discovered this about six o'clock and about half-past six they apparently decided to move up town to avenge the effrontery. About a dozen of them proceeded into the square in extended form, all armed with rifles and revolvers and obviously unconscious of the impending attack. They halted by a telegraph pole on which another of the notices had been posted. Immediately a whistle sounded and fire was opened on them from the adjoining houses. Taken completely by surprise, the Black and Tans paused momentarily before dashing for the shelter of their barracks. Some returned fire as they retreated, and Constable Jolly was killed, whilst some others were wounded. In a few minutes the IRA were out in the street to retrieve weapons abandoned by the enemy. Several shots were fired into the barracks and then the column made an orderly retreat by the Newcastlewest road. Whilst the IRA was still on the outskirts of the town the Tans emerged from their barracks and fired after them repeatedly but without effect. The IRA was in the charge of Jimmy Collins.

BURNING OF NEWCASTLEWEST COURTHOUSE

In April 1921, battalion columns were formed under the command of vice-commandants and to strengthen these, members of the flying columns were distributed amongst them. Following this development the courthouse at Newcastlewest was burned one night, under the noses of a strong garrison. Amongst those who took part in the operation were Con and Ned Cregan, Jim Liston, Owen McAuliffe, Tadhg Collins, the O'Mahonys, Amos Reidy, Jeremiah Kiely and P. Mulcahy. The customary reprisals were vented on the inhabitants when the IRA withdrew from the town.

The capture near Broadford of a spy, who was executed at Clonmore, Broadford, after trial, was due largely to the activity of Lieutenant P. Aherne, of Templeglantine.

BLACK AND TANS AMBUSHED IN DROMCOLLOGHER, BURNING OF COURTHOUSE

IN MAY 1921, an IRA column attached to the 3rd battalion under Con Foley and which included Ben Sullivan, Mick Sheehy, Jim Doody, Mick Devane, Martin Cussen amongst others from Dromcollogher, successfully occupied the town of Dromcollogher and ambushed a patrol of Black and Tans who lost one killed and several wounded. That night was one of terror in the town and several houses were burned as reprisals. Earlier in the war four Volunteers lost their lives and others were badly disfigured in the burning of Dromcollogher courthouse. The fatal casualties included Buckley, Duggan, Brennan and Stokes. Jack Farrell, who was badly burned, barely escaped with his life.

During the month of June several weeks were taken up preparing plans to ambush military lorries which frequently plied between Abbeyfeale and Newcastlewest. The help of the North Cork men was again requisitioned and Paddy O'Brien and Michael Sullivan, of Cork, with Mossie Harnett, Jimmy Collins, T. Sexton and T. Bouchier of West Limerick, studied the country around Templeglantine and

Barnagh. It was ultimately decided that the ambush should take place on the west side of Barnagh Hill. Larry Harnett and Denis Collins, who had been in Cork for instruction in mine-laying, prepared mines in the forge at Kingwilliamstown. Early in July forty men of the North Cork column arrived at Kilaculleen, Tournafulla and were billeted at Kelly's. There they met the West Limerick column in full strength and final preparations were made to attack the British next day, as it was learned that about sixty military and Black and Tans travelling from Newcastlewest to Abbeyfeale, would pass Barnagh.

Eight mines were laid on the road and signallers were posted on the hillside. The engineers had wired the mines for a distance of one hundred yards and controlled them from inside a fence running parallel to the road. This fence, which was covered with furze, extended for over a mile and was the main IRA position. It had not yet been occupied when suddenly the sound of British transport vehicles could be heard approaching earlier than expected, and before steps could be taken to deal with them, four lorries of military and a private car dashed over the mined road towards Abbeyfeale. Arrangements were then made to ambush the British on their way back to Newcastlewest but, contrary to usual routine, they did not return. At noon on their third day in the ambush positions the IRA withdrew as the Truce had been proclaimed between the British and the Irish Republic. It was a glorious and heartening sight on that summer morning to see the soldiers of West Limerick and North Cork drawn up in line whilst they were addressed by Commandant O'Brien, who read the dispatch announcing the cessation of hostilities. The commandant asked the men to observe the Truce in a soldierly manner and if necessary to be ready again for a further fight in the defence of the Republic.

Amongst the West Limerick men who fell in the fight for freedom was Tim Madigan, well-loved captain of the Shanagolden company. He was shot dead by British forces whilst leaving his house, which he occasionally visited to see his mother and people. Another fatal

West Limerick casualty was John O'Brien of Coolcappa, who was mortally wounded following an explosion of an enemy booby trap when a party of IRA men attempted to break down a bridge which had been temporarily repaired by the Black and Tans in the spring of 1921.

BLACK AND TANS IN WEST LIMERICK

by J.D.H.

IT WAS A quiet evening in Abbeyfeale when the first Black and Tan entered the town. A good deal had been heard of his savage methods elsewhere, so that his arrival was not devoid of interest. He came in the afternoon train and made his way leisurely towards the Royal Irish Constabulary barracks, wearing that mixed uniform, shortly to become such a familiar and unwelcome sight. He was a tall fellow, well set up in his khaki pants black coat and peaked cap. His arrival portended the gathering of the clouds.

Some time afterwards when the autumn twilight of a September evening had become lost in the darkening night, the sharp crack of rifle shots startled the inhabitants of Abbeyfeale. Everybody knew that something out of the ordinary was taking place, but it was not until morning that it was learned that a police patrol had been ambushed on the outskirts of the town, and that Constable Mahony of the Royal Irish Constabulary had been killed in the encounter. The next day and, in fact, the week that followed will not be readily forgotten in Abbeyfeale. It was then that the town had its first experience of Black and Tan reprisals. Early in the morning the local garrison of Royal Irish Constabulary and Black and Tans was reinforced by a detachment of the Yorkshire Regiment and the combined British forces immediately proceeded to make things as unpleasant as possible for everybody. They opened the proceedings by terrorising the congregation leaving Mass. Shots were fired into the air and men, women and children were interrogated as they left the church. Some young men were beaten up and threatened with death, and many houses were searched for arms. The detail of the Yorkshire Regiment withdrew before nightfall and then began a flight of men, women and children from the town as though from a plague-stricken area. No mercy was expected from police and Black and Tan thugs capable of firing on little children, as they did at Croyle Hill near the Kerry bridge some time previously, when little Peggy Brosnan was wounded and several other children had narrow escapes.

Only a small number of inhabitants, grouped together in neighbours' houses, remained in Abbeyfeale town that night to face the anticipated terror. In the streets Black and Tans fired their rifles and exploded grenades almost continuously throughout the evening and after nightfall. In the early hours of the morning armed men marched in military formation from the Royal Irish Constabulary barracks, and having turned off the main street, halted between the licensed premises of P. Enright and T. Scannell. There were knocks on the hall-door of one of the adjoining houses, but nobody could possibly have answered before the door was smashed in about the house. Appeals and expostulations from the inmates of the raided house followed, as one or two of the Black and Tans were advocating the shooting out-of-hand of a youth of sixteen years, because his brother was out with the republican army. Whilst the officer in charge prevented their dastardly design, he curtly informed the lady of the house that she had a quarter of an hour to clear out before his men set her place on fire. Before the Black and Tans withdrew they saturated clothes and furniture with petrol, and placed them in the centre of one of the rooms, all set for conflagration. The officer then directed his men down Church Street, towards the local Temperance Hall, erected fifteen years previously by Fr Casey, PP, of revered and popular memory. The police smashed down the entrance gate, and whilst doing so, awakened Dan Harnett, publican, who appealed to them to spare the building. This man was forcefully pulled out of his own house, placed against a wall to be shot, and was only saved by the appeals of his family. The Temperance Hall was soon a mass of flames, volumes of smoke and cinders flying down Church Street as the Black and Tans returned to finish the work which they had originally commenced.

Meanwhile, Mrs Maggie O'Neill had sent word to the Very Rev. Dr Ned Leen, home on a few days visit from Blackrock, County Dublin, and asked him to appeal to the officer in charge not to burn her house. Doctor Ned got the family on their knees to say the Rosary which had not been completed when the Black and Tans returned and again knocked at the door. Dr Leen's appeal was successful, largely because the officer in charge did not appear to relish the job as did his subordinates, who expressed their disappointment when the burning was called off. Fifty yards away the Black and Tans halted again in the middle of Main Street outside the home of Dr Ned whose prayers had only just saved from destruction the home of a neighbour. Petrol tins in hands, they tried the gate leading to the back entrance of the house. Finding that it was locked and barred on the inside the Tans withdrew to the middle of the road and, joining hands, they charged against it, using their heavy boots as battering rams. The gate was sent splintering from its fastenings and the hooligans dashed into the yard. Dr Ned Leen was a silent witness to what was going on, but the ladies in the house were terrified. Having saved one house by his appeal Dr Ned remained dumb when his own turn came and never uttered a word to the destroyers. During his noble work in the wilds of West Africa, to win souls to God, he had faced death in many forms, and that night he stood there calmly facing the drunken rabble.

The Black and Tans surprisingly withdrew again without setting fire to the house, having first of all threatened its future destruction.

Later in the night, however, they exploded a bomb in the house of the late John Collins, Bridge Street, who was then nearly eighty years of age. Two of his sons were out with the IRA, and before the actual bombing of his home a Black and Tan named Huckerbery threatened to blow the old man up with his house unless he evacuated. Old Collins pluckily told the Tan, who all the while played about with the explosive, to fire away as he did not intend to leave. It was later in the night that the bomb was thrown into Collins.'

The days which followed were packed with minor aggressions. On the excuse of seeking the head which was supposed to have worn a cap found at the scene of the ambush, certain drapers were subjected to blackguardism, and bombs were left on some of the premises visited. An envelope on which the name of a young townsman had been written, and which was also supposed to have been discovered at the scene of the ambush, provided reason for interviewing all and sundry as the police searched for a victim. Several people were taken to the barracks, where they were subjected to third degree measures. One Black and Tan named Huckerbery threatened a young man named Johnny O'Connor who refused to deny or admit connection with the IRA. 'I will shoot you if you don't tell me what you know,' the Black and Tan threatened.

'Shoot away,' replied the young man, 'I will tell you nothing.'

'You are a brave fellow,' sarcastically declared the Tan, who strangely enough did not shoot. He was reported to have murdered a number of people in similar circumstances, and next day he shot to death two young Abbeyfeale men who never had any connection with the IRA. This shooting took place about six o'clock on the evening of 20 September in a field a short distance outside the town. It transpired that shortly before the Angelus bell rang out on the calm of that autumn evening, Patrick Harnett, a young rural post-man and son of a shopkeeper residing opposite the police barracks, decided to visit his uncle's house at Kilconlea, a little over a mile outside the town. From the barrack gate, Huckerbery, who bore a sinister reputation, watched him set out from his home. Harnett was joined by Jeremiah Healy, a blacksmith's apprentice then employed by Batt Begley. Emerging from the forge, Healy called on young Harnett to wait for him, and together they walked the footpath out the Castleisland road. Huckerbery followed them, and later both were found shot to death in a field not far from the town. When he learned of the foul deed Rev. Fr Fitzgerald, CC, called at the barracks and declared to the Black and Tans that if innocent young men could be shot down like that in cold blood and for no apparent reason, then the earlier everyone else prepared to meet a similar fate the better.

On Wednesday 22 September, Major Lloyd presided at a military inquiry into the Abbeyfeale shooting. It was held in the day-room of the old police barracks, and turned out to be a most remarkable affair. Two hundred military in full war kit with rifles, fixed bayonets and machine-guns were drafted into the town and took up positions round the barracks before the court opened at eleven o'clock in the morning. It was the first time in the Abbeyfeale district that the ordinary coroner's inquest was superseded by a military inquiry, and the proceedings opened with long technical discussions. Instructions were issued to the press urging the necessity for care in the matter of excluding the names of certain witnesses, and, in fact, it was stressed that no evidence contrary to the interests of the British government should be published. Pressed for further elucidation of these instructions the court told Mr J.D. Harnett that publication was not desired of the names of the officers of the court, the prosecutor, the military witnesses and particularly the name of the Black and Tan who shot the young men. District Inspector Lynn, who was subsequently promoted in the six counties, prosecuted, and Mr Maurice J. Woulfe represented the next-of-kin of the deceased boys. Whilst the proceedings took place young Harnett was 'waked' in his father's house across the road.

Dan Healy, farmer and father of the dead blacksmith, told the court that he last saw his son alive on Monday morning when he left his home a short distance outside the town to go to work as usual at Batt Begley's forge. He was dead when he next saw him at ten o'clock on Tuesday morning. As his son did not return home on Monday evening he made enquiries without avail. About six o'clock on the same evening he heard three shots in the direction in which the bodies were subsequently found, and a few minutes later he saw a man in a khaki coat walk inside the fence parallel to the road. The man got on the road and went in the direction of Abbeyfeale. A short while afterwards five or six Black and Tans came out from Abbeyfeale to the place where he had first observed the man in the khaki coat. When they reached the gap where the bodies were found they crossed the road and one of them looked into the field, after which they all returned towards Abbeyfeale. Shortly afterwards two men in the uniforms of the regular Royal Irish Constabulary came from Abbeyfeale to the same place. Healy had no idea of what had happened as he thought the shots which he had heard had been fired into the air.

In reply to the president, Healy stated that he first learned of the death of his son from his employer, Batt Begley, and went immediately to the police barracks, where he saw the bodies of both young men. His son made no remark at any time that his life was in danger. Healy said that he could not recognise the first Black and Tan whom he saw coming from the scene of the murder as he was more than a quarter of a mile distant at the time.

The head constable deposed that he was in temporary charge of the barracks about 7.30 p.m. on Monday evening. He was in his office when it was reported to him that two men had been shot some distance outside the town. He took a sergeant with him to the scene of the shooting which was about three hundred yards from the barracks, and there in a field they found the dead bodies of two young men, both of whom had apparently been shot through the head. He examined the bodies but found nothing to assist identification. At that time there were also present at the scene of the shooting a sergeant and some other constables. He returned to the barracks and had the bodies brought in by ambulance. They were identified next morning by Mr B. Begley.

Replying to Mr Woulfe, solicitor, the head constable said that the Black and Tan named Huckerbery had been in his office on the evening of the shooting and left about five minutes to seven. He did not know where he went then, but later he saw him about eight o'clock when Huckerbery said he was going to Newcastlewest. The head constable added that the cadet corps or Auxiliaries wore breeches and that the Black and Tans wore pants and puttees sometimes.

Sergeant Lattimer stated that he was a member of the cadet corps and that about 19.15 hours, or about 7.15 old time, the Black and Tan, Huckerbery came to him in the barrack yard and said, 'I have just shot two men. I was standing at the barrack gate and said "good evening" to two young men who were passing. They took no notice and as they looked suspicious I followed them. The men kept looking back and then broke into a run. I dashed after them and they ran through a gap in a hedge to the right of the road. I called on them to halt and as they would not do so I shot them.' Lattimer told the court that he asked the Black and Tan if the men were dead and he replied 'dead'. Lattimer then asked if he were sure, and the Black and Tan replied, 'I know when a man is dead.' Lattimer further told the court that he asked Huckerbery to show him the bodies as they might be only wounded. Huckerbery replied, '*They* are dead right enough.' Lattimer then called two constables and they went with Huckerbery to a point about three hundred yards west of the barracks. There, through a gap in the hedge Huckerbery showed him two civilians lying on their backs inside the field and about three yards from the road. They were about a yard apart and the younger of the two had a soft hat clutched in his left hand as though he had taken it off to enable him to run faster. They had climbed through the hedge before they had been shot. There was no sign of a struggle and he could not tell from what direction the shots had come. There was a great deal of blood.

In reply to Mr Woulfe, solicitor, Lattimer said that the men had no arms and that the shooting struck him as being drastic under the circumstances.

When he had seen the bodies Lattimer returned to the barracks, sent a few men to picket the scene and reported the matter to the head constable. All the while Huckerbery remained perfectly cool and collected. He voluntarily produced his pistol and called attention to the fact that he had expended only three rounds. He did not belong to Lattimer's command. In reply to Mr Woulfe, Lattimer said that the Black and Tan, Huckerbery, remained absolutely quiet when looking at the bodies. He did not refer to the hat in the man's hand. Lattimer did not engage Huckerbery in conversation as he did not wish to speak to him. He also declared that he knew nothing of Huckerbery's previous history.

As Miss Kitty Cronin, a shop assistant, since deceased, was going to the country on the night of the shooting, she passed the courthouse about five minutes to six old time, and saw Pat Harnett standing at his own door opposite the police barracks. A little nearer the courthouse, and between it and Harnett's, Jeremiah Healy emerged from the forge. There were some Black and Tans about at the time. Miss Healy told the court that a girl cousin was with her and that Healy asked them to wait for him. She replied 'No', as it was already getting late. They walked about one hundred or two hundred yards and looking back they saw both Healy and Harnett walk the footpath in the same direction as themselves. Later they observed two Black and Tans follow the young men – a tall one and a small one. The tall man was somewhat in advance of his comrade.

A little later the girls again looked back and saw nobody on the road. When they got as far as Moloney's cottage they heard shots and then delayed as they were afraid to proceed further. From that position they observed the tall Black and Tan walk back to the town. They knew that the time was then about five or six minutes past six old time, as they had heard the Angelus bell a short while previously.

John Harnett, father of one of the murdered men, told the court that he was standing in his own doorway when Healy came out of the forge, putting on his coat. Healy called young Harnett and they both went along together. He saw the Black and Tan, Huckerbery, who was then armed with a revolver strapped to his leg, and whom he knew well, walking about one hundred yards behind the young men. They disappeared round the bend of the road and he returned to his house. He did not hear shots as he was removing furniture at the time. His son had not been connected with any political society and neither he nor Healy had ever harmed anybody in their lives. In reply to Mr Woulfe, John Harnett told the court that the house of John Collins, next door to his own, was bombed on Sunday night, that the people of Abbeyfeale had been terrorised, and that a general exodus to the country had taken place.

Further witnesses were then examined and the proceedings adjourned. That was the last heard of the inquiry. It had been going against the British and almost immediately Mr Woulfe, the solicitor who defended the interests of the next-of-kin, was arrested on a trumped-up charge of possessing firearms without a current permit. He was conveyed to William Street barracks, Limerick, and amongst his escort was the Black and Tan Huckerbery. Mr Woulfe, incidentally, was one of the many Irishmen who fought, as he thought, in defence of small nations in France. When discharged from the British army he retained his service revolver, possession of which was made the excuse for his arrest during the inquiry.

Early in the morning of 5 June 1921, a second ambush took place in Abbeyfeale and a Black and Tan named Jolly was killed and several others wounded. When the IRA withdrew from the town many of the inhabitants had narrow escapes from being shot. Head Constable Casey saved the writer from a Black and Tan named Nolan, who, seemingly insane, discharged his rifle repeatedly into the wall of Jimmy Joy's house before being disarmed by his comrades. He was carried away, still shouting in frenzy that he would have revenge for his chum Jolly. Some time previously an old age pensioner was murdered at Shanagolden by the Black and Tans, from whom old age commanded neither respect nor humanity. Young men were frequently held up, beaten and searched; the houses of men believed to be operating with the republican forces were regularly searched, furniture knocked about and the maximum annoyance caused the inmates. In most cases ladies were not molested, but the terror produced by a visit of the Black and Tans was in itself a refined form of cruelty which left its mark on many. Mr O'Mahony, then manager of the Devon Road creamery, was placed against a wall to be shot with members of his staff whilst the creamery was set on fire by Black and Tans. The men escaped, however, and the greater part of the creamery was subsequently saved, when the forces representing British law and order had withdrawn.

Parson W.E. Bentley was probably the only Protestant rector to be arrested by the Black and Tans, while being conveyed in a lorry along the 'Black Banks', between Brosna and Castleisland, Black and Tans threatened to shoot him. Bentley faced up to them and pointed out that it would be difficult to justify the 'shot whilst trying to escape' excuse when applied to a member of the Church of Ireland. 'If you shoot me, my brave,' said the parson to one of the Black and Tans, 'you will find yourself dangling at the rope's end some fine morning.' Close to the parsonage is the thriving business then conducted by Robert Browne, whose brother was killed in the first attack on an RIC barrack in Ireland, that at Gortatlea, County Kerry. Bob, as he was popularly known, was compelled to abandon his business and go 'on the run' because of the keen interest which the Tans maintained in his activities. He was ultimately surprised by a party of the police from the Listowel district and murdered.

Because of his association with the Volunteers and the IRA in their initial stages, Dr Edward Hartnett was carried about the country as a hostage in a Black and Tan lorry for nearly a month. Near the village of Ashford he was compelled to witness the cold-blooded murder of a young man named Boyle, who was shot down on his farm by one of the gang of uniformed thugs in whose charge the doctor was paraded throughout West Limerick. Dr Hartnett later undertook heavy risk whilst professionally attending Volunteers wounded in action against the British forces.

BRIGADE COMMANDANT SEÁN FINN OF THE WEST LIMERICK COLUMN

by S.B.

AMONGST THE YOUNG men who fell in the fight for Irish freedom none occupied a higher place in the esteem and affection of his comrades, and of the people of the area over which he was brigade commandant, than the boy-patriot, Seán Finn. He was little more than twenty-two years of age when he fell in action at Ballyhahill, gallantly defending the cause he has espoused when, as a young schoolboy, he had joined the Fianna Éireann in his native town of Rathkeale. Like the brothers Pádraig and Willie Pearse, Seán Finn had dedicated his life to the freedom of his native land from his earliest years, and whilst still a schoolboy he became a member of the Gaelic League, of Sinn Féin and of the GAA. Tall, well-built and singularly handsome, he was an athlete of no mean attainment, and hurled with the famous Rathkeale team in its heyday. Above all, he was a young man of the noblest character.

Fr Michael Hayes, patriotic Limerick priest, described how one morning he was particularly impressed by the piety of a young boy who served his Mass in Rathkeale parish church. The altar boy was young Seán Finn. Years afterwards when the noble-minded priest and the young boy who had served his Mass, were destined to give distinguished service to their native land, a close friendship developed between them. When Brigade Commandant Finn fell in the Ballyhahill fight Fr Hayes gave expression to his sorrow in a touching little poem which appeared anonymously in *The Observer*. An extract indicates clearly the admiration which the scholarly and patriotic priest felt towards the young IRA commandant:

> He gave to Ireland's call his all,
> His heart's best love, his service high;
> To break her chain – to end her thrall
> He gave his love without a sigh.

Nor was it alone in that last fight at Ballyhahill that Seán Finn had proved his heroism. During the successful siege of the Kilmallock RIC barracks he played a leading and gallant part, and in many other engagements his personal fearlessness was an inspiration to his men. But for all that he was far from being the typical gunman. Seán was by nature gentle and kindly, and ever thoughtful for others. Although twenty-seven years have passed, I recall, as if it were only yesterday, walking with him along the mountain road to the house of a good priest who offered us the hospitality of the parochial house. It was before the first flying column was formed. We were both 'on the run', and night had fallen on the western hills. There had been considerable enemy, activity during the day, and the priest who befriended us probably knew this and was endeavouring to protect us by inviting us to his house which, at that early period in the fight, would almost certainly be immune from police or military raids. On arrival at our destination we went immediately to the room assigned us, and Seán, having placed his gun on the table, knelt down beside his bed and recited the Rosary with that manly Catholic piety which became him so well. When he awoke next morning he said to me, 'Fr —— did not sleep at all during the night; I heard him walking in the corridor. He was obviously keeping guard for us, and if I thought he would thus deprive himself of his night's rest to safeguard us, I certainly would not have come.' Thus, even in peril, did Seán's consideration for others come first.

Brigade Commandant Seán Finn was endowed with exceptional intelligence. He was widely read and uncommonly well informed on most of the important questions of the day. Many heavy responsibilities weighed upon his young shoulders. His intervention at a critical stage in 1920 saved a great Limerick Co-operative Agricultural industry from internal collapse. That the industry survived to flourish today was due largely to the action of the brigade commandant. When Seán Finn fell on the threshold of his young manhood I believe that Ireland lost a son whose character and personality would have been of great value when matured in the days of peace. Those of us who were his comrades shall never forget him. At the end of the Civil War his comrades and the people of West Limerick erected a noble monument to his memory, and it stands over his grave in his native Rathkeale.

THE HONOURABLE MARY SPRING-RICE

by S.B.

In ANY RECORD of West Limerick's part in the fight for freedom the name of the Honourable Mary Spring-Rice should have an honoured place. Miss Spring-Rice, who belonged to the landlord and ascendancy class, was daughter of Lord Mounteagle of Mount Trenchard, Foynes. The family had long association with British government in this country, and the first Lord Mounteagle was British secretary of state in the 1830s. The Spring-Rice family was also noted for the liberal opinions and independence of thought of its members. It was an ancestor of Miss Spring-Rice who insisted on the arrest of the influential man who murdered the Colleen Bawn. The first Lord Mounteagle's sister was the mother of Aubrey de Vere whose deep love of country and race is reflected so feelingly in his poetry.

The Honourable Mary Spring-Rice, who obviously inherited most of the best qualities of her ancestors, associated herself with the Irish-Ireland movement while still a young girl. I remember seeing her on the platform at an open-air Gaelic League meeting which Dr Douglas Hyde addressed at Foynes early in the century. When the Carson gun-running took place without interference by the British, her generous sympathies were all with her unarmed countrymen in the south. With her friends, Mrs Alice Stopford Green, the distinguished historian, Erskine and Mrs Childers, and others, she not only helped to provide funds to purchase the Hamburg rifles, but she also set out aboard the *Asgard* for the rendezvous in the North Sea where the rifles were taken on board Mr Childer's yacht. The story of the Howth gun-running by the *Asgard*, and that of Kilcoole by Conor O'Brien's yacht, the *Kelpie*, are well known. Not so well known, however, is the part which Miss Spring-Rice took in the subsequent fight for freedom. As the struggle became more intensive and danger grew, she stepped quietly into the front line. At all times prepared to back the Irish Republican Army in its desperate struggle, she undertook many dangerous missions to headquarters in Dublin. I remember the morning in the autumn of 1920, when Commandant Finn and members of the West Limerick staff were staying at a farmhouse near Foynes, and Miss Spring-Rice, accompanied by her cousin, Miss Knox, crossed the fields from Mount Trenchard, to offer the hospitality of her stately home to the men 'on the run' any time they might need rest or shelter. Not only that, but she also conveyed to the officers in her quiet, lady-like way, her eagerness to give any assistance of which the brigade might be in need, no matter how dangerous or difficult. It was then that both ladies volunteered to convey messages to headquarters in Dublin, or to any other part of the country, as required. Furthermore, Miss Spring-Rice also told the officers that she had arranged to maintain a boat in readiness between Loughill and Foynes, near her home by the Shannon, so that it would be available to the brigade in case there was necessity to contact the Clare brigades across the broad river. Later she put Mount Trenchard at the disposal of the late Dr Con Lucy of the first Cork brigade, and the 1st southern division staff, so that they could give lectures to the ladies of Cumann na mBan.

The national activities of the Honourable Mary Spring-Rice embraced a still wider field. By virtue of family ties she naturally had many acquaintances in distinguished and liberal-minded English circles, and when the terror in Ireland was at its worst she brought many such influential English people to Mount Trenchard where, by arrangement, they met the late Con Collins, TD for West Limerick, and others, who told them first-hand of the outrages which Hamar Greenwood was then denying so vigorously in the British House of commons. Mrs Stopford Green, author of *Irish Nationality* and *The Making of Ireland and Its Undoing*, was with her at these interviews.

The Honourable Mary Spring-Rice was still a young woman when she died shortly after the outbreak of the Civil War. She had dear friends on both sides during the conflict, and she felt the tragedy all the more keenly. She was laid to rest amongst her ancestors, her coffin wrapped in the flag of her country, the land she loved so well and served so faithfully in its time of danger.

FATHER MICHAEL HAYES, PRIEST AND PATRIOT

by ONE WHO KNEW HIM

WHEN IN 1935 Fr Michael Hayes was laid to rest beneath the shadow of his parish church at Ardagh, County Limerick, leaders of church and state vied with one another in paying tribute to the memory of one of Ireland's most illustrious priests and patriots. For nearly a quarter of a century before his death he had thrown himself wholeheartedly into the movement for the revival of a Gaelic and freedom-loving spirit amongst a people whom he loved and honoured as his own. While never for a single moment departing from the saintly dignity that characterised his role as a churchman, he was in the vanguard of the struggle for freedom during the most difficult and dangerous period of the fight for independence.

His noble contribution to the establishment of the Volunteer movement and his active association with the glorious epoch of the Easter Rising of 1916 are well known far outside the confines of his native Limerick. Irish history, as is also well known, has recorded with triumph and satisfaction the ignominious failure of the brutal General Maxwell to have Fr Hayes and his equally patriotic confrere, Fr Tomás de Bhall (now Very Reverend Canon Wall, PP, Ballingarry), removed from their respective parishes in furtherance of the British commander-in-chief's campaign 'to stamp out Irish sedition for a hundred years'. Elsewhere in these pages will be found the dramatic story of how Maxwell failed miserably to accomplish that end, thanks to the historic national stand taken by the lion-hearted Bishop O'Dwyer of Limerick.

The story of Fr Hayes is largely the story of Ireland's struggle for liberty from the earliest days of the Volunteers. Member of a distinguished West Limerick family which was prominently identified with the national movement, he was endowed with exceptionally high cultural attainments. When he came to Newcastlewest as curate he immediately won the esteem and respect of the parishioners who honoured him for his dignified personality and his saintly qualities as a minister of the church. Speaking of his work for the national movement in West Limerick, one of his closest and most intimate friends said of Fr Hayes: 'Fr Michael Hayes was, with Fr Tomás Wall and the late Fr John Kelly, the founder of the new spirit that led to the ultimate triumph of 1921. Apart from his clerical duties he hated the limelight, yet his fine personality and outstanding qualities as a public speaker were ever at the disposal of the cause, into which he threw all his high intellectual energy and untiring efforts.' It was a fitting tribute from one who knew him intimately in life and mourned with thousands of others his unexpected and premature passing.

Fr Hayes was a native of Bruree, famed in history and song for its great Gaelic and national sons and daughters. He was son of Mr John Hayes, NT, Bruree, who subsequently moved to Rathkeale to take up the position of principal teacher in the national school there. Of the large family, two, including Fr Michael, answered the call of the church. Another brother, Rev. James Hayes, while acting as a curate in Limerick city, volunteered for the Maynooth mission in the United States, where he is still engaged in the work of the Divine Master. Fr Hayes is also survived by another distinguished brother, Dr Richard Hayes, film censor, who fought with Thomas Ashe at Swords in the 1916 Rebellion and for a number of years after the Treaty represented Limerick as a Dáil deputy. No fewer than five of the sons followed the father's footsteps in the teaching profession. Of these Mr Edward Hayes, BA, principal, Kilfinane, and Mr Joseph Hayes, principal, Rockhill, are now living in retirement. Three of Fr Hayes' remaining teacher brothers have passed away – Mr Garrett Hayes, who was principal at Bruree; Mr John Hayes, who was principal at Rathkeale, where he succeeded his late father; and Mr Patrick Hayes, who acted as assistant teacher in the home town. Two of the sisters also entered religion, while a third, Miss Mary Hayes, has been acting as county public health nurse in Limerick for a long number of years.

Such, in brief outline, was the family background of the patriot priest of West Limerick who invoked the wrath of Britain's commander-in-chief in Ireland during the darkest days of the struggle for independence. He came to Newcastlewest as curate in 1913 and in a short time he proved the shining light in the gloom that overshadowed the country during that period. He was the host of such patriots as Seán MacDermott when they came to West Limerick to lead the way for that glorious epoch that began in 1916 and ended with the victory over the Black and Tans. He was the heart and soul and inspiration of the movement. His public speeches, while retaining all the dignity and profound thought of his sacred calling, did much to arouse the people to a true sense of their nationality. Writing of Fr Hayes another old friend, who was intimately associated with him during those stirring days, says:

Now that he is no longer with us it is possible to write more freely of his national work. Having been associated with him as secretary of the many national organisations of which he was president, such as Sinn Féin, Gaelic League, and some more, I was accordingly in the position to know something of his great work for the independence movement, of his burning zeal for the cause which he espoused, and of his calm in the face of danger. Great and zealous priest as he was, the duties of his sacred office naturally came first with him at all times; and his labours in a large and exacting parish like Newcastlewest permitted little spare time. Despite that he was able to preside at meetings, often as frequently as three times a week according to the exigencies of the situation. He drafted the agenda for most meetings and whenever the occasion called for the issue of a circular he prepared the manuscript himself. His work of organisation not only embraced his own locality, but the county at large. It was he who thought of and personally organised the first Sinn Féin court, before the regular courts of the first Dáil Éireann were established. When the British threatened conscription it was he who brought together Newcastlewest men of divergent political views, and persuaded them all to guarantee funds to provide the local financial backing for the great fight against Lloyd George's Blood Tax, then in imminent danger of enforcement. He spoke at proclaimed meetings throughout West Limerick in defiance of trench-helmeted soldiers of Britain. When the Irish Republican Army was formed he kept in close touch with that organisation, and provided funds to arm the men. He was largely responsible for the establishment of a newspaper in support of the cause, and when another newspaper which also supported the movement was threatened with a change of ownership, which might have resulted in an alteration of policy, it was he who came to its rescue.

When subscriptions to the first Dáil Éireann Loan began to reach the then Minister for Finance, that department marvelled greatly at the large number of subscriptions from West Limerick. These resulted directed from Fr Hayes' work of organisation in the area. Calmness in the face of danger was, perhaps, Fr Hayes' greatest attribute. Although a marked man by virtue of his nationalist and IRA sympathies, Fr Hayes stood his ground manfully when Hamar Greenwood poured Black and Tans and Auxiliaries into Newcastlewest town; and when most of the prominent men in the movement were compelled to go on the run. It was, indeed, a miracle that he survived the terror. Living with Fr Kelly in the curate's house, then the only dwelling house in that secluded countryside near the main Limerick–Newcastlewest road, armoured cars and lorries loaded with British military and police rumbled past outside by day and by night, not infrequently after their occupants had indulged in drunken orgies, either in Newcastlewest town or Limerick city. There is evidence, in fact, that groups of these brutal hordes contemplated his assassination; and it is known that on at least one occasion an attempt was made to lure him out of the house to his death, as was done with Fr Griffin of Galway.

The story of that incident is told by Fr John Kelly who related how one night at the height of the terror Fr Kelly was himself awakened by a noise outside the house which sounded like somebody moaning in great agony. He dressed himself and having listened again became suspicious that the cry was not genuine. He left his room and met Fr Hayes, fully dressed, coming along the landing towards the stairway. In response to his enquiries as to where he was going Fr Hayes replied that he was going out to attend to 'one of the boys', who appeared to be badly wounded outside. Fr Kelly, who was senior curate, said he felt that it was a trap, and that in his opinion there was none of the boys wounded outside. It was with the greatest difficulty that Fr Kelly succeeded in convincing Fr Hayes that the moaning sound was a decoy to draw him out of the house. These suspicions were confirmed in the morning when the grounds showed no trace of the impressions that a wounded man would naturally make on the gravel of the drive, or on the grounds of the lawn.

Such is the pen picture of Fr Michael Hayes by a comrade, friend and confidante during those years of tragedy and triumph for the cause of Irish freedom. Yet how much more could be written of this great patriot sagart who stood boldly in the vanguard at a time when it was both dangerous and unpopular to do so; who sacrificed practically every moment of his spare time to what he sincerely believed to be a just and noble cause; who flung back defiance at the challenge of the imperial military and political power of Britain.

But Fr Hayes asked for and expected no greater reward than the ultimate triumph of the cause he loved so well; and it was but fitting that he should have lived to see the defeat of the Black and Tans and to watch Ireland rise phoenix-like from the ashes of 1916. Like many another patriotic Irishman, too, he must have wept bitter, if silent tears, over the national tragedy of the Civil War. Eventually he was transferred to Stonehall and was later elevated to the parochial charge of Ardagh, where he was one of the best beloved and revered of pastors. Eventually, in 1934, his health failed and in June of that year he travelled to Dublin for hospital treatment. A few days later Limerick and Ireland heard the sad tidings of his premature and widely lamented passing. He was laid to final rest in the grounds of his parish church at Ardagh and in due course his parishioners raised a fitting memorial over the last resting place of a distinguished churchman and illustrious patriot.

Michael Keane, of Feohenagh, who was a prominent officer of the 3rd battalion, West Limerick brigade, played an active and gallant part in the activities of the East Cork brigade, following his appointment as creamery manager in East Cork. He once had a remarkable escape from a British murder gang who took him from his lodgings at Castlelyons. They were carrying him towards a lorry about midnight when he made a dash for freedom and got clean away although hotly pursued; Michael Keane emigrated to Australia, after the Civil War, and died there in exile.

WITH THE MID-LIMERICK BRIGADE 2ND BATTALION

by PATRICK MALONEY

IN THE EARLY days of 1917 the reformation of an active Volunteer body began to take shape in Limerick city. Meetings were addressed by Ernest Blythe and organisers from Dublin, who included the late chief of staff of the National Army, Peadar McMahon, and Peadar Dunne, who became the first O/C Mid-Limerick brigade, were actively engaged recruiting Volunteers and forming them into companies. A number of city junior hurling clubs hailing from the different districts, and each with a large band of enthusiastic followers, proved fertile ground in which to sow the seed of the new Volunteer movement. Each hurling club became identified with a Sinn Féin club and each Sinn Féin club sponsored a new company of Volunteers. In that manner the Star hurling club from the Irishtown district, its clubroom sheltered'neath the famous old walls of Limerick, affiliated with the Roger Casement Sinn Féin club and resulted in 'C' company Volunteers. St Patrick and Claughaun clubs which covered the Pennywell and Park areas created the Tomás Ashe Sinn Féin club and sponsored 'B' company Volunteers. Treaty, on the Thomond side of the city, Shamrock, in the Boherbuidhe district, and Faughs from the Ballysimon-Blackboy-Pike areas sponsored Sinn Féin clubs bearing the names of Limerick Easter Week Patriots, Ned Daly, Con Colbert and Thomas Clarke. Their Adjunct Volunteer units were respectively designated 'A', 'D' and 'E' companies. The foundation stone having thus been laid the companies were each merged into a battalion while still retaining their district headquarters. Drilling and route marches were enthusiastically taken up and became very popular. Many members of the old guard, pioneers of the republican movement in Limerick, and men who had been actively associated with the Limerick City Volunteer regiment before and during 1916 threw themselves heart and soul into the work of training the new Volunteers. They were ably supported by a number of ex-British soldiers who were invaluable as instructors.

Of the pioneers of those early days, it may not be out of place to recall a few: Martin Barry, Bill Keane and Mick McCann of 'A' company; Paddy Doyle, Paddy Ryan (Lacken), Johnnie Sweeney and D. Maher of 'B' company; Davy Dundon, Thomas Keane, Jack Cronin, Tommy McInerney, Henry Meany of 'C' company; Joe O'Brien, Arthur Johnson, P. Ryan, 'D' company; Mick Doyle, Michael Hartney and E. Punch of 'E' company. Mainly due to the efforts and sacrifice of those men the Limerick city 2nd battalion IRA became an active force in the fight for Irish freedom. Peadar Dunne, first O/C of the new battalion was later appointed brigade O/C over an area which comprised Limerick city; Castleconnell and Murroe, 3rd battalion; Caherconlish and Fedamore, 4th battalion; Patrickswell and Adare, 5th battalion. The new area was called the Mid-Limerick brigade area.

During the early stages of the war of Independence Peadar Dunne was arrested by the crown forces and was succeeded as brigade O/C by Liam Forde. Forde had been one of the ablest and most active of the officers of the Limerick City regiment, 1st battalion, prior to and during 1916. At the time of his appointment as brigade O/C he was a most successful Volunteer organiser.

Early in 1918 a strong contingent of Volunteers from the new battalion was sent to Waterford under the command of Captain Henry Meany to undertake protection duty in the Sinn Féin interest during the hectic by-election campaign between Dr White and

Captain Redmond. Later an intensive campaign to procure arms was launched, and specially concealed dumps were constructed in all battalion areas and company districts. The first clash with the British occupation forces took place in March 1919. The 2nd battalion had been engaged all day in field manoeuvres in the Patrickswell–Kildimo area some miles from the city. At the conclusion of the exercises the Volunteers were led back into the city by the Patrickswell band. Later in the night, as the band was returning home in a 'brake' it was attacked in O'Connell Street by squads of soldiers who destroyed the instruments and seized a tri-colour which they trailed through the streets. Learning of the attack, the Volunteers mobilised in their different districts and converged in groups upon the soldiers, then shouting and singing in O'Connell Street. A regular battle followed in which the tri-colour was recaptured. In the streets, highways and byways of the city, batons, hurleys, sticks and stones were freely used, until eventually the soldiers were driven back to their barracks. Later the city streets were taken over by large forces of armed military and police accompanied by armoured cars, but by that time the Volunteers had been ordered to their homes by their officers. Numbers of soldiers and civilians were injured in the street fighting and several civilians were subsequently arrested.

The next night the battalion was again mobilised and carrying hurleys the various companies marched in military formation from their own districts into the city. The soldiers were confined to barracks and nothing untoward happened. The Volunteers then marched back to their respective areas where they were addressed by their officers and dismissed.

RESCUE AND DEATH OF ROBERT BYRNE

AT THE UNION Hospital in Limerick city, on 6 April 1919, were exchanged the first shots which presaged the intensive guerrilla warfare of the years which followed, and the first Volunteer to fall in the new fight for freedom was a young Limerick city man, Robert Byrne, then twenty-eight years of age and in the prime of life and manhood. Full of ambition and imbued with fire and energy in espousing and propagating the ideals of the newly formed IRA, 'Bobby' Byrne had barely been elected adjutant of the Limerick City 2nd battalion, when he was arrested at his mother's house, 'Townwall Cottage,' situated beneath the famous old walls of Limerick and on the very spot where the women of 1690 had manned the breach. Charged with being in unlawful possession of firearms, 'Bobby' was sentenced to twelve months imprisonment.

In jail he quickly became the idol of his fellow prisoners whom he led in a fight to secure political treatment. In the course of that campaign he instigated a riot that resulted in the cells being wrecked and considerable damage being caused before the prisoners were overpowered by reinforcements of police specially drafted into the prisons. As a result the prisoners were subjected to barbarous treatment; many had their boots removed and were left bare-footed and handcuffed in their wrecked cells both night and day. Others were held in solitary confinement. Eventually, having exhausted every other means of seeking redress the prisoners went on hunger strike. Vain efforts were made by the prison authorities to induce the men to eat and to break down their morale. After a time some of the prisoners became very weak and Byrne, one of the bad cases, was removed to the hospital at the Limerick Union where he lay in the general ward guarded night and day by a prison warder and by armed police.

Plans were immediately formulated to effect his rescue, and on the orders of Peadar Dunne, the officer commanding the brigade, the battalion officers attended a meeting in the Roger Casement Sinn Féin club which was situated next to Matt Boland's in Gerald Griffin Street, for the purpose of preparing and enrolling Volunteers to make the rescue attempt. So popular was 'Bobby' Byrne that there was difficulty in restraining and holding back would-be rescuers. After a course of instruction in which the rescue was carefully rehearsed a number of men were selected and told to hold themselves in readiness for the attempt which was scheduled to be made on the next visiting day. The general plan provided that the rescuers were to present themselves in pairs at the workhouse to secure admission as visitors.

It was arranged that upward of twenty would be in the ward at three o'clock, the hour on which the rescue was to be attempted. Fifteen or sixteen others were to be in readiness in the corridors and passages and about the precincts of the hospital. According to the plan the Volunteers in the ward were to rush the warder and the police guard, overpower and tie them up, in response to a shrill blast of a whistle at the striking of the hour of three o'clock. At the same time, 'Bobby' Byrne, who was to be made aware of the plans in advance, was to be helped from his bed and escorted to a carriage waiting in the Union grounds, and driven to a previously arranged destination. Curiously enough, although there were close on forty men engaged in the rescue attempt none of the senior battalion or company officers participated, and the leading roles were filled by men who did not become officers until long afterwards. Moreover, only two of the entire party was armed.

Sunday 6 April, dawned bright and sunny, and at two o'clock little groups of men were already on their way to the workhouse by various routes. It was an easy matter to gain admittance on the pretext of seeing a patient. Accordingly, as the hands of the clock approached three, the scheduled hour, twenty volunteers were in the guarded ward mingling with the visitors, many of whom were women, and making sympathetic and anxious glances towards the prisoner patient. An armed guard sat on either side of Byrne's bed, and other armed police who numbered six altogether, occupied vantage positions inside the ward. In the corridors outside, and in the grounds, the remaining Volunteers were on the alert, calmly awaiting the signal for action.

Shortly before the zero hour, the carriage for the prisoner's get-away, lent by a friendly undertaker, rumbled through the main gates into the enclosed grounds, ostensibly to participate in a funeral from the hospital. Inside the carriage was Mary Giltinan, with clothing and disguise for the man about to be rescued.

At three o'clock, the striking of the hour and the shrill blast of the Volunteer whistle were almost simultaneous. A concentrated rush was made at the police. 'Bobby' Byrne, weak and exhausted, attempted to get up, but was frustrated by Constable O'Brien who threw himself bodily across the bed and grimly held down the prisoner while in a kneeling position. Shots rang out and there was general pandemonium as patients jumped panic-stricken from their beds and mingled with terror-stricken visitors in a wild dash towards exits. Volunteers and police were everywhere at handigrips, rolling and struggling. In a few minutes all was over and the ward was empty save for the bound and trussed-up policemen. The raiders had gone, one bearing across stalwart shoulders the limp figure of 'Bobby' Byrne, attired only in pyjamas. 'Bobby' was placed on a commandeered donkey and cart, and driven away. During the journey it was noticed for the first time that he was bleeding profusely, and a hurried examination revealed a hole, almost the size of a halfpenny, on the breast close to the heart. He was immediately wrapped in an overcoat and conveyed by pony trap to the house of John Ryan, Knocklisheen, about three miles from the Union hospital. Byrne was then dying, having been mortally wounded during the struggle in the ward. Medical attention was forthcoming, and the Last Sacraments having also been administered, he expired at 8.30 that evening.

In the general confusion which followed the fatal struggle in the ward, the rescuers failed to contact the carriage and its attendant nurse when they emerged from the building. Actually, the carriage had gone round to the back of the main hospital building, and thus missed the rescuers who came out through the front exit. Accordingly, 'Bobby' Byrne's last journey in life was made under circumstances which added to the agony and poignancy of that sad and memorable day. In the course of the melee Constable O'Brien was also shot dead, Constable Spillane gravely wounded, and Sergeant Goulding, Constables Tierney, Fitzpatrick and Clarke all received slight wounds and minor injuries.

FITTING FUNERAL TRIBUTE

POLICE AND TROOPS were out at once, scouring the countryside, and a number of men were immediately arrested and remanded, charged with being accessories after the fact in connection with the murder of Constable O'Brien. These men included Seán Hurley, cousin of 'Bobby' Byrne, who later became quartermaster of the Mid-Limerick brigade IRA; Arthur Johnson, battalion engineer, whom Byrne had succeeded as adjutant; Thomas Crowe, cousin of 'Bobby' Byrne; Michael Doherty, farmer's boy at Ryan's of Knocklisheen; and Patrick Bray, undertaker's driver. The next day great tension prevailed all over the area, and every approach to the house in which the body of 'Bobby' Byrne, covered with a blood-stained overcoat, lay in an upper room, was held by detachments of the Scottish Horse in full war kit. Later, when the body was handed over by the military, relatives had it laid out in the uniform of a Volunteer officer. Police removed the uniform, an action which led to a protest at the inquest by Mick Brennan, then an officer of the Clare IRA.

The scenes and incidents which followed will forever be remembered by those who witnessed them, the removal of the remains from the quiet farmhouse at the foot of the Clare hills to St John's cathedral, was an occasion of reverence and inspiration, as the coffin, draped in the tri-colour, was borne slowly through the quiet countryside, and then through the silent though crowded city streets. Thousands of Limerick and Clare Volunteers followed the remains that evening, and again next day, when, after Requiem Mass, the coffin was borne on the shoulders of Volunteers through the entire three-mile route to Mount St Laurence cemetery. There were poignant scenes of grief and mourning as the funeral cortège passed through streets thronged with sympathisers. On the streets, too, were lines of steel-helmeted troops with fixed bayonets, who came smartly to the 'present' as the coffin was borne past. Armoured cars were out, their guns trained upon the procession whilst aeroplanes hovered and droned overhead. Surely, it was a fitting funeral tribute to a soldier of Ireland, the first to die in the new fight.

RAIDS FOR ARMS

TOWARDS THE CLOSE of 1919 a small party of IRA from 'A' company whilst engaged in a raid for arms at Greene Barrys, situated near Sheehan's Cross, was surprised by a party of British military officers who happened to be in residence. The IRA were lucky to get away in the running fight which followed, and had barely done so when military reinforcements in lorries arrived on the scene. A few days later Constables Clarke and Mulcahy of the RIC were held up at the junction of the Ballysimon and Patrickswell roads by four members of 'B' company and their carbines taken. That night the Tomás Ashe Sinn Féin club at Claughaun, Pennywell, was attacked by the RIC who smashed up all the furniture and wrecked the building.

SECOND BATTALION ACTIVITIES DURING 1920

THE YEAR 1920 opened briskly with several isolated attacks on members of the crown forces in the city garrison. On 1 February Private Quinn, a British soldier was wounded in O'Connell Avenue and his revolver taken. On 22 February Sergeant Wellwood of the RIC was seriously wounded just as he emerged from the William Street barracks. Constable Murphy was wounded in Thomas Street on 10 March, and Sergeant Conroy of the RIC was seriously wounded on 18 March. During indiscriminate firing by the police which followed the attack on Sergeant Conroy an ex-British soldier named Murphy was seriously wounded. On 5 February a force of IRA drawn from all companies of the battalion took up positions at the Limerick railway station to ambush a party of RIC escorting the mails. The attack was abandoned because of the unexpected arrival on the scene of strong military forces, supported by an armoured car. However, on 9 March the mail van was successfully held up by the IRA as it passed through Davis Street on its way to the railway station. The IRA driver took over and the van was driven down a side street where the mails were seized and taken away. Ever afterwards the mail van was escorted by an armoured car and lorries of troops. On 9 April evacuated RIC barracks at Kilmurry, Blackboy Pike and Ballinacurra were burned down by IRA companies operating in the districts in which they were situated. In the burning of Kilmurry barracks Denis Maher of 'B' company, 2nd battalion, was trapped in the flames and received frightful burns which totally incapacitated him for life.

As darkness set in on the night of 3 April 1920, a party of IRA from 'C' company, 2nd battalion, under the command of Company Captain Davy Dundon entered the income tax offices situated in the centre of O'Connell Street, the city's principal and busiest thoroughfare. The staff were held up at the point of revolvers and made prisoners whilst IRA men thoroughly and systematically ransacked the offices. All important papers were placed in sacks and conveyed to waiting cars in the back streets and driven away. The raiding operations lasted several hours during which time the usual military patrols passed up and down the street outside. Once the situation became tense, men on guard fingered their guns, those engaged in sorting and packing desisted from their work and prisoners gazed apprehensively. Reason for all this was an armoured car which stopped directly in front of the building. Everyone breathed a sigh of relief as it moved off after a few seconds delay. When the business on hand was finally finished the raiders withdrew, having first warned the staff not to leave the building for some time. During the same night men from 'D' company under the command of battalion Commandant Joe O'Brien entered the Custom House in Rutland Street and started fires inside the building. The city and military Fire brigades put these out before they had taken firm hold.

WELSH FUSILIERS RUN AMOK

ABOUT THAT TIME the Welsh Fusiliers, one of the regiments of the garrison ran amok, and having armed themselves with entrenching tools and such weapons as bayonets and revolvers, paraded the streets in force. They raided cinemas, public houses and attacked and beat up people in a reckless manner. Groups of civilians retaliated and counter-attacked with bottles, stones, and in fact anything suitable that came to hand. Other troops armed with rifles then emerged from the barracks and indiscriminate firing took place all over the city. A publican in Roche's Street, Mr O'Dwyer, was shot dead behind his shop counter and Miss Johnson, a cinema usherette, was shot dead whilst returning home from her work at the Coliseum Cinema. During the week which followed a tense atmosphere prevailed in the city which had virtually become an armed camp with thousands of steel-helmeted troops in possession of the streets, and armed RIC holding up and searching pedestrians.

A REMARKABLE ESCAPE

TOWARDS THE END of April men of 'C' company had a remarkable escape as they prepared to ambush an RIC patrol that occasionally

passed along the Clare Street road under the shelter of the Good
Shepherd convent wall. On the opposite side of the convent wall
was a large sally grove swamp, and the IRA were actually coming
through the canal on the other side of the grove to take up their
positions when lorries and soldiers suddenly descended upon the
scene. It was obvious that the crown forces were acting on supplied
information and the IRA commandant immediately observing that
something had gone wrong ordered his men to retire at once. Under
cover of darkness they hastily bundled themselves with their arms
and equipment into boats and having crossed the canal all got away
through the swamps, hedges and fields on the opposite side. The get-
away was completed as the military cordons occupied the bridges
at both canal ends to complete an encircling operation. All through
the night the crown forces carried out an intensive comb-out of the
locality and the search was not given up until after dawn.

DAYLIGHT ATTACK ON BLACK AND TANS
IN HENRY STREET

A PARTICULARLY DARING attack on three Black and Tans was carried
out in broad daylight on 22 June 1920, by a small party of Volunteers
of 'E' company under the command of Lieutenant William Barrett.
The Black and Tans were Constables Oakley, E.T. Jones and H.
Jones and the attack took place in Henry Street in the heart of the
city, with military and RIC barracks in close proximity all round.
Constable Oakley was shot dead and the two others were disarmed.
The attackers, faced with the problem of retreating through crowded
streets with their own arms and those captured from the Black and
Tans, decided to separate, and made their way to their own areas as
best they could. One of them dropped his revolver in a post office
pillar-box at a street corner and casually mingled with the people
plying their usual business in the streets. Next morning, when the

postman opened the box, he was confronted by members of the IRA, who recovered possession of their weapon.

BRUTAL VENGEANCE BY BLACK AND TANS

THE ATTACK ON the Black and Tans in Henry Street had a tragic sequel. Some time afterwards two ex-soldiers of the British army, Patrick Blake and James O'Neill, both of Rossbrien, were arrested and charged with the murder of Constable Oakley. Conveyed to Dublin they were tried by military court martial at which they were defended by P. Lynch, KC, instructed by H. O'B. Moran, solicitor. The parents of the arrested men, relatives and a number of other witnesses for the defence travelled to Dublin for the trial. When the case was heard it was proved conclusively that neither men charged was near the scene of the shooting on 22 June and their innocence having been established beyond doubt the court had no alternative but to order their acquittal.

Accordingly, on the evening of the 20 November 1920, the Saturday preceding 'Bloody Sunday', the two men, accompanied by their parents and some relatives, were escorted to an open char-a-banc[††] by members of the RIC and set out on their journey home. When the party arrived at Limerick Junction the police procured a motor-car for Patrick Blake, his father and his brother, Michael, to continue the last lap to Limerick city. During that stage of the journey the brothers had occasion to change seats and Patrick, then beginning to show signs of strain from the ordeal of his imprisonment and trial, felt the effect of the cold, bitter, wet night. Michael, good-naturedly made him get out on the road, gave him his own overcoat and pushed him back into the centre seat where he would be more warm and comfortable.

---

††   A horse-drawn vehicle, usually open-topped.

As the car approached Oola, a number of men suddenly jumped from behind a ditch and halted it. Without hesitation one of them approached Michael Blake, then seated on the outside without his overcoat, placed a revolver to his head and shot him dead. They then ordered the driver to proceed. Michael Blake, shot through the mouth from which he bled profusely, fell across his brother's knees into the arms of his horror-stricken father. Thus the innocent victim of the vengeance intended to be vented upon his brother by the Black and Tans was brought to the Limerick County Infirmary by that brother whose place he had taken in death and by his sorrowing father, their clothes soaking with his life's blood. The murdered Michael Blake was the father of three young children. It was obvious that his murderers were British police.

Meanwhile, Jimmy O'Neill, seated beside his mother, was continuing his journey in the char-a-banc, which was boarded outside Limerick Junction by a party of men who asked for him. It is thought that Jimmy had some premonition of their mission and that he wished to spare his mother the sight of bloodshed, for he promptly answered their summons. Despite the pleadings of his almost distracted mother, whom the raiders assured he would come to no harm, he was taken away into the darkness of the night. Mrs O'Neill was never to see her son alive again, for when his body was found the following morning it was literally cut to pieces by bullets. These brutal murders by Black and Tans filled the city with gloom, and the double funeral cortège was a sorrowful, yet memorable occasion. Practically the entire population turned out to pay tribute to the dead and to show their sympathy with the bereaved relatives.

AN ORGY OF TERRORISM

FEW LIMERICK FOLK will forget the orgy of terrorism indulged in by crown forces on 15 August 1920. Early that day a strong force of 'B' company under the command of company Captain Michael Hartney was in the vicinity of the People's Park, preparing to ambush an RIC patrol that was expected to pass through Reeves' Path, a street avenue running parallel to the park railings. Whilst the ambush preparations were in progress two 'G' men unexpectedly appeared upon the scene and were promptly seized and disarmed by the IRA, who, however, had to abandon their original plan.

A short time afterwards police and military issued forth in great force and attacked the homes and business places of persons suspected of having IRA sympathies. They swept the streets with volleys of rifle fire and numbers of helpless, innocent civilians were seriously injured as the British beat up anyone with whom they came in contact. A Black and Tan was shot dead in the roadway opposite the Limerick station when caught in the cross-fire of the police shooting down Edward Street. Towards evening the police set fire to several houses, and completely burned down the home and business premises of Matthew Griffin, a Sinn Féin member of the Limerick council. The large stores and the home of the Foley brothers of High Street were also burned down.

As a reprisal the furniture of Detective-Sergeant Mahony which lay on the Quayside at Limerick docks awaiting shipment to Liverpool was set on fire by docker members of the IRA and completely destroyed. About that period also, Sergeants Harty and Dunphy of the RIC were shot dead in an encounter with three members of the IRA in Mallow Street. A few weeks later Constable Carroll was unfortunately shot dead by two members of the IRA in the bar attached to the Railway Hotel. The unfortunate shooting of Constable Carroll was the last thing desired by IRA brigade headquarters and from their point of view it was a most regrettable happening.

Whilst being conveyed in military custody to William Street RIC barracks, Limerick during the afternoon of 27 October 1920, Michael Scanlon, NT, of Galbally, commandant of the 1st Galtee battalion IRA, was fatally wounded. As the police lorry drew up outside the barrack gates Commandant Scanlon, knowing that he could expect little mercy from the enemy, decided upon a dash for freedom. Taking his escort unawares he suddenly jumped onto the roadway and raced into Little Catherine Street. Despite a hail of fire and hot pursuit by the British he succeeded in making his way into Thomas Street, where he dashed through an open doorway into the basement of a house. There he was discovered a few minutes later by Auxiliaries, who shot him through the neck and stomach before they dragged him back to the lorry. He was then conveyed to the New barracks, where he died the same evening. On the following day as his funeral passed through William Street on the way to Galbally it was stopped by military, who removed a tri-colour from the coffin. Some distance up the street, however, the coffin was again covered by the national flag.

ATTACK ON GENERAL PRESCOTT DIECES

TOWARDS THE END of 1920 there came to Limerick city one of the most notorious members of the British headquarter staff, Brigadier-General Prescott Dieces, then in charge of British intelligence. His arrival in the city was duly reported to the Mid-Limerick brigade authorities and arrangements were immediately made to keep him under constant observation. Intelligence officers with orderlies and Fianna scouts were detailed to keep in constant touch with Dieces. It was not easy as he seldom moved in a manner that lent itself to effective shadowing. He usually travelled in a well-protected staff car, escorted by an armoured car and Crossley tenders full of soldiers. When he visited clubs or shops he was always protected by G men, some of whom took up posts outside. Despite these difficulties the IRA was kept well informed of his movements and on one occasion he had barely left a house in O'Connell Street, where he had spent the night, when an armed party called to deal with him.

Through the work of Fianna Éireann extensive notes were copied from Dieces' diary and it is conceivable that few more important documents fell into the hands of the IRA. His diary included minute details of his observations of the RIC, British military, IRA, clergy, teachers, etc., over a large area of the southern district. More important still was the insight given into his work and policy regarding the formation of murder gangs within the British forces, a phase of his work which had brought him specially to Limerick. In view of this it was decided to shoot him as quickly as possible, and for that purpose an active service unit was specially detailed to remain in the vicinity of the New barracks, with orders to take advantage of any opportunity that might present itself to end his career.

For several days armed IRA men lurked in O'Connell Avenue despite military patrols which regularly covered the area. After a week's vigil the IRA men had their opportunity. On 26 November 1920, an armoured car, followed by two large staff cars and by a Crossley tender filled with troops, swung into O'Connell Avenue. It was the usual Dieces convoy. In accordance with instructions the men of the active service unit, who were scattered along the street, opened fire with their revolvers on the first staff car. The soldiers in the Crossley tender returned the IRA fire but the armoured car and staff cars continued into the barracks.

The small handful of IRA men reached safety through side-streets and by-streets before the city was filled with steel-helmeted troops in an extensive comb-out for the men who had attacked the general. On the occasion of the attack the usual convoy procedure had not been followed. The first staff car was merely a decoy and Dieces travelled in the second. Two staff officers in the first car were wounded, but though General Dieces escaped he was not again heard of in Limerick. The men engaged in the attack were under the command of Lieutenant Tim Murphy of 'E' company, who was later sentenced to death by field general court martial, but reprieved.

A number of the attackers made their way to Limerick docks where they crossed the Shannon by boat into Clare.

MURDER OF TOM BLAKE

THOMAS BLAKE WAS one of three brothers who resided at No. 1 St Alphonsus Avenue, and who were members of the IRA. Tom was employed at the pharmacy of Messrs Laird and Co., O'Connell Street, Limerick, and was studying to be a pharmaceutical chemist. Owing to his knowledge of chemistry, he was in a position to facilitate the procuring of materials for munitions for the army, and to direct and assist in their preparation.

Apparently some person with an anti-national outlook had, by deduction or otherwise, gained knowledge of these activities and furnished information to the Royal Irish Constabulary, with the result that on three occasions in the month of January 1921, the Blake residence was raided. The different apartments were closely searched, and the three brothers were put through the third degree by Auxiliaries in a futile attempt to get them to confess.

On Friday evening, 28 January 1921, shortly after six o'clock, Tom left the premises of Messrs Laird for his home. He did not reach it alive because less than an hour later his body, riddled with bullets, was found on the Clyde Road.

The funeral, which took place on the following Sunday to Shanavoher, Croom, County Limerick, was accompanied all the way by a great throng of citizens, including most of the men of the IRA. Whilst the interment was actually taking place, the Royal Irish Constabulary gave an exhibition of their 'civilisation' by making a murderous attack on those at the graveside, of whom many received serious injuries. These included Paddy O'Halloran, a young carpenter, who had been an active Volunteer since the inception of the movement, and who had been a member of 'B' company, 1st battalion. He died within a few days as a result of head injuries received.

RAID ON GUNSMITHS

DURING JANUARY 1921, an early morning raid on Nestors' Gunsmiths, of O'Connell Street, yielded a number of sporting rifles and a large quantity of ammunition to supplement IRA reserves. In February Hanrahan's public house in John Square was burned down by IRA.

ATTEMPTED RESCUE OF BRIGADE OFFICERS FROM ORDNANCE MILITARY BARRACKS

DURING MARCH 1921, some of the most prominent officers of the Mid-Limerick brigade, including Peadar Dunne, brigade commandant, and Michael Colivet, brigade vice-commandant, then imprisoned in the detention quarters of the ordnance military barracks, were forced to accompany enemy patrols as hostages. The IRA active service units were then functioning, and in view of plans to intensify hostilities by wholesale attacks on British patrols and convoys, it was felt that the lives of the arrested leaders were in serious danger. Consequently, at a meeting of the Mid-Limerick brigade council it was agreed that an immediate attempt should be made to rescue the men from military custody.

After considerable deliberation, it was decided that the most effective manner in which rescue could be effected would be by tunnelling from the outside into the prisoners' quarters. Accordingly, the barracks was kept under strict surveillance and the movements of the garrison were noted and recorded. Sketches and plans were prepared and investigated, and particular attention, was devoted to the lay-out of a tramway which divided the ordnance barracks from Shaw's Bacon Factory. All details having been thoroughly examined and approved, a party of men from 'A' and 'C' companies of the Limerick City 2nd battalion, led by Captain Dundon and Lieutenant Rahilly, occupied Shaw's Bacon Curing Factory at seven o'clock on the morning of Sunday 13 March. The watchman, together with the resident foreman and his family, were made prisoners, and guards were immediately placed at the different entrances to the factory. Employees of the emergency staff reporting for work at intervals later in the morning, and who were admitted at the outer gates, were made prisoners when they got inside the factory. The first to arrive was the fitter, who enquired of the Volunteer who admitted him if he were the new gate man, and being answered in the affirmative, advised him to be careful of his job, as it was a good one. Next followed the foreman, the jobber to feed the pigs, and later two men to attend the horses. One man, realising that something out of the ordinary was amiss, and believing that he was in danger, created an awful shindy. He violently resisted arrest, and vigorously protested that he had done no harm to anybody. He was some time, with his fellow employees, in their temporary prison in the Boiler House before he could be pacified.

The fact that it was Sunday morning, and that the factory was closed down and few people about, greatly facilitated the work of the IRA. As the gates which led to the tramway were closed, they became an effective screen to cover the operations of the men inside, who were thus permitted to work with a greater degree of confidence, as they were safe, from interrogation or interference from sources which in the circumstances would not have been welcome.

On the other hand, should the military or Black and Tans discover the presence of the Volunteers, these men would be in an extremely tight corner, especially those engaged in the passage between the barrack wall and Shaw's, who would be caught like rats in a trap unless given timely warning. As a precaution against such eventuality Battalion Commandant J. O'Brien, who had charge of the operations in the vicinity immediately outside the barracks, had a chain of men posted at different points covering the entire area. Each man was in sight of his neighbour at a convenient distance, and with definite instructions as to the method to be employed to pass on warning of suspicious activities by the enemy. The entire area was thus effectively covered off, and arrangements perfected for the speedy transmission of news of threatened danger. Meanwhile, a number of men working under the instructions of J. Grant, battalion engineer, had set about preparations for boring and tunnelling inside the factory precincts.

In a short time communication by means of a tapping system was established between the prisoners and the intending rescuers. Progress which thus gave early indication of success then assumed a definite shape. Practically all available members of the brigade and battalion staffs were then in the vicinity of the ordnance barracks. Scouting was tightened up, and armed patrols were sent out to cover the roads converging on the district. In the vicinity of the cemetery, a motor car was seized to be used as a decoy in case of emergency.

Another party entered the garage of a well-known and popular medical doctor, and were about to seize his car when he unexpectedly came on the scene and indignantly told them to put their guns down. He said that he had taken more lead out of their fellows than most of them had ever seen, and pointed out that taking his car might, in an emergency, mean the difference between life and death to a patient. Realising the situation, the men apologised and withdrew. In the event of the rescue turning out successful, it had been arranged that the escaping prisoners would join the brigade flying column, then quartered round Inch St Laurence. As an additional precaution, an ambush party, under the command of the captain of 'A' company occupied positions on the railway bridge skirting the road, in order to cover retreat and prevent pursuit.

MELODY INSIDE THE BARRACKS

MEANWHILE, INSIDE THE barracks the prisoners commenced to sing lustily to drown the noise caused by the men engaged in the boring operations, and strains of 'Whack Fol the Diddle', 'Wrap The Green Flag Round Me', 'Ireland Over All', 'The Soldier's Song', and, by way of change, 'Bonny Mary of Argyle', floated through the air to the accompaniment of impromptu 'music' given on such instruments as enamel mugs and plates, with knives and forks as tuning rods and drumsticks. The hours passed and work proceeded steadily, nothing of an untoward nature occurring to arouse suspicion. Suspense was eased somewhat by the prisoners' choral efforts as they continued to entertain the rescuers working outside, and the military listening inside, with exhibitions of their 'musical' abilities.

Suddenly, close on one o'clock, an armoured car and some tenders unexpectedly appeared in the barrack square, and squads of fully equipped soldiers 'fell in' on parade. Notification was immediately transmitted to the commandant and brigade adjutant, who ordered a suspension of all operations. The rescue enterprise was in the ordinary course an extremely hazardous and dangerous undertaking at any time; with armoured cars and troops in full war kit standing by, it became doubly so. Various reasons were advanced to account for the sudden appearance of the troops. One was that the sentries posted on the wall adjacent to Shaws' Factory had heard the noise of the tunnelling and reported the matter; another was that soldiers in the building situated in the market opposite had their suspicions aroused by observing some of the brigade officers enter and leave the factory. It was also thought that the prisoners themselves might have aroused suspicion of the military authorities by their sudden and sustained outburst of song, and that the troops were mobilised to conduct a search. Whatever the reason for the appearance of the military, the rescue attempt was finally abandoned, and Colivet, Dunne and the other leaders remained in captivity. Their places were filled, and as the war entered its vital stages, the forces of the Mid-Limerick brigade in city and county continued to give outstanding service.

JOHN STREET AMBUSH

By THE TIME the annual retreat for the St John's division of the Arch-Confraternity opened on Monday, 4 April 1921, rampaging Black and Tans had established a veritable reign of terror in Limerick city, so much so that some of the more timid citizens were fearful to perform their ordinary avocations in life. Not a day passed without incidents of brutality being recorded, whilst night, which should in the normal course bring rest and repose, became an occasion for the creation of panic and suspense. Victims of the terror were mostly inoffensive and helpless people. Curfew was in force, and people confined to their homes since nine o'clock, would often lie awake in their beds all through the night, afraid to sleep. Some of the more venturesome would peer through windows of darkened rooms to observe the troops move stealthily and silently through the streets. Everybody was on the alert for the dread sound of military lorries patrolling the streets, and for the loud knocking of search parties on the doors of houses marked down for investigation and possible destruction.

It was indeed a time for reflection, as nobody knew what would happen during those agonising nights. On the other hand, outwardly at all events, IRA activities did not appear to be moving well, and it seemed as if the Tans, having thought they had established a permanent ascendancy, intensified their campaign of terror against the unfortunate people. What the enemy did not realise, however, was that the IRA had been merely marking time whilst taking stock of their position. A new order had been issued from GHQ, whereby many existing officers were systematically replaced by younger men with initiative and a desire for action. General headquarters had swept away the old system by which officers, sometimes without qualifications, had been elected by popular choice on the votes of their subordinates. It had been directed that for the future all commissions in the Irish Republican Army would be filled by appointment, after due consideration had been given to the qualifications and merits of the candidates As a result of this order, several changes took place in the staffs of the different units of the Mid-Limerick brigade. Officers 'on the run', in hospital, or in prison, were replaced, and in most cases by young men not previously in the limelight. At a meeting of the newly created battalion and company officers, the formulation of a fresh policy towards the conduct of active service operations had the effect of giving each company the opportunity to distinguish itself within its own area. As a result, things began to take more lively shape in the city, and it was soon apparent that the activities of the Black and Tans were about to receive a check.

Because of the limited number of serviceable arms available to the City battalion, and the scarcity of suitable ammunition, it was not possible to plan a general attack upon the enemy, or to commence operations on a large scale. It was, accordingly, arranged that each company or group of companies would assume the offensive in turn, and as matters went, it was 'C' company which initiated the new campaign. The new brigade O/C, Liam Forde, attended a mobilisation of the company active service unit, at a place called 'Paddy's Hedge' on the canal, on Friday night, 8 April. All available arms having been procured from dumps nearby, a patrol of ten men set out to comb the area in search of members of the crown forces.

Having patrolled almost the entire district, without contacting the enemy, for whom they also searched every public house unsuccessfully, the men returned to the Irishtown, and were about to give up for the night, when six Black and Tans, armed with carbines and revolvers, emerged from a public house at the junction of John Street, Broad Street and Mungret Street. At that stage some of the IRA had already moved through White's Laneway on their way home. The police had come upon the scene so suddenly and so unexpectedly that no advance preparation for an ambush could be made. Accordingly, without more ado, the battalion commandant, who was with the party, advanced to within fifteen or twenty yards of the enemy, and threw a bomb into their midst, whilst the remainder of the IRA opened a barrage of revolver fire. As the police scattered, two of them fell on the pathway and others ran towards their barracks, a hundred yards away, firing indiscriminately as they went. The street being thickly filled at the time, the scenes of uproar and panic which followed the explosion of the bomb and the subsequent retreat of the enemy are beyond description.

Sergeant McCarthy, of the Royal Irish Constabulary, lay where he had fallen, badly wounded, and the other fallen Royal Irish Constabulary man crawled to the safety of a nearby house. One unfortunate civilian was killed outright, and two were wounded. The attackers having scattered immediately, retreated into the network of alleyways in the vicinity of Clare Street, only Commandant Dundon being slightly wounded in the hand, from which he bled profusely.

BLACK AND TAN SHOT DEAD

ON THE SAME night, 'A' company active service unit, having divided into two sections, also patrolled their company area. They, too, were in the act of demobilising without making contact with the enemy, when they were informed that there was an armed Black and Tan at the junction of Church Street and Palmerstown, close to the Royal Irish Constabulary barracks. They immediately proceeded there, and the Black and Tan, Constable Wiggins, was shot dead. This shooting took place about five minutes before the John Street attack, and it is presumed that the Black and Tan party engaged in the latter street was about to return to the barracks prior to engaging in reprisals for the death of Wiggins.

REPRISALS — OFFICIAL AND UNOFFICIAL

MEANWHILE, SOME MEMBERS of 'C' company, having retreated into Clare Street, three of them, Dundon, Downey and McGrath, entered an unoccupied furnished house in Lelia Street, on either side of which resided Royal Irish Constabulary sergeants and their families. Consequently, when the reprisals commenced a short time later in the night, these men felt comparatively safe in what was probably the most dangerous, yet the safest position, in the city. It was most unlikely that the Black and Tans would seek their attackers on the veritable doorstep of their own sergeants' quarters. The three IRA men had ample opportunity to study the situation as they peered through a window. Below them in the roadway were Black and Tans, all set for a campaign of terror and vengeance.

Further down the street, crown forces could be seen entering the home of Jack Madigan, another member of 'C' company. That house was wrecked completely. Led by a drunken ex-soldier, who had informed them of the attackers' line of retreat, and whom they subsequently forced to accompany them, the Black and Tans attacked many other houses in the 'C' company area. In Clare Street, they attacked the house of Andy and Paddy Egan, two of the ambushing party; thence they proceeded to Roxton Terrace, where their first visit was to the house of M. Wrenn, who was also one of the ambushers that night. The houses of the Harringtons, O'Briens, O'Halloran's and Shinners were then visited in turn. A brother of Mick Harrington, who was in prison at the time, was taken out of his house and, having been brutally beaten up, was placed against a wall and threatened with shooting.

The occupants of all houses raided were roughly handled, and most articles of furniture were systematically broken up and destroyed. Ranges and fire grates were torn from their settings, and strewn about floors, whilst bed-clothes and bedding were set on fire. Women, half demented by fear, strove vainly to calm children clad only in night attire, and crying with terror. In John Street, Black and Tans raided and wrecked the homes of two other members of the ambushing party, Ringrose and Downey. There the orgy of destruction and fury knew no bounds, as having completely wrecked the inside of the house and maltreated the occupants, they demonstrated to the horror-stricken families the manner in which they would take vengeance on the IRA men, should they capture them alive. Three weeks later the same Black and Tans backed up their threats when they captured Henry Clancy, an ex-British soldier, who was also a member of the attacking party.

It is scarcely possible, nor is it intended, to detail the houses visited by the Black and Tans, nor to describe the happenings in the houses visited during the course of these reprisals. Such details as have been given are intended to show the accuracy of the information supplied to the authorities by the ex-soldier. After the night of the attack he disappeared from his usual 'haunts' for several weeks, but on his return, he was arrested by the IRA, tried by court martial, convicted and condemned to death. The last rites of the church having been administered by a priest, he fell before a firing party of his countrymen.

Following a night of reprisals, the grey light of dawn brought a meagre ray of hope to partially allay the fears of stricken families, and people looked forward to a brief respite at least. But the forces of the British crown had other plans. A proclamation was posted throughout the lower end of the city, ordering all persons indoors at two o'clock on 9 April. The previous night's orgy of destruction was regarded by the authorities as merely justifiable revenge by the Black and Tans; now the military were to extort their satisfaction. One may readily visualise the effect of this new order on citizens already harassed almost beyond endurance. There was much hustle and bustle in business houses, factories and workshops, in order to release employees in time to reach the refuge of their homes before the latest reign of terror was launched in the shape of official reprisals. By two o'clock on that very fine Saturday afternoon, the city was desolate, its streets deserted, as entire families imprisoned in their homes waited and wondered.

The suspense did not continue long, for soon the roads were occupied by a veritable army corps, which included steel-helmeted infantry with fixed bayonets and rifles at the ready; engineers in white overalls; heavy trucks, lorries, Lancia cars, armoured cars, Crossley tenders and ambulances. In fact, all the paraphernalia of war was there, including General Cameron and his staff in a large touring car. The military proceeded to Lock Quay and John Street, where they selected for destruction the houses of prominent IRA officers, then in prison. All residents of the particular streets in which these houses were situated were promptly ordered out. Then began a parade of refugees, as distracted women and children marched along the streets, not knowing where they were going, nor what would be the end of it all. The windows of 'Liberty Hall' and the 'Chamber of Commerce', pet names the boys had for the large tenement houses at Nos 2 and 3 Lock Quay, were thronged with men, women and children who shouted encouragement and sympathy, and offered succour and shelter to the band of refugees.

As the enemy engineers set about their work, the whole area in or about McInerney's public house at 9 and 10 Lock Quay was cleared; even the occupants of the houses opposite on the Sand Mall, across the river were ordered out. All preparations having been completed the fuses were laid, and at a signal from an officer, an explosion took place which shook half the city. The entire frontage of McInerney's seemed to float *en masse* through space, and deposit itself at the base of the wall across the river on the Sand Mall side. The remainder of the building crumpled and collapsed, leaving but a smouldering ruin, the skeleton of what had been a fine business premises a few minutes previously. This was the home and business premises of Tommy McInerney, brigade transport officer, Mid-Limerick brigade, who accidentally lost his life during the Truce. He was the driver of the car that went over Ballykissane Pier, County Kerry, in Holy Week 1916. The troops having completed their work in that locality, proceeded to John Street, where in a similar manner, they blew up the shop and residence of Mrs Nealon (aunt of Henry Meany then in jail).

No sooner had the crown forces departed from Lock Quay than the residents of 'Liberty Hall' and the 'Chamber of Commerce' flocked down to the scene of the reprisals. Though very poor people, they were the best of neighbours, and even after curfew, they risked life and limb as they worked heroically amidst tottering and crumbling walls and masonry to save what they could of the belongings and property of a family for which they had the greatest admiration, and full sympathy. That was the way by which these women and girls gave expression to their feelings of loyalty to a cause of which they knew but little, because of their environment. Drink, which was available in the ruins of the shop, was left untouched. At the height of the salvage operations, a Crossley tender, laden with Black and Tans, appeared on the scene, and a sergeant of the Royal Irish Constabulary, who already bore an unenviable name, added to his notorious reputation by mercilessly lashing old women and girls with a horse whip, as though he were driving cattle before him.

Squads of soldiers, off duty, visited the scene of the day's operations, and the opportunity to indulge in an orgy of free drinking amidst the ruins of the wrecked public house, was indulged to the fullest by the men. The drunken soldiers then carried on a concert amidst the ruins of McInerney's premises, and in the early hours of the morning they terminated the proceedings by setting the place on fire. With a stiff breeze, the rising flames quickly grew in intensity, and spread rapidly until the entire block of buildings became endangered. Mick Noonan and another neighbour were knocking up the residents in the adjoining buildings, when the fire brigade arrived. One of the male residents was assisting Lieutenant Barry and Andy Kelly to lay lines of hose, when a military curfew patrol appeared on the scene. As he did not get indoors quickly enough to satisfy the NCO in charge of the soldiers, a revolver was pressed against his forehead to the accompaniment of choice language and warnings as to what would happen should he resume his work as a good Samaritan.

During April a mixed force of city and county members of the column, under the command of brigade O/C Liam Forde, shot two Black and Tans dead in an ambush at Fedamore, County Limerick.

ATTACKS ON ROYAL IRISH CONSTABULARY AT CAREY'S ROAD AND SINGLAND BRIDGE

ON SATURDAY NIGHT, 25 April 1921, a group of IRA active service men under the command of Paddy Barry, battalion adjutant, and which included D. Dundon, battalion commandant, left brigade headquarters in Transport Union Hall, O'Connell Street, to attack Black and Tans reported to be in Dunne's public house, Little Catherine Street, close to William Street barracks, headquarters of the Royal Irish Constabulary in Limerick city. On their way to Dunne's the IRA were intercepted by scouts from 'E' company, who reported that preparations were under way for a similar attack at Carey's Road. As the IRA party mostly comprised men from the Carey's Road area, under the command of their company O/C, Joe Saunders, the original plan was cancelled and all retraced their steps to the Carey's Road district. On the stroke of curfew bombs were thrown at Black and Tans in Hickey's public house, and Constable Redfern was seriously injured. The attackers got safely away before the customary terrifying reprisals were started by crown forces. The Rangers club, Boberbuoy bandroom, Birmingham's, Davern's, and the houses of several IRA men and republican sympathisers were attacked and ruthlessly smashed up by the police.

On the following day, Sunday 24 April, whilst the brigade adjutant and some of the staff were again engaged at brigade headquarters, word was conveyed to them that over twenty Royal Irish Constabulary men, armed with carbines and revolvers, had passed through the canal, apparently bound for an evening walk along the banks of the Shannon at Plassy. The adjutant and a couple of men standing-to immediately set out to make hurried preparations to intercept the enemy on their return. Scouts were sent to contact the active service unit men in 'C' and 'B' company areas, which bordered on the canal and Plassy.

The Royal Irish Constabulary had the choice of three different routes by which to return. They could come back the Plassy bank, or across the Black bridge on the upper reaches of the river, then through Stravakee and back through Corbally on the Clare side. They could also reach the main Dublin road on the Limerick side by walking through the woods. The railway line from Limerick to Ennis covered all three return routes close to the city, the difference between them being approximately one mile either way.

A patrol from 'B' company, under Captain P. Troy, took up position at Corbally on the Clare side. The mixed patrol of 'C' and 'B' company, under J. Kelly, officer commanding 'C' company, covered the canal route, and the battalion adjutant, battalion commandant and three or four members of the active service unit took up position on the railway bridge at Singland, astride the main road to Limerick. Cycle scouts returning from a tour of the area reported that the Royal Irish Constabulary returning by the Limerick road were then only a short distance away. The small party on the railway bridge soon had the enemy under observation, about two hundred yards distant. The police walked in pairs, laughing and joking, nonchalantly swinging their carbines. The IRA, crouching beneath the parapet of the bridge, held their breath and waited. The tenseness of the waiting minutes was terrific, and the only sounds in the still air of that glorious summer's evening were the tramp of the marching policemen and their merry chatter. Suddenly, the atmosphere changed.

As the unsuspecting Royal Irish Constabulary men were about to pass under the bridge a sharp command rang out and the air became filled with the banging and crashing of exploding bombs. The police scattered along both sides of the roadway, clutched their carbines, and sought what cover they could find. Some injured lay moaning on the pathway. In a few seconds the quiet countryside re-echoed to the crack of rifle and revolver fire, as the frenzied police, recovering from their initial surprise, blazed away at their unseen foes.

By that time the IRA had retreated down the railway line, through hedges and fields, and into the shelter of boreens of the neighbourhood. In their haste some waded through the nearby river at Groody. All believed that they had struck a smashing blow and inflicted serious casualties on the cream of the Royal Irish Constabulary garrison in Limerick. Unfortunately, such was not the case. The bombs used, a new pattern issued by general headquarters and tried for the first time in Limerick, were practically useless. Apart from their loud detonation they merely wounded Sergeant Crowley seriously, and four other policemen slightly. Had the bombs been of the normal type, the Royal Irish Constabulary party would almost certainly have been wiped out.

Following the attack Lieutenant Patrick Dawnen of 'B' company, 2nd battalion, who lived in the vicinity of Singland Bridge, was taken from his home in the middle of the night by Auxiliaries and Black and Tans, and brutally tortured in the presence of his wife and very young family. He was finally left for dead on a refuse-heap, but survived his terrible ordeal. Dawnen was one of the outstanding men of the active service unit, and participated in the actions at The Union, Dromkeen, Shraharla, Lackelly, Pennywell, and in the attack on Prescott Dieces.

PENNYWELL AMBUSH

CURFEW RESTRICTIONS RIGIDLY enforced in Limerick city made it extremely difficult for the active service units of the various IRA companies to effectively pursue the plan of campaign which provided for intensification of the fight against the British. Under curfew regulations the entire population was compelled to be indoors by ten o'clock each night during the summer months. Sharp to time the forces of the British crown took over the streets of the deserted city each night, and armoured cars, lorries filled with troops, and police patrols on foot were continuously on the move to ensure that no civilian was out of doors and that no lights were shown from dwellings. The military governor had ordered family lists to be posted nightly on the back of each doorway. Raids to check these lists were frequent, and families were paraded in their night attire any time it became the whim of some officer or policeman to make a check. Thus, the unfortunate citizens were kept constantly on edge.

The moment ten o'clock struck each night a special squad in charge of an intelligence officer swept out of the New barracks in a fast Crossley tender to make a preliminary tour of the entire city in order to pick up stragglers getting to their homes and to scout the way for military and police patrols which followed. The IRA noted this custom, and plans were laid to ambush the scouting car during one of its operations. The job had a special appeal to the IRA as it was known that an intelligence officer associated with the murder of the mayors was usually an occupant of the Crossley. The ambush was a difficult and hazardous operation as for obvious reasons the men engaged in it had only a matter of seconds in which to work. The IRA men could not take up positions until the people had left the streets, and the speeding Crossley would have to be ambushed and the attackers dispersed before the streets were filled with the usual curfew patrols a few minutes later. Accordingly it was arranged to engage the scouting car with rifle and revolver fire, as it sped from

Pennywell, near the junction of the Dublin road bordering on the canal and Plassy, where boats were in readiness to take the ambush party across the Shannon into Clare.

On the night of 18 June a small party from 'B' company, under the command of Captain P. Troy, took up positions in a gateway screened by houses. The position commanded a full view of the narrow roadway, and faced the blank wall of the Good Shepherd convent. Curfew chimes had scarcely died away before the Crossley tender came sweeping up the road, and the ambush party blazed away at it for all they were worth. The military returned the fire, and the tender sped on. Carrying their rifles, used for the first time in a city street ambush, the little band of IRA men retreated by the banks of the canal and at Plassy they crossed the Shannon to safety. It was later announced that the military casualties were two wounded, one of whom was the lieutenant of the intelligence staff already referred to. He was subsequently taken prisoner by the IRA elsewhere, and during the Truce he was shot dead in the streets of Cork whilst attempting to escape from custody.

TRAGIC DAYS FOR THE
MID-LIMERICK BRIGADE

A DATE THAT I can never eradicate from memory is 1 May 1921, for the happenings of that day and of the week which followed must ever hold a special significance for me. I have often wondered since if it were merely in the order of things that the call of duty to another sphere should be the main factor in my being alive today to record these events. The quiet and apparently peaceful countryside was bathed in sunshine as May Sunday ushered in the summer of 1921 in all its splendour and glory. Yet, beneath the outward calm and peacefulness, tragedy and death walked hand-in-hand through highways and byways in County Limerick. Far away on the North

Cork border a little column of the Mid-Limerick brigade was that very day battling with greatly superior forces of the British crown; a fight which went on almost continuously for two days and which extended from Shaherloe in North Cork to Lackelly in East Limerick.

In these engagements death took a heavy toll of some of the bravest and best of Limerick's fighting men under circumstances that will ever be recalled with pride. At Shraharla a small Mid-Limerick column under the command of Liam Forde, brigade O/C and Seán Carroll, column commandant, about to take up positions for an ambush, were unexpectedly confronted by four Crossley tenders filled with military and Black and Tans and supported by an armoured car. With all the advantages in their favour the enemy opened a withering fire with machine-guns and rifles on the exposed IRA men. A running fight of savage intensity followed as the column fought grimly to extricate itself from an almost impossible situation. Captain Paddy Starr was shot dead as he lay flat on the road side, sheltered only by a slight rise near the Catholic church, whilst fighting a rearguard action with his commanding officer, to cover their comrades who sought better positions. Captains James Horan and Tim Hennessy, having been isolated from the main body, were also killed after an epic fight, and Patrick Casey was wounded and taken prisoner when his ammunition was exhausted. Casey was tried by drumhead court martial on the same day and executed on the following morning. Next day, the same little band of Mid-Limerick men, together with members of the East and West Limerick brigade columns, were again engaged by the enemy at Lackelly, in East Limerick, where Jim Frahill, Pat Ryan and Riordan of Mid-Limerick and T. Howard of East Limerick, lost their lives.

Meanwhile, on Sunday, 1 May, when coming from eleven o'clock Mass in St John's cathedral, Tom Keane, who had a short time previously been appointed captain 'C' company, Limerick City 2nd battalion, informed me that he was going to Ballysimon to meet Captain Casey of 'A' company. His purpose was to secure the return of two guns belonging to 'C' company which had been left in 'A' company dumps since the unsuccessful attempt to rescue Peadar Dunne and M.P. Colivet from the ordnance barracks. I agreed to Captain Keane's suggestion to accompany him to Ballysimon and having arranged to meet again half-an-hour later we parted at the street junction on our different ways home. On arrival home I was met by a scout with a communication from Paddy Hegarty, brigade intelligence officer, instructing me to report to brigade headquarters, Transport Union, for a meeting of the intelligence staff. Accordingly, when Captain Keane turned up at our arranged rendezvous sharp on time I had to explain the circumstances and suggest another companion, who was immediately forthcoming in Henry Clancy. As the men set out in what all thought would be just a country walk, none knew how tragic would be the ending nor realised that we should never meet again in this life.

On arrival at Ballysimon, Captain Keane and Henry Clancy met Casey as arranged and having secured the two revolvers from the dumps but without ammunition, were returning across the fields towards the roadway when suddenly a Crossley tender and cage car, with armed Black and Tans appeared on the main road, travelling very fast in the direction of the IRA men. Casey, the first to sight the enemy, started to run, whilst Keane and Clancy threw themselves flat on the ground, hoping that they had not been observed. Their hopes were futile, however, for in a matter of seconds they were surrounded by notorious men whose names were a by-word in every Limerick household. Every one of them was known to Clancy and most of them knew him. Having first been clubbed with rifles, kicked and punched about, the IRA men were handcuffed and placed in the tender, which then continued back towards the city. The Black and Tans taunted and jeered Clancy about his association with the Star hurling club, and he, defiant to the last and knowing that he could expect no mercy from his captors, vowed that he would have sold his life dearly if he had ammunition. He was then subjected to further brutal treatment and finally driven to desperation he made a wild, defiant bid for freedom by plunging from the speeding Crossley, handcuffed though he was. Bruised and shaken when he struck the road, he had no sooner staggered to his feet than he fell, literally riddled with bullets. So died one of Ireland's daring and dauntless soldiers. Having fought with the Warwickshire Regiment for the freedom of small nations in the 1914–18 war and having come unscathed through the fighting in Italy, France and Flanders, he had returned home to give his life's blood for the freedom of his own country. He had enthusiastically thrown in his lot with the IRA and was one of the most valued members of 'C' company, 2nd battalion, to the active service unit of which he was attached. As a fighter and instructor he was without equal in the battalion and did not know the meaning of fear. The Black and Tans in John Street barracks knew him as one of the 'Star Boys' (members of the Star hurling club) for whom they had an intense hatred and wholesome dread. The fact that he was an ex-soldier with war experience and trained to the use of modern weapons made them all the more anxious to bring about his death. The brutal torture and taunts to which he was subjected in the lorry were deliberately intended to goad him to a desperate escape attempt so that they could kill him without awaiting the formality and mockery of a military court martial.

The body of Henry Clancy was first placed in the morgue near the New barracks and later handed over to his sorrowing people. It was conveyed to St John's cathedral, his parish church, to await burial. Meanwhile Captain Tom Keane, who was witness to the gruesome tragedy, was placed in the detention prison within the New barracks.

In a previous sketch, reference is made to military tributes paid at the funeral of 'Bobby' Byrne. Two years later the situation was different, and Henry Clancy was denied even Christian burial although the Warwickshire Regiment with which he had fought in the Great War then formed the garrison of Limerick. Respect for the dead and facilities for burial were all set aside in a vendetta of hatred, and so debased had become the forces of the British crown that they could not permit the funeral of their victim pass without making it the occasion of a further orgy of terror and bloodshed. Before the cortège had moved off from the cathedral Crossley tenders filled with Black and Tans appeared in the square in front of the church, their rifles pointed menacingly at the mourners.

Later, when the funeral had reached the fountain in Upper William Street, the Black and Tans again appeared in their Crossley tenders and halted the cortège whilst a police sergeant got down and read a proclamation to the bereaved, sorrow-stricken father and brother. Then the police proceeded to break up the cortège. Mourners and sympathisers were assaulted with rifle butts and threatened with shooting, whilst carriages and cars were sent careering away. When the funeral was permitted to continue on its way, it comprised the hearse, one carriage and five mourners – the bereaved father, two relatives and two one-armed men. On arrival at the cemetery it was necessary for the hearse to proceed to the graveside as there was not sufficient help available to shoulder the coffin. At that time the Black and Tans again appeared and their fury became like hell let loose. The air re-echoed to the rattle of musketry as they fired indiscriminately in all directions. P. Shanny, Lieutenant of 'B' company, had a narrow escape, throwing him into a dyke as bullets whistled over his head. Michael Downey, a Volunteer of 'B' company, 2nd battalion, was shot dead whilst crossing the fair green.

The Rev. Fr McNamara, who officiated at the graveside, had to break off the burial service to minister to the unfortunate victims, amidst a hail of bullets. The bodies of Michael Downey and Gerald Nunan were thrown into Crossley tenders and conveyed to the dead-house in the New barracks. Accordingly, amidst scenes of death and desolation the remains of Henry Clancy, soldier of Ireland and soldier in France, were laid to rest.

Meanwhile, Michael Downey's corpse and Gerald Nunan lay

on slabs covered with sheets in the morgue in the New barracks. During the night when the orderly was going his rounds he was amazed to hear moans coming from the interior of the dead-house. Going inside to investigate he heard further cries and saw movement beneath one of the sheets covering the slabs. Almost petrified by fear the orderly dashed out of the dead-house to report that ghosts of dead Sinn Féiners were haunting the morgue. The guard turned out and medical officers who removed the sheets revealed Gerald Nunan coming out of a dazed stupor. Only grazed by a bullet he had been left for dead and covered up alive beside the corpse of Michael Downey.

EXECUTION OF CAPTAIN TOM KEANE

Captain Thomas Keane, gentle father of a young family, who had been taken prisoner by the Black and Tans at Ballysimon on Sunday 1 May, was subsequently tried by field general court martial, charged with being unlawfully in possession of arms and with waging war against the crown forces. He was sentenced to death though ably defended by the late Patrick Lynch, KC, instructed by H. O'B. Moran, solicitor, now registrar for County Limerick. Keane's execution took place in the detention prison, New barracks, on 4 June 1921.

As the hour of execution approached crowds kneeling on the roadside reciting the Rosary outside the barracks were attacked and scattered by the Black and Tans. Many were brutally beaten and a number were seriously injured. Keane's body was buried in the county jail, but during the Truce it was taken up by his comrades of 'C' company, reverently re-coffined and after a fitting public funeral was finally laid to rest beside his comrade Henry Clancy in the republican plot at Mount Saint Laurence cemetery. Michael Downey's body is also buried in the plot. A wayside cross erected to his memory on the road facing his homestead near St Patrick's Well, a few yards from where he was killed, reminds pilgrims to the holy well to pray for the victims of the tragic early days of May 1921.

PLAN TO RESCUE IRA MEN

TOWARDS THE END of May three members of the Limerick City 2nd battalion, Captain Thomas Keane of 'C' company, Captain Edward Punch of 'F' company, and Lieutenant Timothy Murphy, of 'E' company, were in the county jail under sentence of death. The brigade and battalion staffs had under consideration plans to effect their rescue, although the jail was heavily guarded by military and armoured cars were constantly within its precincts or immediate vicinity. Furthermore, the ordnance military barracks was but a short distance from the road. Two military officers' uniforms were seized during a raid made on Cleeves, and plans to kidnap two officers of the jail guard and substitute two IRA men in the captured uniforms were taking shape when it was announced that Punch and Murphy had been reprieved. It was believed in IRA circles that Keane would also be reprieved, and on that account and in order not to prejudice the situation the battalion staff suspended all activities temporarily. In spite of this, however, Keane was executed on 4 June.

Meantime an RIC sergeant was shot dead at Corbally in the early hours of the morning. He had been out with the usual patrol at Park Bridge, Corbally, during the previous night and had left his tobacco pouch on a seat. He did not miss it until his return to the barracks and set out to retrieve it at daybreak on the following morning. On his way he was accosted by IRA men 'on the run' who, thinking that he belonged to a party out to secure their arrest, opened fire and shot him dead.

On 22 March a civilian named Creamer was killed and a Volunteer slightly wounded during an exchange of rifle fire across the River Shannon at Plassy, between RIC and men of 'C' company.

AUXILIARY TRAIN'S NARROW ESCAPE

SOME TIME LATER a train carrying Auxiliaries narrowly escaped destruction at Canters Bridge, where members of the brigade staff with Bob de Courcy, divisional engineer, 2nd southern division IRA, were engaged in testing new guns and explosives. The train in which the Auxiliaries travelled was saved by a pilot engine which preceded it and exploded the mines laid upon the track. The bridge was thus blown up prematurely just as the police train appeared in the offing. Members of the brigade staff present on that occasion included Liam Forde, brigade O/C; Patrick Barry, brigade adjutant; Owen O'Brien, brigade vice-commandant; Seán Carroll, column commandant; Bob de Courcy, divisional engineer, 2nd southern division; D. Dundon, O/C 2nd battalion; and John Vaughan, quartermaster, 3rd battalion.

THRILLS BY SHANNON SHORE

THE RESIDENCE, YARD and stores of Stephen Kennedy, in Michael Street, an out-of-the-way part of the city, was a virtual IRA arsenal during the entire Anglo-Irish war. Large quantities of gelignite, 'war flour', explosives, arms and ammunition for the use of the brigade active service units were stored away in the premises in cleverly concealed dumps and secret passages known only to Stephen, who was assistant brigade quartermaster. Stephen was an old soldier of the Boer War, and as officer commanding the Castle barracks during the Civil War he emulated the exploits of the famous Boer General de Witt, in the manner in which he safely extricated his forces from almost impossible positions. Once he brought them through miles of occupied country, by forced night marches, in order to link up with the main body of the Mid-Limerick brigade, then in County Cork.

On 11 June 1921, quantities of explosives urgently needed in the country areas were loaded into carts by Stephen and his brother,

Dominick, a Volunteer in 'C' company, 2nd battalion. The explosives were cleverly concealed in camouflaged loads, and despite police and military patrols, were driven through the city streets to Park Bridge, Corbally, about a mile-and-a-half on the outskirts. There they were transferred to a waiting boat which was rowed up the Shannon towards Plassy by members of the IRA, preceded by armed scouts who walked the banks on both sides of the river. As the boat approached McMahon's house, 'C' company's headquarters, situated at the head of the canal facing Plassy, its occupants were attracted by frantic signalling and gesticulating by two men on the bank. As something was obviously amiss the boat was pulled ashore on the Clare side of the river. No sooner had it been grounded on a sandy stretch than military in full war kit appeared on the opposite side. Down the river towards Corbally more troops disembarked from lorries and came swarming up the opposite bank. Crawling through the thick sedge undergrowth the IRA boatmen made their way to the shelter of a hedge without being observed, and thence through dykes and ditches they reached the heart of a countryside well protected by nature. There they were safe from the encircling British forces but, meanwhile, the unattended boat with its precious cargo was wedged on the sandy beach.

Every male person within the area cordoned off by the military was taken prisoner and marched away with hands above heads, to be interrogated by British officers. The two men who had given the alarm to the IRA, not responding quickly enough by putting their hands up, were threatened with shooting by a British officer who was calmly told that each had left an arm in the battlefields of France, fighting for the freedom of small nations. They were one-armed ex-British soldiers, one of whom had already lost a soldier brother killed fighting with the IRA. Somewhat nettled by the unexpected turn of events the British officer hinted that the ex-soldiers were in France at a time when bombs were made by troops, and accused them of using their knowledge of the manufacture of these bombs to help the IRA.

During the interrogation troops were conducting a vigorous search of the surrounding fields. Finally, an officer produced a hand paddle and getting into the only boat available, a fisherman's small *brecaun*, or flat-bottomed boat, began to paddle into the middle of the Shannon towards the boat beached some distance away on the opposite shore. Knowing its cargo, the ex-soldiers began to make their peace with God, for they knew what would happen should the officer reach it. They breathed a sigh of relief when the *brecaun* stopped within fifty yards of the boat and the officer paddled back as though for dear life. It subsequently transpired that the *brecaun* had been leaking badly and that the officer became nervous that it might capsize in the centre of the river.

Some hours afterwards all persons interrogated were released and the military left the locality. Brigade Quartermaster Seán Hurley arrived on the scene and the boat with its important cargo resumed the journey through the picturesque river stretch from Plassy to Doonass. There members of the column took away all explosives which were used to good effect some days later when Annacotty bridge on the main road from Limerick to Dublin was blown up by forces of the Mid-Limerick brigade. The two ex-soldiers in the confidence of the IRA, subsequently realised how near they had been to death; but the British officer in the boat probably never knew how close he had been to making an important capture.

ATTACKS ON RIC

ON THE 25 June 1921, an RIC patrol was fired on in Patrick Street by members of the IRA, who escaped through Arthur's Quay. On 27 June members of 'D' company, City 2nd battalion, under the command of Company Captain M. Danford, later killed in the Civil War, and Lieutenant Edward Doran, attacked an RIC patrol at Nicholas Street, close to Mary Street barracks. Shortly after leaving the Boot Shop of Mick Healy, an officer of the company, where they had made their preparations, the attackers encountered the patrol at Nicholas Street corner, opposite St Mary's cathedral. In the exchange of firing Dan Gallagher, section commander of 'D' company, was wounded. The British casualties in this engagement, and in the Patrick Street ambush, were unknown.

Just before the advent of the Truce, Constable Beamish of the Royal Irish Constabulary was fired upon by two members of 'C' company in the vicinity of Baal's bridge, and shot through the hand. On the same night as reprisal, the Royal Irish Constabulary brutally beat up several civilians and threw one man into the locks at the canal. They left him to drown but he was rescued by members of the IRA in the vicinity.

A TRIBUTE TO LABOUR

DURING THE CAMPAIGN against the forces of the British crown in Limerick the IRA received magnificent support and co-operation from labour. As already stated the headquarters of the Mid-Limerick brigade was situated in the Transport Union Hall in O'Connell Street. That IRA activities were directed from the building must have been obvious to numbers of the workers who occupied the rooms for union meetings, card playing and other activities. Situated in a back attic at the top of this four-storey building, the brigade headquarters was almost always occupied by a small complement of staff officers, sending and receiving dispatches and communications from all parts of the country, covering the movements and activities of IRA and British forces, alike. Although the building was frequently raided by Auxiliaries, police and military, at no time was anything discovered by the British which would give them an indication as to what went on in the top attic. At the same time the IRA officers on duty had some narrow escapes, but they were always given the necessary 'split' second in which to disappear. In the front hallway a bell-push that connected with the attic at the top of the building was ingeniously concealed and an orderly was always on duty beside the bell in order to warn the IRA officers upstairs of impending danger. A light ladder gave access to the roof through a cunningly disguised trap-door which, in position, looked like an ordinary part of the ceiling, Whenever the warning bell sounded the occupants of the attic immediately went on the rooftop, taking all papers in their brief cases and drawing the ladder up before replacing the false ceiling in position. On the roof they could make their way along the entire block of buildings, protected and screened from observation from the street below by a high brick-built parapet. They felt doubly safe on the rooftop of the building at the end of the block, as that was the residence of the British crown solicitor.

FIANNA ÉIREANN IN LIMERICK CITY

by VOLUNTEER

SHORTLY AFTER THE foundation of the Fianna Éireann in Dublin in 1909 a branch formed in Limerick city under the guidance of Seán Heuston, one of the executed 1916 leaders, soon became firmly established. Its members paraded with the Irish Volunteers in Limerick on Easter Sunday, 1916, from which period onwards the boys, who had been devoted to their organisation since its foundation, organised and trained with renewed enthusiasm. When the British made Limerick city a military area in 1919, following the rescue of Robert Byrne from the Royal Irish Constabulary, nobody over sixteen years was permitted to enter or leave the city without a permit from the British authorities. In such circumstances the services of the Fianna were particularly useful, and the boys made many journeys to the country to bring back foodstuffs to the beleaguered townspeople. From that time onwards the scope of the organisation was greatly extended, and the Fianna participated in raids for arms and seizures of mails, whilst they also carried dispatches, kept police and military posts under observation, and conducted general intelligence work. No risk was too great for the boys and no hardship too big. Whether cycling miles in the rain with dispatches for Clare or County Limerick, or standing for hours in the cold whilst keeping a barracks under observation, all tasks were carried out so cheerfully and with such enthusiasm that it was freely admitted by Volunteer headquarters that the Fianna Éireann played a major part in the struggle in Limerick. Bicycles were necessary to carry dispatches, so thirty enemy machines were duly 'requisitioned'. Every opportunity, too, was taken to secure firearms. One Sunday a British officer, armed with a service revolver, was held up in O'Connell Street by two Fianna boys, one of whom was armed with a small revolver slightly larger than a toy pistol and just about as effective. They ordered the officer to put up his hands, but he promptly responded by attempting to draw his revolver. Both boys pounced on him before he could do so and all three fell to the ground, struggled and rolled off the footpath. A hard fight followed, but the boys were beginning to get the better of the officer when a spectator of the loyalist persuasion decided to intervene on his side. Using his walking stick the loyalist proceeded to beat the boys but, fortunately, by that stage the officer was about done up, and his revolver wrested from him. It was but necessary to fade out of the picture, a movement which the two Fianna boys promptly effected, taking their prize with them.

In 1920 Limerick City Volunteer headquarters was established on the top floor of the Transport Workers' Hall in O'Connell Street. A member of the Fianna was always on duty at the street entrance. Apparently leaning casually against the door post with his hands behind his back, his finger never left the electric bell-push, so that timely warning of a raid could be given and thus enable the Volunteers upstairs to escape by the roof. Although a number of raids did take place on Volunteer headquarters neither personnel nor documents were ever captured there.

Members of the Fianna were regularly on duty outside the post office, and copies of all telegrams in code for British military or police were passed out to them by Volunteer intelligence men working inside. The keys to the various codes were in the possession of the Volunteers, who received them from headquarters in Dublin.

Scouting in the vicinity of the British military headquarters at the New barracks, Fianna boys found a means of entering the fortress through a skylight in the roof of one of the store rooms, through which they were able to remove large quantities of motor tubes, sparking plugs and electrical equipment. Such hauls were repeated on several occasions, and although only a wall divided the store from the guardroom the boys always got safely away with their loot.

Before and during attacks on British forces the Fianna were on duty to inform the attackers about enemy dispositions, and to assist the getaway afterwards. During a raid on enemy mails by the Fianna a letter was intercepted from a Black and Tan stationed in a country barracks, to his brother in England. The Black and Tan expressed fear for the safety of his barracks if it were attacked, and gave details of a weak spot in the walls which, he said, a 'Guy Fawkes' squib' would be sufficient to send it sky-high. The information was passed on and shortly afterwards the barracks was attacked and captured by local Volunteers. It is not known whether the writer of the letter ever discovered the damage caused by his indiscretion.

In May 1921 the Fianna lost several officers when a large force of Black and Tans surrounded a small wood near Limerick where the boys were holding a parade. Amongst those captured were Gus Gabbett, commandant; Patrick Tubridy, shot accidentally some time after his release; Gerard Corr, Thomas Dargan, Bill Bourke, Paddy Tuttle, Tom Kearns, P. O'Driscoll, and Frank Cooney. Each received a sentence of three years. Also arrested on that occasion was Seán Keane, who had just served a sentence of six months for having IRA dispatches in his possession. He was then sentenced to ten years. Previously arrested Fianna boys included the former commandant, Patrick McSweeney, then interned at Ballykinlar; Gerard Wharton, sentenced to two years for a 'hold-up' of British soldiers, and Patrick O'Mahony, sentenced to three years for firing at a Black and Tan. Although these losses were a great handicap the Fianna did not relax their activities, but under their new commandant, Joe Crowe they continued to organise and give all the help possible to the national movement. Amongst the more active officers at that period were: Patrick Deegan, Liam McInerney, K. Bradshaw, P. O'Brien, Thomas Lowe, Joe McMahon, P. Shinners, Patrick O'Sullivan, Val Forde, Liam Barry, T. Crowe, S. Reen and T. Bray.

GALLANT CUMANN NA MBAN OF LIMERICK

by MADGE DALY

SOON AFTER THE formation of the Volunteers, a branch of Cumann na mBan was started in Limerick city. The first meeting was held in the Gaelic League rooms, and the majority of those in attendance were members of the Gaelic League, or were girls belonging to families who had carried on the Fenian tradition. A provisional committee was elected, and I had the honour of being made president, an office which I held until 1924, except for one year, 1921, when we unanimously asked Mrs O'Callaghan to accept the position. She insisted on resigning at the end of a year of office.

Following the inauguration, Mrs Dermot O'Donovan was vice-president; Miss Mollie Kileen, honorary secretary; Miss Annie O'Dwyer, honorary treasurer, and the Misses Tessie Punch, Maggie Tierney, Laura Daly, Una O'Donoghue and Mrs Michael O'Callaghan were on the committee. I am quoting these names from memory, so that it is possible that I may have omitted some. From its inception, ours was a large and active branch, and I can recall over seventy girls who were active members to the end. Classes were immediately started for first aid, home nursing, drill, signalling, and for instruction in the care and use of arms. For military matters we had the services of Captain Montieth and other Volunteer officers, whilst we had four city doctors and two nurses who gave the First

Aid and nursing lectures voluntarily. In 1911, my uncle, John Daly, and some Fenian friends were responsible for the erection of a Fianna Hall on the grounds at the back of our house, 15 Barrington Street, and there most of our activities were carried on. Designed by the late Maurice Fitzgerald of Richmond Street, it was a lovely little hall complete with stage and seating accommodation. We arranged lectures, Irish dances and concerts, while many of our honoured martyrs came there to teach us the way to freedom. Terry MacSwiney, Seán MacDermott, Mary MacSwiney, P.H. Pearse, Roger Casement and many others, gave lectures which helped to keep active the various organisations, the Fianna, the Volunteers and the Cumann na mBan, during the black days which followed the outbreak of the European war. We always charged admission to these functions, and all members, except the Fianna, had to pay; in this way we helped the Volunteer Arms' Fund. Our classes were held in the hall, and we also had the use of a room from my uncle at 26 William Street, where the committee met every week.

When John Redmond forced his nominees on the Dublin executive of the Irish Volunteers, the word went around that the women of his ideas should join, and, if possible, gain control of the Cumann na mBan. Accordingly, in Limerick, as elsewhere, large numbers joined who, if they held any national opinions, were supporters of the Parliamentary Party and had nothing in common with the original members. Soon after this development an election for a new committee was held, and some of these new members made an all-out effort to secure election; a few succeeded. A short time prior to this, we had made over £130 from a fête in aid of the Arms' Fund. At our first committee meeting following the election, the Redmondite members enquired about our funds. They were informed that our collections were for the Volunteers' Arms' Fund, and that we had handed over all the money to the Irish Volunteers for that purpose. The new members were very disappointed. We had the big majority on the committee, however, and co-opted additional members of our way of thinking, so that we had full control. Following a few meetings, the opposition became dispirited by the course of events, and resigned in a body. They immediately started the National Volunteer Ladies' Association, and set up in great style in expensive rooms in O'Connell Street. They soon faded away, however, as they had neither the faith nor the enthusiasm of Cumann na mBan. During this upheaval, we lost only one of our original members, and she returned a few months later. Our committee remained practically unchanged during these years up to 1924. We got some additional members, but those whose names I have mentioned were there to the end. Mrs Clancy resigned the honorary secretaryship, and the Misses E. Murphy and Tessie Punch took over her duties.

The friendships formed with the members of the committee are most precious to me. We worked together as one, each one doing all possible to help the organisation and to forward the cause, whilst never counting the cost. This applies equally to the rank and file, in which each girl not only carried out the task allotted her, but, in addition, let pass no opportunity of doing any national work that came to hand. As time passed, and the difficulties and dangers multiplied, the girls rose gallantly to the occasion, so that it was joy to work with them.

A practice which caused us much fun was initiated soon after the outbreak of the European war. We started First-Aid classes under the department of education, and a number of our members passed the examinations. For each of our members who passed we were given a grant from the department, and in this way we earned £48 which, as usual, was transmitted to the Arms' Fund of the Irish Volunteers. In that way the British government was unwillingly subscribing to the funds of its enemies. The classes were confined to Cumann na mBan, and were held in the Gaelic League rooms and in the Fianna Hall. The home nursing classes were sometimes held in private houses.

As the Rising approached, work went ahead with great energy and enthusiasm, and for a few weeks a group of girls was constantly busy in our house making first aid outfits. Wholesale arrests followed the suppression of the Rising, and the Cumann na mBan then began collecting for the Volunteers' Dependants' Fund (later the National Aid Fund), attending to the welfare of the prisoners and their families, and helping in every way to maintain the national morale.

Crowds thronged the churches to attend the Requiem Masses for the 1916 martyrs arranged by the Cumann na mBan. The memory of one Requiem Mass stands out. On my suggestion, it was arranged by the Cumann na mBan, and through the special permission of the late Bishop O'Dwyer, it was celebrated in St John's cathedral at dawn on 4 May 1917, the first anniversary of the Rising. Hours before daylight St John's square was packed by a dense crowd of people, which swelled as others joined it from the farthest ends of the town; from streets and lanes and the suburbs they came to honour the memory of our latest martyrs. As we hurried along in the darkness, most houses were lit up, and every family seemed to be about and moving. When we arrived at the church it was densely packed, and there was an immense crowd outside which could not gain admittance. The Volunteers were unable to get us to our specially reserved seats, and we had to hear Mass in the sanctuary. The altar was crowded with young priests, the choir was splendid, and the impressive ceremony was altogether unforgettable.

Some Volunteers were released in the autumn of 1916, and internees in Frongoch and other English jails were released on Christmas Eve 1917. Limerick Cumann na mBan had collected a large sum of money to send parcels to these men. Those under sentence were not allowed any parcels. We got about 500-weight of butter from local creameries, and this was sent with hampers of cakes, ham and all kinds of Christmas fare. I had been in touch with Michael Staines, who was in charge of parcels in Frongoch, and he asked me not to expend any more money on food, as huge parcels had reached them from all parts of Ireland. Accordingly, following the releases, we sent the balance, over £80, to Dublin, to be spent on the prisoners. We also sent regular parcels to the women prisoners in England. When release came unexpectedly, a few volunteers had to remain in Frongoch to re-pack the food and send it to Dublin for re-distribution amongst the 'prisoners' families.

In June 1917, all the sentenced prisoners were released, and then work started on the Sinn Féin campaign for the general elections, in which members of the Cumann na mBan were busy helping in all constituencies. Soon the jails began to fill again, as Sinn Féin and the latest resistance movement gathered impetus, and the Limerick branch of Cumann na mBan had much to do attending to the needs of the prisoners and their families, visiting the jails, arranging for meals, and writing to prisoners' relatives. Sometimes, men arrested in the neighbouring counties of Kerry, Limerick and Tipperary were brought to Limerick, and their people never knew where they had been taken until our members reported to them, a step we always took as rapidly as possible. A sergeant in William Street barracks always sent word to me when prisoners arrived there. Then Maura O'Halloran would prepare meals in our house and take them to the barracks. Strangely, she was never refused permission to see the prisoners or to give them meals, and stranger still, I never learned the name of the friendly sergeant.

Time went on, and our activities became intensified as the men in the columns and on the run had to receive attention; safe houses had to be found in which they could rest, and clothes and other necessities provided. Eventually, this part of our work was organised systematically. Our committee met weekly, examined reports of all cases, received collections and, where needed, made grants to families of men in jail and on the run. The workers of Limerick gave splendid support to our fund during those terrible years. Every week we received considerable sums from the employees of Messrs Clunes Factory, Dennys Factory, Evans and Company, Limerick Wagons Builders and Railway men, Bannatyne & Company, Abbey Boatmen, Shaws & Company, McMahon & Son, carmen at Messrs

Russells, and the workers at the Limerick Clothing Factory. We had a grand group of girls at this factory, in which the workers had a grand national tradition. From these working groups we got regular weekly collections from £13 downwards. Cleeves Factory always headed the list. This money was generally handed into our shop in Sarsfield Street by Mr Reddan. We also received help from individual workers and generous subscriptions from some sympathetic merchants and business people. On the whole, however, I must agree with John Mitchel's assertion 'that merchant make bad revolutionists'. The Sinn Féin clubs also helped us by collections, some very generously. Many of our members were also in these clubs.

Early in 1920, the Fianna Hall was burned down by crown forces, and from that time onwards it was difficult to arrange general meetings. Still we maintained contact with all of our members and could mobilise them at a moment's notice. At the time of the burning of the Fianna Hall, we were not living in Barrington Street, but as I had rented from Messrs Nash the plot of ground on which it was built, I was the nominal owner. I made a claim for compensation which came before Judge Pigot, who was very sarcastic and rude to me, and gave a decree for the smallest possible amount, £288. This sum, with interest, I returned to the Fianna later on. It was subsequently taken by the Free State government in lieu of income tax which we had refused to pay to the British government, and which we had paid over and over again to the republican authorities.

The Fianna Hall was a loss to us and to the other city republican societies. We issued appeals for funds to the general public from time to time, calling on all the business houses, private houses and professional people. The response was generous and willing, and I can only remember one businessman refusing to give me a subscription. One such drive for funds, made in October 1920, realised over £542 17s 6d. Each pair of girl collectors was given a collecting book and a particular district to canvass. They worked hard, and always with good results. This was not easy, especially during the height of the Black and Tan war. We organised flag days in October 1921, which realised £439 11s 3d for the White Cross. Through these activities alone we were able to assist the families of the prisoners and meet all of our other obligations, until the Truce. In July 1921, we received over £200 from the American Celtic Cross through Mrs O'Callaghan, and, in 1923, we got over £200 from the White Cross. I also got further large sums from the Limerick Women's Association in America.

I think it was in 1921 that Cumann na mBan changed the constitution and arranged for more active co-operation with the IRA. Each branch needed a captain, who was specially trained for this work. In Limerick, we appointed Miss Mary McInery, and she proved a very satisfactory choice. She gave her whole time to the work until the finish, and was always cool and practical. She had a number of young girls working with her. During the years of the campaign we regularly got bundles of posters, leaflets and other literature from headquarters. These parcels generally arrived by rail at our house, and were later distributed amongst the members of each district. They were then posted on walls or otherwise published by night. We often went into the country and put posters on chapel gates. We also had our own special propaganda, and in this connection Desmond Fitzgerald gave me a list of people outside of Ireland, to whom we used send reports of local atrocities committed by the British. I got a duplicator and, with Tessie Punch's help, sent out a large volume of propaganda. Later on I got a typewriter which I lent to Tessie Punch. This was taken from her house by Free State raiders and that was the last I heard of it.

The British had a special hatred of Cumann na mBan, and well known members of the organisation had little rest. My own case was typical. We were raided regularly, our business place was set on fire and our furniture seized for unpaid fines imposed by courts-martial. My sister was dragged out of the house one night, her hair shorn off and her hand cut with a razor. She was later court martialled and fined £40 for tearing down a military proclamation which the Black and Tans had put up inside our shop window. Still this treatment was mild when compared with the desolation and sorrow dealt to other members. In March 1921, Michael O'Callaghan, ex-mayor of Limerick, was shot dead in the presence of his wife. George Clancy, the mayor, was also killed the same night in his wife's presence, and Mrs Clancy was wounded in the wrist in a fruitless effort to save her husband. Thus two of our foundation members were dealt the cruelest blow that the Black and Tan fiends could devise. In 1921, we proposed Mrs O'Callaghan as TD for the city, and her nomination was acclaimed with great enthusiasm. She was elected with a huge vote, and proved a grand representative, incapable of being deflected from her high ideals. Rev. Dr I. Cotter, a distinguished American priest and author, aptly wrote of her:

> Mrs O'Callaghan, refined, cultured and learned, has ever employed all her great powers before her martyr's death, as well as since, in the emancipation of her country from the yoke of the despot. She does honour over much to historic Limerick … I was never in a home where husband and wife so supplemented intellectual activities on behalf of their dear country.

Mrs Clancy had not been married many years at the time of her husband's murder. Both had always worked for the cause, and though life was then strenuous and dangerous, they had a lovely and a happy home shattered in a moment by the devilry of the British forces.

Cumann na mBan did not waver under the increased terror, and the work went on as before. Sometimes wounded Volunteers were brought to the Limerick hospitals and, to the credit of the staffs, the men were sheltered and nursed, and never a word or hint of their presence reached the British. Whenever the hospitals were raided by the Black and Tans, the wounded men were safely hidden. The nuns of St John's hospital were particularly kind and helpful, and the Limerick doctors were also splendid. Irrespective of their political opinions, they went to the relief of our wounded, often at great inconvenience, and to the most out-of-the-way places. There was never a question of fees, nor was there idle talk which would have led to the capture of the wounded.

When the Treaty was carried, Limerick Cumann na mBan lost some of its members, but the majority remained loyal to the Republic. During the Civil War the republican forces in the New barracks were joined by Cumann na mBan who helped them in many ways. The hospital was in the charge of Nurse Laffan and Nurse Connerty, a Limerick girl home from New York on holiday. These nurses, with the nursing section of Cumann na mBan, attended to the sick and wounded, whilst other girls helped with the cooking of meals and maintenance. When the republicans evacuated the city, the girls remained in the barrack until the men had got clear, and then returned to their homes, still ready to undertake any duty required of them. Mrs Hartney, an early and most active member, who went to Adare to help the IRA, was shot dead by Free State troops when crossing the yard of the hotel there. Her husband was serving with the republican forces at the time. She was a fine woman, with a definite Fenian outlook, and was a great worker. Some time previously, her home and shop in Davis Street were burned down. She left two lovely little girls to mourn her loss with her husband. Cumann na mBan arranged High Mass and a public funeral, and she was buried in the republican plot in the New Cemetery.

From that stage onwards Cumann na mBan made the arrangements for the burial of the Limerick republicans killed in the fight, as all the men were with the armed forces. It was the saddest period in our history, the comrades of yesterday fighting and killing one another. I was trustee for the republican burial plot. The other trustees were both on the Free State side. I had the plot opened for the burial of all republicans killed in the Civil War, and the Free State trustees never made an effort to stop me, or to have Free State soldiers buried there – and admission that they had no right to do so, having deserted the Republic they had sworn to defend. Soon the jails were filled with republican prisoners, and conditions in Limerick jail were deplorable. Our girls did all they could to help the prisoners. In 1922 a number of members of Cumann na mBan were arrested outside Limerick jail, where they had been waiting for prisoners who were supposed to be allowed escape. It later transpired that this was a plot to capture the girls and, as far as I can remember, those arrested included Maura O'Halloran, Nellie Blackwell, N. O'Rahilly, Nellie Fennell, Josie O'Brien and Nannie Hogan of Cratloe. They were held in Dublin jails for a long time, and went through hunger strike with Mary MacSwiney and Mrs O'Callaghan, who had also been arrested. The conditions under which they were held in custody in Kilmainham and Mountjoy were appalling. I have a number of letters sent out secretly by Nannie Hogan which describe vividly the brutality to which they were subjected. That was the most terrible and depressing period since the start of the fight. Yet our branch continued to function until 1924, by which time most of the prisoners had been released. I look back now with pride and pleasure to my long association with these grand women of the Limerick branch of the Cumann na mBan. I never observed a sign of pettiness, jealously or personal ambition amongst them. All worked for the cause to the utmost of their abilities, giving of their time and means willingly, and upholding their principles regardless of consequences.

INDEX

Powell, Molly Joe 148
Power, John J. 122, 150, 151
Power, Paddy 148
Punch, Edward 314, 351
Punch, Tessie 361, 363, 367
Purcell, Joseph 32
Purcell, Liam T. 191
Purcell, Willie 148

Q

Quaid, Sonny 254
Quane, Ned 121, 171, 279, 280, 281
Quigley, James 32, 33
Quin, Stephen 20
Quinlan, John 196, 198
Quinlivan, Anne 81
Quinn, Dan 273
Quinn, James 50
Quinn, Maurice 273
Quinn, Stephen 98
Quirke, M. 148
Quirke, Seán 266
Quirke, Timothy 272

R

Raheenagh 251, 259
Rathkeale 130, 254, 257, 258, 259, 260,
        269, 273, 274, 276, 301, 303, 308,
        309
Rearden, Willie 181
Redfern, Constable 341
Redmond, Captain 315
Redmond, John 33, 34, 36, 37, 71, 87, 217,
        218, 362
Reen, S. 360
Regan, J. 264
Reidy, 'Slope' 253, 254, 264, 269
Reidy, Amos 254, 275, 283, 287
Reidy, J. 258
Reidy, S. 267
Reilly, Constable 67, 68, 105, 106, 111,
        114, 115, 116, 117
Reilly, Sergeant 122
Richmond Barracks 59
Ring, Constable 105, 106, 111, 114, 115,
        116
Riordan, Seán (Ballintubber) 195
Roberts, Constable 149
Roberts, Dr 243, 244
Robinson, Seamus 103, 104, 105, 106, 107,

        108, 110, 111, 116, 117, 118, 119,
        120, 121, 254, 255
Roche, James 254, 262
Roche, Jim 266
Roche, Jimmy 254, 258, 260, 269
Roche, P. 258
Roche, Paddy 254, 269, 275, 278
Rockhill 167, 309
Rockmills 178, 179
Rogers, W. 175
Rooney, William 216
Roskeen 105, 106
Rossbrien 324
Rossmore 104, 108
Royal Irish Constabulary (RIC) 20, 21,
        22, 23, 25, 43, 44, 105, 111, 122,
        128, 129, 139, 144, 145, 146, 147,
        149, 150, 151, 152, 157, 158, 159,
        160, 161, 162, 163, 166, 169, 174,
        176, 178, 179, 192, 198, 203, 210,
        221, 222, 223, 237, 247, 248, 253,
        254, 255, 256, 257, 258, 259, 260,
        263, 264, 265, 266, 267, 268, 271,
        272, 290, 291, 295, 299, 302, 320,
        321, 322, 323, 324, 326, 328, 329,
        336, 337, 340, 341, 342, 343, 351,
        354, 355, 357
Ryan, Con 147
Ryan, John 318
Ryan, P. 51, 314
Ryan, Paddy 314
Ryan, Pat 213, 346
Ryan, Robert (Bob) 183, 186, 196, 198
Ryan, Thomas 32, 33

S

Sarsfield (New) barracks 41, 327, 328, 344,
        348, 349, 350, 359, 369
Sarsfield Street 39, 161, 162, 164, 366
Saunders, Joe 341
Scanlon, Debbie 148
Scanlon, Jim 110, 114, 115, 116, 119, 120,
        121, 149
Scanlon, Michael 23, 122, 148, 149, 150,
        276, 326, 327
Scannell, T. 291
Scully, Liam 139, 147, 155, 158, 166, 257,
        260, 261
Sexton, T. 287
Shanagolden 74, 265, 267, 268, 269, 274,
        288, 299